Palgrave Studies in Prisons and Penology

This is a unique and innovative series, the first of its kind dedicated entirely to prison scholarship. At a historical point in which the prison population has reached an all-time high, the series seeks to analyse the form, nature and consequences of incarceration and related forms of punishment. Palgrave Studies in Prisons and Penology provides an important forum for burgeoning prison research across the world.

More information about this series at
http://www.springer.com/series/14596

Maggie Hall

The Lived Sentence

Rethinking Sentencing, Risk and Rehabilitation

palgrave
macmillan

Maggie Hall
Independent Academic
Sydney, Australia

Palgrave Studies in Prisons and Penology
ISBN 978-3-319-45037-7 ISBN 978-3-319-45038-4 (eBook)
DOI 10.1007/978-3-319-45038-4

Library of Congress Control Number: 2016950019

Printed on acid-free paper

This Palgrave Macmillan imprint is published by Springer Nature
The registered company is Springer International Publishing AG
The registered company address is: Gewerbestrasse 11, 6330 Cham, Switzerland

Contents

List of Abbreviations

AVL	Audio-visual link
CALD	Culturally and linguistically diverse
CORE	Low-risk sex offender programme
CSNSW	Corrective Services NSW (formerly Department of Corrective Services NSW)
CUBIT	Custody-based intensive therapeutic programme (high risk)
DPP	Office of the Director of Public Prosecutions NSW
EHR	Extreme high risk
EPRD	Earliest possible release date
HRMU	High-risk management unit
NESB	Non-English speaking
OPM	Operations procedure manual, DCNSW
PRLC	Program review leave committee (a division of SORC)
SMART (SMART RECOVERY (TM))	US self-help drug and alcohol programme designed as an alternative to 12-step programmes
SORC	Serious offenders review council
VOTP	Violent offenders therapeutic programme

1

Introduction

The atmosphere in the Parole Authority hearing room was heavy, the screen on which the prisoner appeared was fuzzy and crackling, the prisoner's halting speech intensified by the poor reception. The judge, having listened to the prisoner's legal representative list the litany of prisons he had occupied over the past eight years, the lack of opportunities to participate in rehabilitation programmes and the fracturing of already tenuous family relationships by the constant movements, frowned. Suddenly he exclaimed, "Goodness, what have they done to my sentence?!" The prisoner peered through the screen, recognising the judge who had sentenced him eight years before. In the sentencing remarks the judge had made a comprehensive list of recommendations as to how this young man was to be assisted to appreciate the wrong he had done, and left a long period on parole for him to be integrated into the community. The judge could see how little had been implemented and the Authority had no choice but to refuse parole. Even if the prisoner was able to complete the rehabilitation which was recommended and was successful in gaining release, he would have no time left for a period of parole to reintegrate him into the community.

M. Hall, *The Lived Sentence*, Palgrave Studies in Prisons and Penology, DOI 10.1007/978-3-319-45038-4_1

The shock on the face of the judge on realising that "his" sentence, carefully crafted and thought out, bore no resemblance to the sentence which had been experienced by the prisoner reflects the everyday experience of imprisonment. It is as if the prisoner disappears from the bright lights of the sentencing court into the black hole of imprisonment, only to surface at the point of parole consideration. The minutiae of the sentence, the daily actions and interactions which make up the sentence as a lived experience are not viewed as relevant to a consideration of sentencing, whether as a legal construct or as a way of assessing compliance by the prisoner. This book invites a broader conception of sentencing as an ongoing process requiring certain actions and reactions on the part of the sentenced person, the criminal justice system and the broader community.

The lay observer would assume that there is a close relationship between the judicial act of sentencing and the resulting subsequent processes of punishment. In reality, discussion of the aims of sentencing often occurs at a highly philosophical level and as a way of justifying the sentence to appellate courts with little attention paid to how these aims are carried out in practice. Despite this disconnection sentencing is clearly invested with a real structural and physical content.

The concept of the "lived sentence" arises primarily from the somewhat trite and obvious observation that "the sentence" as conceptualised by legal practitioners and academics and correctional staff, as opposed to "the sentence" experienced by the sentenced person manifests real and concrete differences. Lack of attention to this difference leads to a real and significant "lacuna" (McNeill et al. 2009) in theories of sentencing and in penality more generally. The sentence as a real, visceral experience contains processes and procedures, as well as expectations and subjective reactions. From this perspective, failure to consider the perceptions and understandings of those living the sentence is not just a question of fairness but leads to a form of "imaginary penality" (Carlen 2008) by omitting a crucial view of the process from examination and theorising.

Is it so controversial to contend that sentencing has meaning? This assertion is different from the normative argument that sentencing should have meaning. Rather, the idea is that whether we like it or not or whether we acknowledge it or not, the sentence does transmit meaning. To the sentenced person this meaning engenders both prescriptions for action and expectations for fulfilment of obligations. These arise both from the imposition and living of the sentence. The actions and reactions of sentenced people, judicial officers, correctional workers and others constitute the sentence in action.

A consequence of the acknowledgement that

> the discrepancy between the general assumptions about a disposition (held by criminal justice professionals) and the day to day reality of such decisions among criminal justice workers, makes examining the local culture of punishment important (Grey and Salole 2006, p. 661).

is that attention must be paid to the experiences of the sentenced. This "governmentality gap", that is,

> the lacuna in the existing penological scholarship which concerns the contingent relationships between changing governmental rationales and technologies, on the one hand and the construction of penality in practice on the other (McNeill et al. 2009, p. 419).

can only be illuminated by a close examination of not only the practices of criminal justice but also the experience of the subjects of criminal justice dispositions.

This book seeks to link the sentence and the result of that sentence: in particular in how it relates to risk and opportunities for rehabilitation. The main argument is that the aims of sentencing provide not only a philosophical guide to judicial officers but also an overarching rationale for the processes and practices which constitute the lived sentence. A primary contention is that the aims of sentencing contain significant subjective elements. In order to fulfil the aims of the sentence and satisfy the release authority, the sentenced person must demonstrate certain subjective states connected with and implicit in the aims of sentencing. The "subjective" requirements of sentencing, those often unsaid and non-explicit expectations that the prisoner demonstrate appropriately that he feel not only punished, denounced and separated from the community, but also feel rehabilitated, accountable to the community and attentive to the needs of victims, are the crux of what we expect the sentence to be about.

The use of the word "subjective" requires clarification. This concept is used here to describe the internal thoughts and consciousness of the individual being sentenced, not the narrower meaning of "subjective factors" used in sentencing. In addition, a distinction must be made between the "subjectivist" arguments about punishment (e.g., Kolber 2009; and for a rebuttal of this perspective, Gray 2010) and the theoretical position proposed here. The term is used in this work to illustrate the fact that, for example, the condition of being remanded in custody is little different for the prisoner to being sentenced, despite the legal difference in their status arising from the presumption of innocence. In other words, the lived experience of the subject must be taken into account in the analysis. This is different from asserting that because of individual differences, punishments should be calibrated accordingly. Feeley (1979) has already noted the "seamlessness" of process and substantive law in criminal justice; this perspective is explored as it applies to the relationship between in-court sentencing and the experience of the sentence of imprisonment by the prisoner.

Much attention has recently been paid to public perceptions of sentencing, as it is felt that a lack of confidence in the process can diminish important aims of sentencing such as deterrence. The "community" clearly does not include the sentenced person whose views are rarely sought. Asking prisoners about their experience of sentencing and imprisonment is important from a practical point of view to assess efficacy; further, it is a matter of fairness that if sentencing is a communicative process, the communication is fully understood by all involved parties, particularly those who are subject to scrutiny and assessment as to their compliance with the strictures contained therein.

Imprisonment is the focus of this book, as it provides an opportunity to view the practical manifestation of sentencing in its most restrictive, powerful incarnation.[1] The question of the legitimacy of our instruments of punishment is inextricably related to the way the aims of sentencing are linked with the resulting structural and physical aspects (Sparks and Bottoms 1996). Perhaps more central to the main

[1] This is not to deny the punitive effects of other forms of punishment such as fines and probation.

argument, the importance of subjectivity in sentencing, the "meaningfulness of punishment" (Weaver and Armstrong 2011) requires the offender to be "accepting of the punishment in order to be able to respond and be receptive to the reproach communicated through the act of punishment" (Weaver and Armstrong 2011, p. 29). Concomitantly, the responsibility arguably cuts both ways, with the expectation of the provision of the means to fulfil these obligations. If prisoners are to be held to account, then it is incumbent on the sentencing and imprisoning body to first communicate clearly what these obligations are and, second, to provide the conditions under which this can be done.

The criminal justice system in NSW consists of a number of related but independent agencies. When it comes to sentencing, the courts operate as the lead agency. Clearly they do not have available to them "choices about the general purposes of punishment" (Duff and Garland, 1994, p. 16), having to choose from a limited menu of sanctions constrained by bureaucratic and political choices as enshrined in legislation and case law. Nevertheless the judicial officer, on the basis of an abundance of information about the offence and the offender (often not available to others concerned with implementing the sentence), hands down a sentence which, if one of imprisonment, comprises not only a term of years but also often includes recommendations as to treatment, rehabilitation and reparation to the victim as well as fulfilment of the other aims of sentencing.

Philosophy must be translated into action in sentencing and it is in the operationalisation of these aims that the true nature of the sentence is revealed. The relationship between the act of sentencing and the implementation of the sentence would appear straightforward and the aims of each agency should thus be in accordance with each other. Each step, however, has its own internal managerial "habitus" (Bourdieu 1980, p. 52) with adherence to internal priorities and exigencies unrelated to the other and, perhaps uniquely for public sector bodies with overlapping roles, very little communication between them. The Department of Corrective Services NSW (henceforth CSNSW) views itself as a "downstream" agency with little control over the flow of people through its doors (Sotiri 2003,

p. 173) and generally as the passive recipient of the waves of prisoners sent there each year. If an agency can be evaluated by the way it assesses itself, it would appear that the goals of CSNSW are more about security and safety, tangible and measurable goals, and not so much about implementing the philosophical aims of sentencing. The courts may similarly view themselves as having little agency in dealing with matters investigated by the police and prosecuted by the Department of Public Prosecutions (DPP) (and police in the Local Courts). They have also maintained a "hands off" policy when it comes to the serving of the sentence, holding that their role does not include interfering with the job of the executive (Edney 2002).

1.1 Core Hypotheses

The aim of this book is to document and theorise about the way that sentencing is operationalised. By relating what prisoners say about their experience of sentencing and imprisonment to official policy around the aims of sentencing and other related themes such as risk and rehabilitation, the result is an account of the way in which a group of prisoners reflect on their experiences of sentencing and imprisonment.

The central ideas arise from the contention that the sentence should be viewed in its totality, not just as a legal artefact but as a lived experience continuing throughout incarceration, conditional liberty and sometimes beyond. Another important premise is that the sentence contains certain conditions and expectations of the sentenced person. If sentencing is meant to be a communicative enterprise, the underpinnings of that communication are contained in the aims of sentencing. Further the communicative aspects of the sentence continue past the courtroom into the requirement that the sentenced person respond to the strictures of the sentence. A fundamental albeit unarticulated condition or expectation of sentencing is the requirement that the sentenced person undergo some kind of personal, transformative experience in response to the sentence. In the light of these expectations of personal transformation an understanding of the environment of the prison from the prisoners' point of view is important in identifying the barriers to redemption, restoration or rehabilitation.

Little attention is generally paid to the perceptions and understandings of the subjects of criminal justice processing. While it is important to identify the philosophy and practice of correctional authorities, it is in the voices of those who are the subjects of these processes that a fuller understanding of the barriers to the fulfilment of the aims of sentencing is to be found. In seeking to identify the elements of subjectivity contained in sentencing law, the experiences of prisoners of sentencing and imprisonment were sought. Semi-structured interviews were conducted with 30 prisoners serving medium to long sentences, in seven prisons which were mostly maximum security with one medium security wing.[2] In an open-ended but basically chronological interview process, prisoners were encouraged to speak about the sentencing process and their subsequent experience of the processes of imprisonment. Methodological perspectives which emphasise subjectivity were useful in preparing for interviews and analysing data.

One of the major aims is to emphasise the continuous and related nature of the sentencing process and the serving of the sentence. The difficult task of bringing together the "habitus" of law with that of corrections was therefore attempted. Beginning with a socio-political analysis of criminal justice in NSW (Chap. 2), legal analysis of sentencing law (Chap. 3), a degree of policy analysis (Chap. 5) and theoretical and policy analysis of the influential paradigms of risk and rehabilitation throughout, the book utilises a mixed method approach, placing interview data in context, together with an examination of sentencing law and correctional policy in NSW.

Care was taken in the data collection phase of the project to allow prisoners to express those matters which they perceived as important to them, and although a broad question guide was used the open-ended nature of the process allowed them to focus on what was important to them. Although there was a high level of consistency among their comments in many areas, some emphasised the "in-court" phase of

[2] Although for the visitor, it is often difficult to tell the difference as medium-security prisons in NSW still have a high-security wall and similar restrictions on access.

their sentence, some were more interested in talking about the way the sentence was operationalised.

Only male prisoners were interviewed as the aim was to provide a picture of mainstream imprisonment in NSW, women constituting only a small minority of prisoners. Women suffer particular and specific disadvantage in the NSW prison system and it was felt that the scope of the project would not allow a proper analysis of their position.[3] There was also no attempt to check what prisoners said against the official record as the aim was to foreground their concerns. Their responses have been placed in the context of an examination of the aims of sentencing and the sentencing process in the light of the subjective elements therein: the local context of criminal justice in NSW, the managerial and individualistic focus of CSNSW and the conceptualisations of risk and rehabilitation which substantially inform the way the sentence is operationalised.

As a highly contextualised practice, the meaning of sentencing and imprisonment is temporally determined and is a product of the time and place in which they occur. As the culmination of a process of assessment of information about the offence and the offender, sentencing is the most visible and controversial aspect of modern criminal justice. Thus, an essential part of the analysis is consideration of the socio-political context of sentencing and imprisonment as practised specifically within NSW.

Rather than a legally constrained event, the sentence is also a collection of socially mediated and constructed practices carried out by various criminal justice functionaries as well as by the prisoner himself. These practices have an empirical character in that they can be seen, experienced and assessed. In relating the sentence as handed down by the court to the sentence as experienced by the prisoner, it is necessary to examine the social institutions such as the prison and those who work within it to conceive of the way in which the sentence is operationalised and made into a real, experiential artefact.

---

[3] The pronoun 'he' is used throughout for this reason.

As Garland and Young (1984b, p. 15) point out, it is important to note that the penal realm "is not a singular coherent unit". The multiplicities of different practices undertaken within the prison are carried out by a range of different occupational groups and institutions within the criminal justice system, with different habitus (Bourdieu 1980). All of these function to transform the sentence from legal artefact to a lived experience with content and consequences for those living it. Further, rather than analysing these practices in their own terms it is important to consider "their operative function, their strategic effects and conditions which allowed these and not other knowledges to become empowered" (Garland and Young 1984b, p. 170).

Linking the practice of sentencing as it is conceived and practised in the courts as a discrete event beginning and ending in the confines of the courtroom, and the actual visceral, experienced sentence as served by the prisoner, a number of preliminary steps must be carried out. The first step in the analysis is an examination of the connection between the content and meaning of the aims of sentencing to the serving of the sentence. A distinction between this perspective and the justification for the sentence by the judicial officer or the philosophical underpinnings of sentencing is made. Chapter 3 commences with an examination of each of the aims of sentencing with particular attention to the subjective requirements contained therein. By drawing out some of the implicit but perhaps unacknowledged expectations which arise from the general normative principles of sentencing and which underpin the ultimate assessment of the success or failure of the individual prisoner, it is hoped that a more realistic and reciprocal picture can be drawn of the serving of the sentence. It is recognised, however, that drawing a direct line between the criteria in section 3A of the *Crimes (Sentencing Procedure) Act* 1999 NSW (which reflect the kind of philosophical principles used to justify punishment in general) and the types of processes and procedures involved in imprisonment would ignore the socially mediated nature of imprisonment.

It is argued that these general principles not only embody societal justifications for punishment but also a whole set of expectations of the prisoner that need to be articulated and explained. Despite recognition of the complex and mediated nature of the relationship between the aims of sentencing and their implementation, it is important to make the "subjective" expectations arising from the philosophical/normative aims of punishment/sentencing more explicit as the prisoner is ultimately assessed on the basis of his capacity to address them.

The operationalised aims of sentencing constitute the process by which meaning is invested in the legal sanction. To conceive of the means of punishment as somehow independent of the legal process that not only precedes them temporally but also gives them meaning and content is to disembody punishment and deny it meaning beyond the limited managerial aims of custodial organisations. This is evident in the trend towards "warehousing" of prisoners so prevalent in high imprisoning nations like the USA (Irwin 2004) and is arguably the logical result of uncoupling the instruments and processes of punishment from their philosophical and, thus, moral basis. Conversely, to disconnect the formal legal process of sentencing from the sentence as served, underpinned as it is by philosophical aims and principles, is to deprive it of a material, visceral "real-world" form, leaving empty, abstract words without real meaning beyond the time and place in which they are spoken. This is not to say that the disconnection of the judicial act of sentencing from its consequences does not have some functional purpose. Apart from the constitutional aspects of the separation of powers, this disconnection allows the courts to practise a type of "imaginary sentencing" (Tombs in Carlen 2008, p. 84) by which sentencers can prescribe remedies to be carried out without any thought to the practical consequences or any need to monitor or evaluate their efficacy.

Weaving through judicial statements on sentencing are the elements of risk and dangerousness which, while always a part of sentencing, have acquired new meaning and prominence due to the wholesale adoption of actuarial measurement in the correctional system and the enactment of preventive detention legislation (see discussion in Chap. 2). Considerations of risk run through the sentencing process, and it is important to attempt to gauge the effect on the way the aims of sentencing are operationalised, particularly on the aim of "rehabilitation". Assessing the effect of actuarial risk assessment on the practices of sentencers in NSW is a difficult task, and leads to the following questions: if risk assessment has changed the form of rehabilitation (as argued later in Chap. 7), have sentencers caught up with this change? Is there any dissonance between the way rehabilitation is conceived by the courts and what is practised as a result of their sentences?

While sentencers may feel that they have balanced the aims of sentencing in a way which reflects the individual and the case before them, factors beyond the control of either the courts or the sentenced person can tip the balance in ways that are not monitored or officially recognised. For example, while appeal courts may give limited recognition to the conditions in which the prisoner serves the sentence, a sentence served in strict protection with limited access to programmes and services will emphasise the punitive and denunciatory goals while often interfering with the rehabilitative and victim-awareness goals. Those non-citizen prisoners who will be deported at the end of the custodial portion of their sentence may be denied access to rehabilitative services thus making their sentences more about denunciation and incapacitation than any of the more restorative goals. In the light of the subjective expectations which sentencing places on prisoners, it is instructive to examine how they perceive the processes to which they are subjected during imprisonment and how they impact the prisoner's ability to negotiate the system.

The subjective experiences of the prisoner in the sentencing process, including the issue of "remorse" which, it is argued, persists as an important consideration throughout the sentencing and imprisonment process, are then examined. In a practical sense, the requirements identified in the previous chapter need to be communicated to the sentenced person in order that they can attend to those parts of the sentence which require action on their part. Obvious though this may seem, the way that courts and trials are structured often militates against this and the practical difficulties experienced by sentenced people in apprehending what is required of them are magnified where the penalty is imprisonment.

It is in the way that the system communicates with the prisoner and the way that the prisoner responds that the sentence is really carried out. Communicative theories of punishment (most notably Duff 2004) highlight the importance of a reciprocal understanding of the reasons for the punishment and clear communication of what is expected from the subject of the punishment in response to it. This places the obligation as a reciprocal one—if the punished person is required to perform certain acts and undergo certain internal transformations, then the State in its turn is obliged to make these expectations clear and unequivocal and further, provide conditions which foster the achievement of these aims. The important but little considered role of remorse and its demonstration is highly relevant to these subjective expectations and provides a continuous link between the subjective requirements of the sentencing process and those of the subsequent processes of imprisonment.

While sentencers routinely speak of the conflicting nature of the goals of sentencing, there is little acknowledgement of how confusing this can be for the individual prisoner who is often suffering from a myriad of social if not mental or physical disabilities. Any failure is the prisoner's and the prisoner's alone. The high level of discretion practised within prisons and the lack of oversight and accountability as to the processes of discipline and management contributes to the invisibility of the processes of imprisonment.

Release is not automatic in NSW for prisoners with sentences over 3 years and relies inter alia on a process by which the individual prisoner and the sentence as served is examined as to the compliance of the individual with the objects of the sentence. In fact, although strictly speaking indeterminate sentences in NSW are now restricted to those found not guilty by virtue of mental illness,[4] the way the parole system operates may lead to a similar indeterminacy given the uncertainty as to release, expressed in the term "earliest possible release date" or EPRD currently used by CSNSW staff to refer to the end of the non-parole period. While prisoners cannot be detained beyond the upper level of the sentence, many do not obtain release at the EPRD. The relatively recent and comparatively rare implementation of preventive detention for sex offenders provides another exception to determinate sentencing and, as in the case of the existence of high security "supermax" units, provides a powerful disciplinary tool in the abstract for use by correctional authorities with prisoners who otherwise may be reluctant to comply with compulsory "rehabilitative" programming.

[4] Outside of a small number of life sentence prisoners under s18 *Crimes Act 1900.*

Many of the prisoners' comments related to the processes and procedures of the system and the way in which these either facilitated or hindered the carrying out of the sentence. The importance of an examination of the actual practices carried out as a result of the legal event of sentencing, as opposed to the official rhetoric around which the legal sentencing process is arranged, is placed in sharp relief when the subject of the sentence is assessed as to his compliance with the strictures of the sentence. It is then that the legal artefact of the sentence becomes transformed by the decision-making body. It becomes a checklist where the compliance of the prisoner or sentenced person with the instructions implicit in the judge's words is made, with the reward being release from incarceration. This highlights the necessity of viewing the sentence as a complex range of interrelated, but also at times conflicting events and practices, arising from the practical consequences of the act of being sentenced, serving the sentence and being released from the sentence. The sentence is often conceptualised as an onward journey, where the prisoner passes through a number of stages, culminating in minimum security, day or work release and eventual conditional release on parole. In reality, many of the managerial practices, and the interpersonal or relational factors, can be conceptualised as bumps in the road or sometimes outright detours in this metaphorical journey.

When the prisoner begins serving a sentence of imprisonment there is little or no oversight until the approach of the earliest release date. Internal processes such as classification and case management (and the Serious Offenders Review Council for serious offenders) provide the only mechanisms by which the ongoing progress of the sentence is monitored. As these processes may not have as their primary purpose monitoring and ensuring that the sentence reflects and contains the strictures of the sentence as outlined in court (e.g., classification also has a major focus on internal management matters such as security), it cannot be assumed without examining the actual practices of sentencing and imprisonment that the sentence as handed down by the courts is related to the sentence as carried out by CSNSW.

In an era of measurement and evaluation, it is surprising that more attention is not paid to the methods by which the sentence is carried out by correctional authorities. The only evaluation appears to be performed in the way the prisoner responds to the strictures of the sentence; any evaluation of the processes by which the sentence is operationalised by correctional authorities is absent. This is not the case with courts based on "therapeutic jurisprudential" principles such as drug courts, where an appreciation of the importance of process has resulted in a type of judicial oversight of the "sentence" (although legally the person may not have been formally sentenced). It remains to be seen whether this innovative type of justice will have any influence on mainstream practices; some of the aims of sentencing in NSW (s3 (e) and (g) of the *Crimes (Sentencing Procedure) Act* NSW 1999 in particular) have a rather "therapeutic jurisprudential" air to them, and may presage some change in this.

While there has been an overall trend towards the evaluation of criminal justice processes in keeping with a managerial focus throughout the public sector since the 1980s, evaluation of the processes of sentencing and imprisonment is at best partial without the input of the people who are the subject of these dispositions. The rise of punitive populism around criminal justice in NSW may underpin the evident reluctance to listen to the subjects of sentencing about the efficacy of the processes to which they are subjected, due to the demonisation and "othering" of prisoners. This failure, however, arguably affects the ability of the criminal justice system to not only undertake appropriate assessment and evaluation but also to develop responses which will be appropriate to carry out the ultimate aims of the system.

This is not to say that the symbolic and expressive functions of our system of justice and punishment should be relegated to a secondary position behind considerations of efficiency and cost, but that any evaluation of the system should be undertaken from a baseline of the overall aims of punishment in NSW and taking into account information from those who are the subject of these dispositions. Thus, issues previously relegated to the status of process issues can be foregrounded, in keeping with the reality that the process is often the punishment (Feeley 1979) and, in the case of imprisonment, the way in which the punishment is carried out. For the prisoner, the sentence may begin in the courtroom but is constituted in reality in a myriad of processes, systems and relationships, which persist throughout incarceration and beyond. In recognising this reality it is necessary to examine the processes of imprisonment through the lens of the prisoner serving the sentence.

Reflecting the findings of other prison researchers, most notably Liebling (2004), prisoners in this study often framed the narratives of their sentencing and imprisonment in interpersonal terms, reflecting the importance of the human aspects of imprisonment in any consideration of the way the sentence is carried out. Prisoners highlighted the importance of the relational aspects of imprisonment. It is in the everyday interactions between prisoners and prison staff, amongst themselves and with their families and friends, that the reality of the sentence is experienced. It is not surprising that Liebling's relationship "dimensions" (Liebling 2004) inflected all of the responses of prisoners, whether the question was asked directly or not, the message is clear—prisoners wish to be treated with respect, humanity and trust and are more likely to respond in kind if they are.

The complexity of dimensions of ethnicity and sexuality in the prison context are also examined. Ethnicity emerged as a prominent theme for many of the prisoners interviewed. The effect of the absence of citizenhood on the way the sentence is served arguably arises from the lack of a rehabilitative narrative for these prisoners. Other dimensions of ethnicity include the formation of ethnic "gangs", officially imposed in one prison and the narratives of prisoners in this study reflect the importance of relationships with people of similar cultural backgrounds in coping with imprisonment.

Bringing together conceptions of risk and rehabilitation with some of the experiences of prisoners, Chap. 7 rounds out the discussion of the transformation of rehabilitation, arguably one of the most important aims of sentencing. Rehabilitation is foundational to the achievement of other aims, such as protection of the community. The way that the rehabilitative ideal has been transformed is one of the most interesting examples of the impact of "science" on punishment. While the impact of Martinson's "nothing works" may have been more muted here than in the USA, reliance on so-called evidence-based practice has seen the ascendance of the "what works" movement[5] which relies on scientific

[5] Characterised by Nutley and Davies (in Nutley 2000, p. 108) as possessing an "evangelical like zeal".

measurement (of re-offending rates) as the gold standard, and referral to programmes on the basis of actuarial risk assessment.

The centrality of risk assessment and the relationship of current conceptions of risk to the way the sentence is operationalised is exemplified by the recent prominence of the relatively new practice of actuarial risk assessment in determining the way that the sentence will be served. This necessitates an examination of the conceptions of risk that underpin current correctional practice and the way that these have been adopted by the courts and the prison and the way that rehabilitation is currently conceived and practised in NSW. Reliance on risk assessment and the provision of generic, offence-specific programmes which aim to reduce risk to the point where release can be recommended is a prominent feature of current correctional administration in NSW. It is argued that both risk and reconfigured notions of rehabilitation are factors that can mould and shape the sentence beyond other considerations and they underpin and dominate the way the aims of sentencing are operationalised.

Thus, the sentence must be conceived as an ongoing series of processes carried out by a range of people and subject to a range of organisational limitations. The aims of sentencing, traditionally expressed in broad philosophical terms, are not only a guide for the judiciary in handing down an appropriate term of years but are also a template for the production of actions and reactions on the part of the penal system and, more importantly for this book, the sentenced person. It is in the operationalisation of the aims of sentencing that the sentence is brought to life as a series of practices, which operate in the life of the sentenced person and which contribute to the success or failure of the response to criminal behaviour.

Somewhat surprisingly, as Garland and Young point out, this philosophical detailing of the aims of punishment "is not in the least concerned with the specifics and mundane details of penal action" (Garland and Young 1984b, p. 11); it is rarely concerned with utilising these principles to "critique the existing system" (Garland and Young 1984b, p. 11). This book attempts such a task, which can only be carried out by observing and recording the actual experience of the "sentence as served" and comparing these accounts with the principles underpinning the sentencing process.

By the same token, it is acknowledged that the complexity and multifaceted nature of the "penal realm" (Garland and Young, 1984b, p. 15) necessitates an acknowledgement of the "institutional differentiation" found within the field of criminal justice. The impossibility of conceiving of a single theory or even a cluster of theories, which could account for the practical manifestation of sentencing and penality however, does not preclude an attempt to draw out and explain the relationship between the different stages and steps in the process. Rather, it provides a cautionary note to any attempt to directly connect the broad philosophical framework, which has been provided in NSW sentencing legislation by the enactment of section 3A of the *Crimes (Sentencing Procedure) Act NSW 1999*, with the actual operation of the processes of punishment such as imprisonment. As Garland explains in his examination of the death penalty in the USA, the aim is to

> understand what is really going on, to learn to see things from the point of view of the participants and the social world they occupy . . . rather than engage in the legal and normative debates that swirl around . . . this approach regards these debates as an intrinsic part of the institution and analyses them accordingly (Garland 2010, p. 14).

In the vast majority of matters dealt with in the courts of NSW, there is a perception that when the court rises, this is the end of the "sentencing process". In reality, if a term of imprisonment is imposed, when the prisoner enters the correctional system to begin serving the sentence he is subjected to processes of sorting, assessment and classification, often now based on a system of risk assessment which relies on actuarial methods.

These techniques have been widely adopted in various sectors of the criminal justice system, including sentencing (to a limited extent), correctional programming and parole. Often occurring quite independently of the courts, these processes are most often related to the organisational imperatives of the correctional system. This means that, rather than being in keeping with the aims of sentencing, the sentence as served may bear little relationship to that envisaged by the judge by the time it has been modified by these mediating processes. To obtain a picture of the operation of the agencies of criminal justice it is sometimes necessary to examine the relationship, or the lack thereof, between the uninterrogated processes of criminal justice. It is in these gaps, these dark places, that the reality of the difference between rhetoric and practice can be perceived.

Documenting the way prisoners experience their sentencing, the managerial processes involved in serving the sentence and their perceptions of the availability of assistance to fulfil the aims of the sentence, including the often unstated but vitally important subjective expectations, has provided another dimension to the discussions around the efficacy of our criminal justice processes. Analysis of the types of factors assisting and hindering access to rehabilitation, the relationship between risk assessment and rehabilitation and the overall relationship between sentencing and the prison system is clearly vital to any proper evaluation of the efficacy of the criminal justice response to crime.

2

The Socio-Political Context of Imprisonment in New South Wales

2.1 Introduction

Criminal justice, and penal policy in particular, is inextricably woven with the particular social, economic and cultural circumstances in which these practices are embedded (Lacey 2008, p. 45). This chapter aims to provide a historical and socio-political background to the discussion of sentencing, risk and rehabilitation undertaken in this book and to place in context the experiences of the prisoners interviewed. The relevance of understanding the socio-legal context in which the sentence is served lies in the need to understand the lived sentence as more than an individual behavioural artefact. As a complex interaction of individuals with various legal and socio-political understandings of punishment present throughout the carceral system, the sentence is a collaborative affair. Attention to the local, to the specific details of the manifestations of criminal justice policy is essential to avoid an overly determined, "sweeping and generalised" account and to reflect the presence of both change and continuity in philosophy and practice (D. Brown 2005, p. 26).

M. Hall, *The Lived Sentence*, Palgrave Studies in Prisons and Penology, DOI 10.1007/978-3-319-45038-4_2

To attempt a synthesis of the various legislative, policy and penal narratives of the past four decades risks emphasising the extraordinary over the more mundane and ordinary continuities. By summarising and decontextualising these events they may lose some of their subtler nuances. Examining the various legislative and policy discourses and practices which have worked to shape criminal justice in NSW within a framework that analyses events and disjunctures in penality necessitates acknowledgement of the continuities and contradictions therein.[1] David Brown points out that accounts of contemporary penality that "accentuate rupture and change" ignore the imperfect nature of the implementation of many policy directions (D. Brown 2003, p. 37). Simplistic notions of social change and deterministic social explanations for the complex phenomena of penal policy and culture can emphasise the extraordinary and particular features of the discontinuities in penal policy and practice at the expense of the often more relevant continuities of the nature of imprisonment.

This chapter begins with an overview of the major enquiries relevant to penal policy, followed by a discussion of some of the major policy changes and socio-political currents impacting these changes, and their effect on penal and criminal justice policy. A summary of the major legislative changes in sentencing, bail and parole is followed by an analysis of the effect of the "risk" paradigm in NSW criminal justice.

Whilst the choice of a starting point must inevitably be somewhat arbitrary, the 1970s represented a turning point in the penal history of Australia due to the confluence of a number of strong social currents, both within and outside prisons, culminating in the Nagle Royal Commission into Prisons in NSW (Chan 1992, p. 28). The comprehensive nature of the resulting *Report of the Royal Commission into the Operation of the Prison System* (1978) chaired by Justice Nagle ("the Nagle Report") and the breadth of the recommendations it contained ensure that it retains relevance even to current criminal justice policy.

[1] For example, the rehabilitative focus strongly identified with the 1970s was present in the practice, if not in official policy, of many who worked in prisons from the 1940s onwards.

2.2 Major Enquiries

The *Report of the Royal Commission into New South Wales Prisons* (1978) was the watershed criminal justice event of this era.[2] The crisis situation in NSW gaols manifested by riots, strikes and allegations of brutality accompanied broader social changes outside the prison, highlighting human rights concerns and creating the opportunity to "turn the violent circumstances of Bathurst in to an inquest . . . on the whole approach of prisons administration" (Finnane and Woodyatt 2002, p. 99). The Nagle Report provided a vindication of prisoners' complaints of brutality, while at the same time disappointing many by the subsequent absence of legal action against the perpetrators of the brutality.

The most immediate positive change was the virtual end of institutionalised violence by prison officers (D. Brown 2005, p. 35). However there was an almost immediate backlash against these improvements by sections of the media, fed by the vehement opposition of the prison officers union. As Zdenkowski and Brown (1982, p. 268) point out, "within a day of the release . . . (of the report) the Daily Telegraph was rewriting the record . . . excusing and legitimating massive acts of state violence". Chan (1992, p. 28) argues that the major significance of the Nagle Report was to legitimise the rhetoric of reform not only for the implementation of the recommendations but also for subsequent policy initiatives.

Justice Nagle devoted just one chapter to women. As Zdenkowski and Brown point out there may have been small numbers of women in prison at the time of Nagle but "the mental institutions are bulging with women" (Zdenkowski and Brown 1982, p. 148). In a climate of political action by women in the early 1980s, assisted by sympathetic bureaucrats, the concerns of the numerically small but vastly disadvantaged women's

[2] Important enquiries on matters ancillary but relating to the prison system were: Woodward in 1979 (*Royal Commission into Drug Trafficking* 1977-9), making limited inroads into police corruption, Wood (*Royal Commission into the NSW Police Service* 1995–7) which finally uncovered some of the deep systemic corruption within the NSW police alleged by prisoners since Nagle and the 1993 ICAC *Police informants: a discussion paper on the nature and management of the relationship between police and informers* (ICAC 1993).

prison population were canvassed thoroughly in the Women in Prison Task Force Report and then largely ignored for almost a decade.

The Task Force found that most women within prison are not violent offenders and therefore pose a lower risk to the community. There were an abnormally high proportion of women on remand (NSW Women in Prison Task Force Report 1985, p. 42) and the Task Force recommended that the number of women inmates should be kept below 100 (Baldry 2004). The rate of female incarceration in NSW increased dramatically between July 1994 and June 1999, reflected in the remand and sentenced population rising from a daily average of 291–412 between January 1995 and January 2000, an increase of 41.6 % (Select Committee on the Increase in Prisoner Population 2001, p. 10).

The implementation of the Richmond Report (NSW Department of Health 1983) recommendations—for the deinstitutionalisation of people with mental illness, the closure of the large psychiatric institutions and the management of the mentally ill in the community—has had far-reaching effects on the criminal justice system (although the process of deinstitutionalisation had begun prior to Richmond). The lack of long-term secure care and support for the most disadvantaged of this group saw many homeless and committing low-level offences. Coupled with decreased tolerance for this type of offence (evidenced by the reintroduction of summary offence type legislation in the late 1980s and increases in police powers), mentally ill people began "cycling" (Baldry et al. 2006) through prisons. The prevalence of intellectual disability among prisoners has also increased, often with coexisting problems of drug use and mental distress, if not mental illness in the legal sense.

A recent review of Chap. 5 of the *Mental Health Act 1990* (NSW) and related matters under the *Mental Health (Criminal Procedure) Act 1990* (NSW) has increased the power of the Mental Health Review Tribunal to authorise release (James 2007); however some of more draconian provisions impacting on those with mental illness remain.[3] Within the correctional

[3] Most notably the lack of any provision for the setting of a non-parole period for those found unfit to plead and given a limiting term under s23(1) after a special hearing under s19(2) of the *Mental Health (Criminal Procedure)* Act 1990. See *R v Mailes* (2004) 62 NSWLR 181 at [22] [43].

system recent improvements to conditions in some areas, the new Justice Health facility at Long Bay in particular, must be balanced against evidence in individual cases of the effects of Supermax conditions on inmates with a mental illness.[4]

The Royal Commission into Aboriginal Deaths in Custody (RCIADC), established in 1987 and reporting in 1991 (RCIADC, 1991), was a national enquiry into the reason for the high numbers of deaths in custody of indigenous people. By default, it became an enquiry into the imprisonment of indigenous people generally and highlighted systemic problems. The Commission found that while Aboriginal people were not dying in custody at a rate greater than non-Aboriginal people, their overrepresentation in custody was a result of disadvantage and inequality (Cunneen 1997, p. 4). The Commission found a culture of racism and neglect of basic human rights in the treatment of indigenous people by police and custodial authorities. One important outcome, which had ramifications for the entire prison population, were the findings regarding breach of duty of care on the part of correctional authorities and police (Cunneen 1997, p. 4). While no charges were laid, some clarity over the responsibility of police and other relevant organisations to ensure that their duty of care is fulfilled was achieved. Cunneen argues that any impetus for reform as discernible in the immediate post-Nagle period was long gone by the time the Commission handed down its report and he assesses most of the reforms resulting from the RCIADC to be "programmatic and administrative" (Cunneen 2004, p. 100).

Despite the exhaustive efforts of the RCIADC, the numbers and rates of indigenous imprisonment throughout Australia continue to climb upwards. The most alarming increase has been among young indigenous women, from 21 % of all women prisoners in 1996 to 30 % in 2006 (Australian Bureau of Statistics, 2006 in Baldry 2009, p. 20). In NSW courts, a distancing from legal doctrines which came some way to recognising the structural

[4] For example, the HREOC submission to the coronial inquest into the death of Scott Ashley Simpson in 2004 http://www.hreoc.gov.au/legal/submissions_court/intervention/simpson.html.

disadvantage experienced by Aboriginal people (known as the *Fernando* principles[5]) has been evident (Anthony 2008, p. 14).

The Legislative Council Inquiry into the Reasons for the Increases in the Prison Population (Legislative Council of NSW 2001) was the first post-Nagle general enquiry into the state's prisons. The Interim report looked specifically at the effectiveness of incarceration as a response to women's criminality and other similar issues (Legislative Council of NSW 2000). Further evidence of the highly disadvantaged backgrounds of female prisoners and the advantages of developing alternatives to incarceration led to the Committee recommending a moratorium on the building of a new women's prison until a serious exploration of ways to reduce the number of women being sent to prison had been completed (Baldry 2004).

The Final Report found that 65 % of inmates in NSW prisons were serving sentences of 6 months or less, recommending that these be abolished completely and the Sentencing Council of NSW echoed these recommendations. Factors responsible for the growth of the NSW prison population were found to be the increased use of remand, longer sentences and increased police activity (Roth 2007, p. 22). As for the political response to this "rational, democratic and well-researched" report, it was "immediately repudiated by both the government and opposition in a bipartisan response which showed clearly the very real political limits to claims of "non-ideological, "evidence-led" policy formation in the law and order area" (Brown and Willkie 2002, p. xxi).

2.3 Popular Sensibilities and Penal Politics

The intensification of the climate of popular punitiveness in the mid-1980s as a "backlash against the reform period" (Brown and Willkie 2002, p. xix) was preceded by a mixed period of limited reform and increasing watering down of political will to temper the rising tide of popular punitiveness. A growing focus on victims addressed strong community concerns about the treatment of, in particular, vulnerable victims such as children and female victims of

[5] *R v Fernando* (1992) 76 A Crim R 58.

male violence. Other currents of popular concern were fanned by concerns about escapes, and a focus on particularly violent and abhorrent crimes. While prison escapes have often fuelled populist cries for stricter security, increasingly the fear of political fallout from such events has become so acute that escapes from custody are much less frequent (since 1980 the rate of escapes has dropped 95 %), but the rate of escapes from maximum security prisons has remained steady between 1979 and 2004 (Clark et al., 2006). As these figures demonstrate, the majority of escapes have always been from medium or minimum security prisons. Despite this, the use of escape numbers as a performance assessment tool has led to increased attention to security by correctional administration.

The media has concerned itself in a highly selective way with the deficiencies of criminal justice. In the "hysteria provoking tone" (Lumby 2002, p. 110) of reporting on the release of high-profile, especially hated categories of prisoners in the latter part of the period, the media has, at many points in the period under study, provided a focal point for the expression of deeper fears. The culmination of this intensification of popular sentiment about crime and punishment came with the election of the Greiner government, heralding the unprecedented dominance of the Minister for Corrective Services, Michael Yabsley, in a radical, ideology-based change of the criminal justice system and sentencing in particular. His "Truth in Sentencing" regime (a misnomer according to Brown and others) and an avowed intention to "put the value back in to punishment" (Michael Yabsley, October 1990, as cited by O'Neill 1990) led to widespread restrictions throughout the prison system for example on property and visits. The abolition of remissions caused huge management problems and the longer sentences that resulted caused critical overcrowding problems. Radical reforms to every aspect of sentencing and criminal justice administration led to an immediate increase in prisoner numbers, and changes in focus from remissions to defined sentences changed the way prisoners were managed in the system. Work was privileged over other forms of activity as the most effective rehabilitative mechanism, just as some of the early programmes, such as the Special Care Unit and the new management regime at

Bathurst, were starting to develop. The effect on the prison system was to "decisively reverse the reforms introduced following the Nagle Royal Commission" (D. Brown 1991, p. 28).

Following the enactment of the *Sentencing Act* in 1989 the influx of prisoners caused yet another near crisis for the department. Correctional staff were simply overwhelmed by the numbers of prisoners. By 1990, levels of community supervision were reduced from 56 % to 31.8 % of offenders (Simpson and Griffith 1999, p. 2). An increase of 50 days in the average sentence led to an increase of 525 prisoners per day (Simpson and Griffith 1999, p. 2).

The continuing absence of a strong, consistent philosophical rationale for the work of the department (Sotiri 2003, p. 394) was also identified by Nagle as a problem (Dawes in Brown and Wilkie 2002, p. 118). Along with the politicisation of criminal justice and the ensuing political pressure on senior management, this absence has resulted in a defensive, closed culture, with an aversion to publicity engendered by escapes, unrest and industrial activity.

This was not a unitary process however, as those techniques of control such as probation supervision began to be seen as ways in which the reach of the prison could be extended. Developing acceptance of so-called sentencing alternatives such as probation, community service, treatment and rehabilitation is evident throughout the 1970s and 1980s. A concomitant movement towards longer sentences, concentration on repeat offenders and restrictions on bail resulted in a huge expansion in the use of prison even as other sentencing options were being developed.

The department, permanently scarred by Nagle and with a difficult relationship with its own past, constantly seeks to redefine itself by virtue of what it is not (Sotiri 2003, p. 249). In the process, lacking a vision of what it is, managerial and security-based concerns have filled the void. A truly "volatile and contradictory" approach (O'Malley 1999) prevailed as the rise of punitive populist sentiments throughout the 1980s led to an increased political sensitivity about crime, with simultaneous implementation of some of the reforms recommended by Nagle. Damage to public confidence in criminal justice generally in NSW clearly grew during this period.

The significance of prisoner activism in the impetus which resulted in the Nagle inquiry and in the many themes and concerns, which coalesce around prisoner rights, must be acknowledged, although such activism is absent from the modern correctional landscape. Industrial action by prison officers has been an important factor in shaping the way prisons are run in NSW, from the concerted campaign in the 1980s to halt the process of reform under Tony Vinson, to the latest moves towards privatisation by the department with the added benefit of reducing the power of the union. Both these extremes represent the central role of those working in the system in the maintenance and reproduction of penality in NSW. The dominance of security concerns which characterises the current regime in part owes its genesis and maintenance to recognition of the undesirable political consequences of losing control over prisoners and prison officers.

Scrutiny by external bodies has recently been reduced, the most notable example being the abolition of the Office of the Inspectorate in 2003. It may be that NSW consequently will be unable to comply with the obligations imposed by the United Nations Optional Protocol against Torture (D. Brown 2009).[6] Privatisation is again on the agenda with the taking over of Parklea Correctional Centre by GEO in 2008, the second privately run prison since Junee opened in 1994. As the Assistant Director Learning and Staff Development, CSNSW points out "In NSW, the Department has used the spectre of privatisation to trial a series of operational reforms in its newly constructed prisons at Kempsey and Windsor" (Griffith and Edwards 2009, p. 4). This illustrates the continued relevance of industrial relations concerns to prison policy.

2.4 Expansion of the Prison Estate

Rates of incarceration have risen higher in each decade since the 1970s, with the exception of a short period in 1972–1973 (NSW Department of Corrective Services Annual Report 1974/1975) and in the early 1980s

[6] The Attorney General, Greg Smith has recently announced that the Inspectorate will be re-established.

(NSW Department of Corrective Services Annual Report 1982/1983). Rates of incarceration rose 51 % in the 3 years prior to 1991. Despite an overall increase since 1991, the rate fell 8 % between 2010 and 2011 to 177.7 per 100,000 (Australian Bureau of Statistics 2011). Recently, prisoner numbers in NSW have again begun to climb, with the Bureau of Crime Statistics and Research predicting a 17 % increase by March 2015 to 12,500 prisoners. (Weatherburn et al. 2014), despite "dramatic falls in the incidence of most major categories of crime" (Weatherburn et al. 2014, p. 6).

While the Nagle Report led to many improvements in prisoner conditions, it was the destruction of Bathurst Gaol, where conditions had been especially harsh, which spurred the biggest rebuilding undertaken in the early part of the period under study. The opening of the starkly modern Katingal Prison which relied on isolation to control troublesome inmates provided a new focus for concern for prison activists and was quickly closed. The need for a woman-specific prison led to the opening of Mulawa in 1980, in a collection of partially renovated former Health Department buildings.

Improvements in physical conditions such as those recommended by Justice Nagle required prison-building programmes and led to a growth in the penal estate. Subsequently, the 1990s saw the biggest prison expansion project in a century following a period of serious overcrowding after the enactment of the Sentencing Act in 1989. Beginning with Parklea in 1985 (the first new prison built in NSW in almost 100 years) and Junee Prison in 1994, new prisons have been constructed regularly in NSW ever since. What Baldry describes as the "reification" of the penal estate at the expense of community services (Baldry 2007, p. 2) is most forcefully demonstrated by the huge expenditure on prison building. The problems created by the construction of prisons in remote country areas (for example, difficulties in recruiting professional staff and in family visits) are reflected by the large number of prisoner complaints to the Ombudsman from these centres (Office of the NSW Ombudsman, 2008, p. 124).

The refurbishment of a section of Goulburn into a "Supermax" prison, recently gazetted as a separate prison, demonstrates the continuation of the practice of segregation of problematic inmates under especially restrictive conditions, not so different from Katingal (Zdenkowski and Brown 1982, p. 218). In recent times, the placement of especially demonised prisoners there (such as Ivan Milat and Bilal Skaf) has arguably diminished the opportunity for mobilisation of public sentiment against such extreme measures.[7] Recently the NSW Ombudsman found that the Department of Corrective Services had instituted a Behaviour Management Unit at the new Wellington Correctional Centre similar to previous programmes where the Ombudsman found that inmates had been "illegally segregated" (Office of the NSW Ombudsman 2008, p. 125). The programme was closed soon after the Ombudsman began the investigation.

2.5 Transmission/Extension of Penal Relations

It would be possible to construct quite disparate dichotomies of intent throughout the past 40 years: a concern with rehabilitation and treatment in the latter part of the 1970s (or earlier according to Chan), alongside more punitive currents developing in the 1980s leading to longer sentences and more bail refusals, an awareness of the need for a human rights-based perspective when dealing with imprisoned populations, alongside a reduction in the actual avenues of action open to prisoners to challenge the conditions of their imprisonment. The situation is much more complex than this and the development of so-called alternatives to imprisonment while a dominant thread throughout the period of study was, in practice, often an instrumental adoption by correctional administration in NSW of the ideology of prison as a last resort.

> Last resort gained prominence in the early 1980's in NSW penal reform discourse because when this ideology was translated in to a policy of reducing the prison population it was beneficial to the political and economic interests of the corrective services (Chan 1992, p. 43).

[7] Although the coronial enquiry into the death of Scott Ashley Simpson in 2001 indicates that vulnerable and mentally ill prisoners are also placed there (NSW Coroner's Office 2006).

Matthews and Young see the problem as not just net widening, but

> a more serious problem is the way in which the proliferation of sentencing options creates a larger self-referential or auto-poietic system which recycles individuals through a more closely linked network of agencies It has also increased the sites of decision making (e.g. prison authorities) (Matthews and Young 2003, p. 226).

This "recycling" process, where prisoners move within a "liminal space" of imprisonment and release has been described in Australia by Baldry et al. (2006) and Peacock (2008). The increasing permeability and blurring of the boundaries of the penal in NSW is evidenced by the types of recent initiatives promulgated by the NSW government in this area, for example, Community Offender Support Schemes (COSPS) represent an extension of penal control into areas hitherto serviced by poorly funded prisoner welfare organisations in the community (Weelands 2009a). The creation of oppressive "regimes" for "pariah" offenders, such as sex offenders, subverts the need for post-release housing into opportunities for increased control (Weelands 2009a). In addition, these strict regimes set up increased possibilities for breach and return to prison.

> Offenders who are released "into the community" are subject to much tighter control than previously, and frequently find themselves returned to custody for failure to comply with the conditions that continue to restrict their freedom (Garland 2001, p. 176).

A feedback effect from conditional release programmes may exist with imprisonment for technical breaches of orders rather than reoffending, leading to reincarceration in "many cases" (Jones et al. 2006, p. 2).[8] Wacquant's "carceral continuum" (Wacquant 2001, p. 97) is thus maintained and extended.

[8] In 2008, the number of parole revocations for reoffending/outstanding charges was 763 while an almost equal number (723) were revoked for breach of conditions (State Parole Authority NSW Annual Report 2000, p. 24).

The notion of a "third space" within which prisoners are trapped, shifting between prison and the community demonstrates the constraints exercised by surveillance and control. Although these constraints are "disguised by notions of reintegration and settlement" (Peacock 2008) the reality for many is that they will never be an included member of the community. The concept of "iterative homelessness" describes the plight of many prisoners (Baldry et al. 2006, p. 20). Linear conceptions of the sentence are common whereas, as Peacock points out, it is more of a "net", a useful concept which reflects the disjunction of the prisoners from their former life and the difficulties of exiting their former status as prisoners when the sentence is finished. As Baldry et al. put it, prisoners are "cycling around in a liminal, marginalised and fluid community-criminal justice space" (Baldry et al. 2006, 2008). This is not to place undue importance on the control aspects of so-called alternatives to imprisonment, as this belies the actuality of the lack of the most basic support services for most prisoners (D. Brown 2005, p. 38). When considered in the context of post-sentence detention, such intrusions of the penal into the community have been part of a broader trend of a risk-orientated "future crime" discourse (McCullough and Pickering 2009), privileging the ostensible prevention of crime by the identification of risky individuals, over the preservation of basic principles of criminal law such as the presumption of innocence.

Bail is another area where an intensification of the extension of the penal into the community is evidenced. From a baseline position which was possibly the most liberal in Australia, NSW, as the first jurisdiction in Australia to codify and extend common law principles of bail, has progressively restricted and reshaped the ideology of bail so as to result in an almost total presumption against bail for all but the least "risky". The development of forms of coercion and control which act to reproduce and multiply the effects of disadvantage by adding a further way to prison, for example revocations of orders, Community Offender Support Services, necessitate the recognition of the role of such initiatives in extending, transmitting and normalising the prison.

2.6 Evaluation and Accountability

A pragmatic appraisal of the capacity of prison to rehabilitate is reflected in Nagle's insistence that prison be seen as punishment and not an opportunity to reprogramme people (Nagle 1978, p. 52). Nagle's criticism of the use of rates of recidivism as a "measure of success" for correctional authorities (Nagle 1978, p. 52) could not be further from the political reality for the current department.[9] The former government's State Plan "aims to keep people safe through reduced rates of crime and reduced re-offending" (NSW Government, 2006).[10] The target is to reduce the proportion of offenders who reoffend within 24 months of being convicted by a court or having been dealt with at a conference by 10 % by 2016. NSW Government policy appears to equate this goal with the performance of rehabilitative programmes "specifically targeted towards offenders addressing the causes of their offending behaviour by participation in programs relevant to their needs" (NSW Sentencing Council 2008, p. 4). Thus, at the highest bureaucratic and political level in NSW, rehabilitation is equated with participation in programmes, which is equated with reduction in recidivism.

In terms of evaluation and accountability, the former Commissioner of CSNSW, Ron Woodham, has acknowledged the difficulties in attributing responsibility for recidivism: "recidivism can never be an absolute measure by which we can evaluate the quality of correctional services provided (Legislative Council of NSW 2010, p. 72). The view that CSNSW is an "end agency" with little control is reflected by his assertion that "recidivism has more to do with policing and sentencing practices than anything else". The existence of a "National Convention" amongst Justice/Corrections Ministers that Corrections departments are not to be held accountable for performance regarding recidivism

[9] "Corrective Services NSW delivers professional correctional services to reduce re-offending and enhance community safety". NSW Department of Corrective Services Statement of Purposes and Values 2009.

[10] NSW state election in 2011, Corrective Services NSW was amalgamated into the Department of Justice. A new Strategic Plan was issued in 2014 – *Strategic Plan 2014 – 2019.*

reflects this view (Legislative Council of NSW 2010, p. 72). "The Committee noted the absence of performance indicators regarding re-entry for either public or private prisons" (Legislative Council of NSW 2010, p. 76).

Data is based on outputs, and no information about evaluation of programmes is available. Even here, for example, regarding sex offender programmes, care must be taken in accepting numbers at face value, as the same participants undertake "prep" and "maintenance" programmes before and after CUBIT respectively. The figures for participation in CUBIT, the programme for high-risk sex offenders, while an improvement on those reviewed by the Audit Office in 2004 (NSW Audit Office 2004), are still low relative to the numbers in custody.

CSNSW measures recidivism in two ways: the national indicator of return to corrective services (custody and community) and the State Government target of reducing the number of offenders who reoffend within 24 months of being convicted. The NSW Department commences its Annual Reports with a section on Offender Management. The primacy of actuarial risk assessment is reflected by the prominence given to the fact that each offender, custodial or community based, is assessed using the LSIR, which "identifies areas of criminogenic need to inform program development" (Department of Corrective Services NSW Annual Report 2008). While the mantra of through care has long been adopted by the NSW Department, this is little more than good practice adopted from social work casework. In any case, patchy and slow implementation means that sentences are rarely coordinated and post-release planning is rare. Many prisoners question the value of through care in that personal information is shared by gaolers (see Chap. 6).

It is difficult to gain a picture of correctional programmes within prisons in NSW as an outsider. Even research organisations such as the Criminology Research Council funded study reported that correctional budget allocations to offender rehabilitation were unavailable and that programme enrolment and completion rates were not available.

> The dilemma for jurisdictions surrounds the political sensitivity of these (evaluation) reports which in turn inhibits dissemination beyond

> the jurisdiction. In some cases, release is only to a select few who are directly associated with program development and management (Heseltine et al. 2011).

In addition, the Productivity Commission report lacked both the methodology and the data to provide an assessment of offender rehabilitation (Productivity Commission 2009). The recent AIC publication on prison-based offender rehabilitation programmes contains no data from prisoners and indeed no evaluations of Australian programmes at all (Heseltine et al. 2011). In this era of accountability, evaluation and professed "evidence-based practice" this omission is significant.

2.7 Legislative Changes

During Attorney General Frank Walker's brief tenure (1979–1983), partly coinciding with the reform period of Commissioner Tony Vinson, progressive steps were taken in the area of bail, summary offences, repeal of many status offences and sentencing. A new focus on the needs of victims began in this era; however, later assessment was that these concerns were harnessed by politicians to "tap the retributive nerve in popular opinion in support of tougher measures" (Hogg and Brown 1998, p. 41) rather than provide actual assistance to victims of crime.

Throughout the 1980s, 1990s and into the new century, a constant political focus on criminal justice has led to a proliferation of legislation, including profound changes in the way certain offences and offenders are dealt with. Interwoven with this frenzied legislative change have been changes in process and legal procedure, including an increasing reliance on technology (CCTV, AVL links). An increasing concern with risk and surveillance, alongside draconian legislation relating to acts of "terror", drug trafficking offences and sex offences has led to the emergence of new discourses around community protection and risk, "future crime" as McCullough and Pickering describe it (McCullough and Pickering 2009), which have come close to infringing the presumption of innocence.

The sheer number of changes to sentencing and bail legislation in NSW over the past 20 years indicates a constant political and legislative focus on these areas. This "uncivil" politics of law and order (Hogg and Brown 1998, p. 41) with an emphasis on more punitive approaches to crime has become a feature of the political, legislative and policy climate in NSW. Simon Bronitt points out the damage to our political processes done by hasty legislation without proper political process (Bronitt 2008, 76).[11] Legislation passed in this way has become a feature of criminal justice in NSW. Loughnan (2010) points to features in offence creation in NSW which evidence a politically driven, over-particularised approach.

The insertion of sections 25A and 25B into the *Crimes Act* 1900 (NSW) in response to public outrage over "one punch" deaths from alcohol-related violence represents the most recent example of the above trend, with the added element of mandatory sentencing for the new offences.

Sentencing

As sentencing is the most public and easily accessible face of the criminal justice system, heightened political recognition of the importance of congruence between the decisions of the judiciary and magistracy and public attitudes towards crime is demonstrated through the constant policy and legislative focus of this era. Longer sentences and the creation of new offences arising from perceptions of public dissatisfaction have been a feature of criminal justice legislation from the mid-1980s to the present. The Sentencing Council of NSW, established in 2000, demonstrates a strong focus on community awareness and the recognition of the importance of ascertaining community attitudes towards sentencing,

[11] Bronitt uses the NSW example of the enactment of legislation in 1 day following the "Cronulla Riots" giving police extraordinary powers. For a detailed analysis of the situation at Cronulla in 2005 see Poynting S. (2008). Thugs and Grubs at Cronulla: From media beat-ups to beating up migrants. In S. Poynting and G. Morgan (Eds.), *Outrageous, moral panics in Australia.* Hobart: ACYS Press.

a development at odds with the traditional legal attitude to sentencing as a purely technical legal task. Throughout the 1980s, significant public concern centred on the need for certainty, indeterminate sentencing and a complex mathematically determined remissions system highlighting problems in the way sentences were administered in NSW.

In 1992, "special circumstances" allowing the court to vary the ratio between the non-parole period and the period of parole were found in 47 % of sentences passed in the higher courts (MacKinnell et al. 1993, p. 3). By 2007, special circumstances were found in 87.3 % of standard non-parole period cases (Poletti 2010, p. 23).

Throughout the 1990s, amendment to sentencing legislation was frequent; there were approximately 49 pieces of legislation related to criminal justice from 1995 to 1998 compared to 23 in Victoria (Simpson and Griffith 1999, pp. 5–15, 28–35). Numerous new offences were created, with prostitution the only area that saw a move away from prohibition towards regulation. In 1996, mandatory life sentences were prescribed for murder and supply of a commercial quantity of heroin or cocaine where culpability was "extreme".[12] Differing attitudes to culpability are demonstrated in reforms to the concepts of intoxication in 1996[13] and diminished responsibility (now substantial impairment) in 1997.[14]

In the context of increasing punitiveness and public concerns about judicial discretion, in 1998 the NSW Court of Criminal Appeal, in an innovative move dubbed "a masterstroke in public relations" (Warner 2003, p. 20) gave a guideline judgement in the case of *Jurisic.* Further characterised as an act by "guerrilla" judges (Freiberg 2000), the impact of guideline judgements has been generally assessed as positive in reducing disparity between sentences but in the case of *Jurisic* and *Henry,* guidelines may have contributed to increased sentence lengths (Barnes 2002; Barnes et al. 2003; Poletti 2005). There was also a "dramatic increase in the number of sentence appeals" between 1996 and 2000 (Poletti and Barnes 2002).

[12] *Crimes Amendment (Mandatory Life Sentences) Act* NSW (1996).

[13] *Criminal Legislation Amendment Act* NSW (1996).

[14] *Crimes Amendment (Diminished Responsibility) Act* NSW (1997).

In 1999, a package of amendments which consolidated sentencing law into three statutes[15] was passed, leaving much of its substance unchanged (Johns 2002a, p. 5). Again in 2002 in the lead up to the State election, further changes were proposed leading to the inclusion of many of the common law principles of sentencing in legislation and the listing of aggravating and mitigating features to be applied in sentencing. A detailed analysis of the aims of sentencing as expressed in section 3A of the *Crimes (Sentencing Procedure) Act NSW* (1999) is undertaken in Chap. 4.

Problems with this codification have included "double counting" of aggravating features by the sentencing court where these features are already elements of the offence (Stratton 2005). A series of standard non-parole periods, which represented "significant increases" in sentence lengths, were introduced in 2002 (D. Brown 2002, p. 71). Whether this has led to increased clarification of the law or simply to complications resulting from the need, for example, to define such concepts as "the mid-range of seriousness" (D. Brown 2002, p. 65) is arguable.[16] What it has achieved are dramatic increases in the length of sentences in matters now subject to the regime (Poletti 2010). Recently, the incoming Attorney General has announced a review of sentencing legislation by the NSWLRC. The High Court decision in the case of *Muldrock*[17] which overturns the decision in *Way* will conceivably lessen the impact of standard non-parole periods while confirming the "instinctive synthesis" approach (*Markarian v the Queen, Veen (no 2) v R).*[18] While generally applauded as a more sensible approach, the decision may necessitate review of numerous sentencing decisions which adopted the now discredited approach in *Way*.

[15] *Crimes (Sentencing Procedure) Act* NSW (1999), *Crimes (Administration of Sentence) Act* 1999, *Crimes Legislation Amendment (Sentencing) Act* NSW 1999.

[16] The case of *Way* (2004) 60 NSWLR 168 was for some years the leading authority on the application of the standard non-parole period provisions.

[17] *Muldrock v R* [2011] HCA 39.

[18] *Markarian v the Queen* (2005) 228 CLR 357;Veen (no 2) v R(1988)164 CLR465.

Bail

The development of bail legislation over the past 30 years can only be seen as a retreat from the proposition that the presumption of innocence is the overriding consideration (as expressed by the then Attorney in enacting the original *Bail Act* in 1979 (Walker 1978, in Simpson 1997, p. 8).[19] Not only has the ambit of offences where there is no entitlement to bail increased, but also a continuing focus on repeat offenders, hand in hand with an increased focus on the prediction of risk, has further limited the availability of bail. Amendments in 2002[20] removed the presumption for those on parole or community-based orders or those who had previously been convicted of an indictable offence. As the *Bail Act* applies equally to juveniles one impact has been a burgeoning of numbers of young people in custody.

As in other criminal justice areas, "many amendments have been a result of political imperatives or moral outrage over a particularly abhorrent high profile case, rather than responses to detailed empirical research or evidence" (Brignell 2002). The significance of political motivation in bail legislation is clear, with NSW amending bail legislation 23 times from 1992.[21] Unable to participate in programmes or work, kept in maximum security, remand prisoners are often merely warehoused.

The long awaited new *Bail Act* 2013 NSW, which sought to replace the complexity of the presumptions in the old Act with a simple test of "unacceptable risk", appears fated to replicate the problems of the old Act (Brown and Quilter 2014). Again, outrage about individual cases fanned by self-appointed community mouthpieces in the popular media has led to ill thought-out modifications to the new regime (Brown and Quilter 2014).

---

[19] The only original exception to the presumption, armed robbery, occurred in response to public concern over a high-profile case.

[20] Bail Amendment (Repeat Offenders) Act 2002.

[21] Compared to six times in Victoria, four in South Australia, seven in Western Australia and the Northern Territory and nine in the ACT (Steel: 24).

Parole

The history of parole in NSW since the 1970s has reflected the limitations on discretion and increasing punitiveness seen elsewhere in the criminal justice process. Initially conceived as part of an individualised sentencing process whereby parole was seen as incentive (Chan 1990, p. 405)[22] and part of a welfarist, rehabilitative framework, parole has arguably been reconceptualised as a process of risk management and prevention involving monitoring and the application of rigid management frameworks. Recommendation 39 of the Nagle Report states that the relevant issue should be whether there are any reasons why the prisoner should not be able to adapt to normal community life (Zdenkowski and Brown 1982, p. 89). In a reversal of this test, the modern Parole Authority must now positively determine that there is sufficient reason to believe that the offender would be able to adapt to normal community life (State Parole Authority of NSW 2008, p. 5).

The *Sentencing Act 1989,* which abolished remissions, provided a further block to the control of prisoner numbers by the department, and provided significant challenges in the management of increasing numbers of prisoners (Chan 1992, p. 416). In the same way that media reports of individual sentences have led to dramatic legislative changes in sentencing and bail, a similar process has applied in the area of parole[23] (Simpson 1999, 1). The current practice of tying parole to the risk assessment process leads to a simplistic tendency to link parole to programme completion. This process privileges inmates who can negotiate the system and disadvantages those who cannot. Other changes that have restricted parole include an amendment in 2004 to the *Crimes (Administration of Sentences) Act 1999*[24] which limited consideration of parole eligibility to an annual event subject to a "manifest injustice"

[22] *Power v R* [1974] HCA 26 "to provide for mitigation of the punishment of the prisoner in favour of his rehabilitation through conditional freedom where appropriate".

[23] Wide publicity given to the case of John Lewthwaite, who in 1999 had served 20 years for the killing of a child and was released on parole, led to further restrictions.

[24] *Crimes (Administration of Sentences) Amendment (Parole)* Bill (2004).

clause (s137B) (Hutchins 2010). The rate of revocation of parole from 1991–1995 averaged 23.4 %, rising to 35.9 % between 1996 and 2003 and has averaged 44.5 % since 2004 (Cunneen et al. 2013).

2.8 Risk + "What Works" = A Limited Version of Rehabilitation

In the 1990s there was a discernible trend towards post-sentence detention in Australia. The case of *Kable*[25] illustrated the first if somewhat unsophisticated move towards a change in the balance between the rights of individuals and the rights of the State. The High Court overturned the *Kable* legislation, which was intended to detain one individual on the basis of his future risk. As is often a feature of developments of criminal law in Australia in other jurisdictions, in this case Queensland provided a template for subsequent legislation in NSW. There has been a revival of interest in the constitutional aspects of the *Kable* decision following the High Court decisions in *South Australia v Totani*[26] and *Wainohu v New South Wales.*[27]

Notions of dangerousness have been supplemented by the scientific, calculable idea of risk. The increase in the use of actuarial methods to calculate risk means that this common sense notion is being transformed into an artefact more compatible with modern penal managerialism. Mark Brown assesses the appeal of the combination of risk with danger as "combining an existential threat with a calculative modality that offers the possibility of quarantining it" (M. Brown 2008a, p. 256). The usefulness of such a modality to a jurisdiction like NSW, in which criminal justice is highly politicised, lies in the comfort given by the attribution of scientific values to quell existential fears.

[25] *Kable v DPP (NSW)* (1996) 189 CLR 51.

[26] *South Australia v*
[2010] HCA 39.

[27] *Wainohu v New South Wales* [2011] HCA 24.

While mainstream sentencing practice in NSW may not routinely (or perhaps explicitly) involve reliance on actuarial assessments, their widespread use in the correctional context and for parole indicates that some impact would be expected on sentencing practice (see further discussion of the role of risk in sentencing in Chap. 4). Community Corrections Officers routinely prepare presentence reports for courts; the same service prepares pre-release reports for parole. Risk assessment, having derived from the practices of parole officers, has professional resonance for them and now pervades their practice, although psychologists have carved out this new area of professional expertise—the administration of risk assessment instruments. The high number of repeat offenders travelling through the court and correctional system means that at some stage these assessments may be used by courts to replace or augment more traditional sources of psychiatric/psychological/human behavioural knowledge.

The Parole Authority in NSW often relies on evidence of predictions of future dangerousness made on the basis of the use of actuarial instruments. Actuarial methods of prediction have been embraced wholeheartedly by CSNSW as part of the re-legitimisation of a new form of rehabilitation, the risk/needs model. The LSIR (used by CSNSW), a Canadian risk assessment instrument using actuarial methods to predict future offending (Andrews et al. 1990) is based on norms established on the basis of Canadian data, although some attempts have been made to adapt it to the local context. As Mihailides et al. point out, "reverse trends in Canada and Australia in terms of crime rates as well as differences in important cultural forensic and macro social political contexts" lead to "concerns regarding the accuracy of norms for the Australian context" (Mihailides et al. 2005, p. 208). Silver and Miller urge caution and note, "insufficient attention has been paid to the negative potential embodied in actuarial social control technologies" (Silver and Miller 2002, p. 157). Questions of adequacy and consistency arise.

Hannah-Moffatt agrees that insufficient attention has been paid to "the subjective, moralistic and disciplinary capacity of actuarial techniques" (Hannah–Moffatt 1999, p. 72). Simon (1993, p. 792) sees political implications for the ability of oppositional groups to "provide identity to members in the kind of political struggle that identity generates", that is "the use of identity to produce political change becomes more difficult" (Simon 1993, p. 794). The emphasis on psychological readjustment in prison rather than provision of citizen rights outside is effected by a translation of welfare need into psychological need. Whereas "need" was previously seen to mean "welfare need" it is nowadays translated into "risk of reoffending", this in official jargon becomes "crimogenic need" requiring psychological reprogramming in prison.

As Sotiri points out, the CSNSW has adopted an approach which, while managerial, relies on notions of objective proof, empiricism, risk, faith in scientific models and rejection of rehabilitation as personal development (Sotiri 2003). Sotiri places CSNSW's "wholesale adoption of the crimogenic needs model in NSW prisons" in the context of "a desire to be professional, objective and scientific" (Sotiri 2003, p. 370).

An important question is whether this new configuration of risk assessment and programme delivery as rehabilitation constitutes an important enough change to signify a paradigm shift. The rhetoric of corrections would have this be so, but on closer inspection the situation is much more complex than this. Is the question of whether there has been a shift or not misguided? (Sotiri 2003, p. 355). Sotiri argues that, in NSW there has been a self-conscious break with the past and a complete rejection of the notion of rehabilitation, to be replaced by a regime of cognitive behavioural programmes linked with risk which, she argues, furthers the disciplinary project a la Foucault.

In NSW courts, far from there being a contest to the death between actuarialism and the modernist psy-knowledge, they appear to be coexisting quite comfortably. When examining the different contexts in which notions of dangerousness are currently used in criminal justice decision making in NSW, it is inevitable that the cultural context will shape the way it is expressed and utilised. Thus, CSNSW has a different focus in their predictions of dangerousness than the criminal courts, but this focus has a subtle but pervasive influence throughout the criminal justice system, partly due to the prevalence of repeat offenders and people incarcerated for breaches of orders.

2.9 Conclusion

Pratt describes five main causes of "penal populism" (Pratt 2008, p. 269) all of which have arguably been present in the recent socio-political context of punishment in NSW, in particular the "decline of deference" and an associated decline in the trust of the community in criminal justice processes. The many legislative attempts to constrain judicial discretion in sentencing and Freiberg's "guerrilla judges" epitomise the kind of complexity of response and resistance that belies direct categorisation and supports a nuanced view (Freiberg 2000). The existence of a level of "ontological insecurity" due to structural changes in society, the role of the media and the impact of the widespread availability of information technology (Pratt 2008, p. 271) has been evident in NSW through the perpetuation of a particular type of populist media reporting about crime. The responsiveness of the legislature to such reporting has at times led to ill-considered, hurried legislation (Loughnan 2010, p. 19). What Pratt calls "democratisation" where the authenticity of lived experience, especially of victimisation, is validated as an authentic and influential part of criminal justice has undoubtedly had an impact on criminal justice discourse in NSW (Pratt 2008, p. 274). Whether the "non-discursive" (D. Brown 2005, p. 29) evidences any real change for victims through the development of a kind of a "zero sum" game between the rights of victims and offenders is another question.

While seeking to avoid the type of "dystopian vision" counselled against by Zedner (2002) and David Brown (2005), this analysis of the various strands of policy, legislation and practice in criminal justice in NSW over the past 40 years leads to the conclusion that, with the exception of the immediate post-Nagle period, legislative and policy development have all moved towards the creation of a large prison estate in NSW. The significance of this fact reflects the way in which imprisonment has become embedded in the criminal justice and penal culture of NSW as the predominant model from which all other sanctions are conceived as "alternatives".

David Brown's argument that "a battered and reconfigured penal welfarism" has survived in NSW and that any critique of the extension of the prison must consider the limited extent to which any kind of proper support has been evident in the community, has some cogency still, although "battered" must be an understatement (D. Brown 2004, p. 36). Post Nagle, improvements to physical conditions for prisoners, a more "social welfare" role for prison officers and the persistence of notions of due process throughout the criminal justice system, are, for David Brown, evidence of continuity rather than rupture and of the persistence of penal welfarism (D. Brown 2005, p. 41). The importance of emphasising "contestation" in criminal justice policy (D. Brown 2005, p. 42) rather than implying any kind of smooth, cohesive, inevitable transformation lies in detailing the actual developments as they occur and the context in which they occurred. As Pratt points out "there is no inevitability about this" and so the development of currents of populist punitiveness in NSW, as elsewhere, must be traced through the specific currents of legislation policy and practice and their socio-cultural context (Pratt 2008, p. 274).

As O'Malley (2008, p. 64) points out, while there has been a discernible shift from "welfare–social policies" towards a more "neo-liberalist political rationality" these currents have a complexity in their aetiology and maintenance. The "volatile and contradictory picture" painted by O'Malley is exemplified in NSW by, for example, the coexistence of punitive trends such as longer sentences and restrictions on bail, with initiatives relying on conceptions of therapeutic jurisprudence, such as the Drug Court. Notions of decarceration may be subsumed by the prominence of conceptions of risk in which the same programmes became less about keeping people out of prison than, in their effect, part of a "carceral continuum" (Wacquant 2001, p. 97) which feeds people back through prison. In addition, the effect of legislation in other related areas, such as anti-terrorism laws, and preventive detention legislation for sex offenders, while constituting a very small part of the operation of the criminal justice system, may in retrospect be seen as an integral part of an overall move towards restrictions on the liberty of individuals falling into specified categories.

This brief sketch of some of the important features of the development of the criminal justice and penal system in NSW since 1970 has been attempted in order to provide a basis for further theorising about the causes and consequences of these phenomena and the implications for those experiencing imprisonment. The next chapter analyses in more detail the specific aims of sentencing in NSW and in particular the obligations of the sentenced person which arise from these aims.

3

Theorising Sentencing

3.1 Introduction

The purpose of this chapter is to examine the aims of sentencing in NSW, not only as guiding philosophical principles influencing judicial decision-making, but also as a baseline to begin to evaluate how the mechanisms of the criminal justice system are working in their practical application. A distinction is made between the aims, which have been codified (in Section 3A [s3A] of the *Crimes (Sentencing Procedure)* Act 1999, NSW) and the principles of sentencing (proportionality, consistency, parsimony[1] etc.) that remain as common law principles in NSW. By analysing the content of the aims, the kind of requirement for action that arises from it and the agency or individual responsible for carrying it out, and the beginning of a feedback loop can be established. A clearer enunciation of the practical consequences and requirements of these aims can then be translated into action. This is important because

[1] Although parsimony appears, with little fanfare, to have disappeared from the law of NSW (NSW Sentencing Bench Book).

M. Hall, *The Lived Sentence,* Palgrave Studies in Prisons and Penology, DOI 10.1007/978-3-319-45038-4_3

subjective expectations, which need to be communicated clearly at sentencing, arise from these aims.

The increasingly important idea of risk introduced in the last chapter in relation to the development of dominant paradigms in NSW criminal justice is examined as it relates to the sentencing practices of judges in NSW. Risk assessment instruments based on actuarial methods to determine the risk of future offending may be attractive to judicial officers increasingly constrained and scrutinised in their sentencing practice. The introduction of legislation empowering courts to authorise post-sentence detention on the basis of future risk arguably elevates these considerations. In addition, the evidence of the "psy"—professions which purport to be able to predict and "treat" it—is raised to an enhanced level of importance in general sentencing practice. This is not to claim that the reliance on medical model psychiatry has been supplanted by this new technology. Clinical psychiatric evidence is considered alongside psychological assessments in the new area of post-sentence detention of sex offenders. The importance of this discussion lies in the way that considerations about risk have permeated each step of the criminal justice process, and in particular, have impacted the way rehabilitation is conceived and practiced. As a ubiquitous, all-encompassing discourse, the question is whether considerations of future dangerousness have changed the way the aims of sentencing have been operationalised throughout imprisonment, and beyond.

Sentencing as a Lived Experience

Any examination of sentencing in a purely legalistic way as something which occurs only in a courtroom will produce an incomplete picture of the process (Hutton and Tata 2002). While sentencing is over in a formal sense when the prisoner leaves the courtroom, for the prisoner and arguably the community, the sentence has only just begun. The consequences of ignoring the ongoing nature of the aims of sentencing are not only to discount the effect on the prisoner of this process but also to short-change the community in the operationalisation of the aims of sentencing. In order to carry out these aims of sentencing, other criminal justice agencies and the sentenced person must themselves transform the sentence into a prescription for action.

An important focus of this book is the element of subjectivity, particularly in relation to the person being sentenced. Many of the aims of sentencing have a requirement that certain subjective states are experienced. Concrete recognition is given to demonstrations of remorse by sentence discounts for guilty pleas. Many of the unstated assumptions within sentencing assume a certain emotional state in the offender, which, if not manifested in a socially recognisable way, can impact significantly on the outcome.

On the other hand, it is also necessary to examine the philosophical underpinnings of the aims in order to gain information about who they are aimed at, what action needs to be taken and what outcome is desired. Communicative theories of punishment posit that a "moral dialogue, a communicative enterprise" is undertaken with the offender (Duff and Garland 1994, p. 15). The idea that, through punishment, an internal transformation is undergone is pervasive "since the possibility of moral repentance and reform depends on how the offender understands and responds to the punishment" (Duff and Garland 1994, p. 15). Once the state has a finding of guilt, there is an expectation that the guilty feel guilty and that they undergo certain subjective states. Implicit in many of the aims of sentencing is the requirement for some kind of internal process, often manifest in outward behavioural signs.[2]

As the penultimate part of the criminal trial process, the sentence brings into the courtroom elements of subjectivity, ostensibly excluded from the examination of evidence required in the determination of guilt. Sentencing requires, of the participants, a level of subjectivity not present (or perhaps not acknowledged) elsewhere in the criminal justice system because of the need to consider "the offender's entire life, including his or her future" (Rotman in Duff and Garland 1994, p. 285). The element of rehabilitation ensures that "a perfected law takes subjectivity into consideration which would otherwise remain largely excluded from the criminal process" (Rotman in Duff and

[2] The importance of demonstrating inner emotional processes in a commonly understood and acceptable way is manifested by the cases of Lindy Chamberlain, and possibly the more recent case of Kathryn Folbigg, convicted of killing all four of her babies. The ambiguities of Folbigg's diary references are transformed into a convincing dialogue of guilt, in the light of evidence of her behaviour, which did not conform to commonly held perceptions of motherhood (Cunliffe 2007, p. 820).

Garland 1994, p. 285). The role of the criminal law in channelling and limiting expressive emotional reactions to crime—"punishment bears the aspect of legitimated vengefulness" (Feinberg in Duff and Garland 1994, p. 76)—implies that there is an inherent subjective emotive aspect which is allowed to enter the sober realm of rational legal thinking at the time of sentencing.

Tata critiques the conception of sentencing as a collection of binary opposites:

> [r]ules versus discretion; reason versus emotion; offence versus offender; normative principles versus incoherence; aggravating versus mitigating factors; and aggregate/tariff consistency versus individualized sentencing. rules versus discretion; reason versus emotion (Tata 2007, p. 245).

Encouraging a view of sentencing as "dynamic, contingent, and synergistic . . . these binaries serve as crucial legitimating reference points in the vocabulary of sentencing account giving" (Tata 2007, p. 425). His argument requires sentencing to be seen as a process involving many different people and agencies (Travers 2006, and in Tata 2007), its agenda often being moulded earlier in the criminal process, shaped collaboratively with other professionals and inextricably bound with guilt-producing processes. Thus, to talk about sentencing craftwork is not to talk only of the craft of judges but of other sentencing professionals, for example prosecutors, defence lawyers, pre-sentence report writers (Tata 2007, p. 434).

Taking Tata's conception further, the sentence in its operationalised form includes prison staff, obviously the prisoner, pre-release staff, the Parole Authority and the family and community into which the prisoner is released after serving the custodial part of the sentence. In this way, a sentence becomes much more than a form of words pronounced in a courtroom or a term of years to be served, but a collection of actions, reactions, subjective states and assessments of subjective states which can last much longer than any formal contact with the criminal justice system.

In examining the aims of sentencing, it must be taken into account that "it is highly questionable that sentencers ever operate or could operate according to philosophical theories of punishment and abstract analytical categories of the case" (Tata 2007, p. 418). Reason giving, as a justificatory enterprise, is "mediated constructed and reconstructed according to the audience" (Tata 2007, p. 419). At the same time, however, sentencing must be viewed not just as a discrete process beginning and ending in the courtroom but as

> [p]art of an extended process which begins when the police or prosecution authorities decide how to process suspects and which extends beyond the formal; stage of sentencing at the trial to such matters as the allocation of prisoners to different kinds of prisons and decisions on early release (Duff and Garland 1994, p. 26).

This extended process includes imprisonment and parole, but arguably reaches even further into the future of the sentenced person, with the effects of punishment, denunciation and retribution often continuing well after the legal sentence has ended.

The prevalence of the discourse of risk and the use of actuarial instruments to predict re-offending raises the question of how this focus has affected the way judges sentence, the way the sentence is operationalised and the way release is negotiated. In relation to the operation of "desert theory"[3] Tata asks, "Yet how in practice are sentencers expected to implement the requirement to ignore the question of expected future behaviour of an offender?" (Tata 2007, p. 412). The prominence of questions of moral culpability in sentencing raises the question of the role of moral assessments of character in the ongoing risk assessment of the prisoner. Tata demonstrates that the risk of future offending and questions of moral culpability are inextricably intertwined. It will be argued in the next chapter that assessments of remorse are a pervasive and ongoing feature of our criminal justice system. Is risk, then, a cipher for moral judgment in the courts and correctional system?

The disconnection between the sentence as served by the prisoner and the perception of a sentence as a legal artefact performed in a courtroom is

---

[3] A full analysis of the different philosophies of punishment is beyond the scope of this book. In NSW, the practice of judges offers few examples of such discussion but a combination of desert (retributive) theory and a form of pragmatic consequentialism appears to prevail.

exemplified and deepened by "(the) tendency for NSW prison administrators to view punishment as taking place in the courts and for the courts to believe that punishment takes place in the prison" (Sotiri 2003, p. 29). While either conception is incomplete, this diffusion in public discourse tends to mean that abrogation of responsibility for the infliction of suffering occasioned by imprisonment is thus complete. If people are not sent to prison for punishment to occur, then there is no reality in the "pains of imprisonment".

Coupled with the movement towards individualisation and responsibilisation, this view leads to the perception that any failure in rehabilitation or preventing recidivism lies in the individual and not in the mechanisms of punishment. Responsibilisation as a process associated with a neo-liberal, individualistic view of crime and which is implicit in assumptions around deterrence, denunciation, retribution and restitution that "only make sense in a world where responsibility or its recourse to agency are given concrete form and taken seriously by various bodies" is, Lacey claims, "the question in normative criminal law" (in Halsey 2008, p. 220). The disavowal of responsibility for the infliction of punishment by the two major elements in the punishment industry, the courts and the prison, leaves only the prisoner to both suffer the consequences and the blame for its failure.

The importance of the prisoner feeling and, importantly, demonstrating that they feel punished, denounced, in need of rehabilitation and have an understanding of the needs of the victim, is underlined at parole, where the sentence itself, as served, is reviewed in the light of these factors. The importance of understanding the meaning and subjective understanding by prisoners of what was said at sentence and more importantly, what is now required to happen is underlined by the element of accountability, thus imposed at the end of a sentence.

Courts and Prisons

Courts in NSW have been reluctant to involve themselves in matters involving the content of imprisonment. An important exception to this is the effect of a sentence served in protective custody in exacerbating the hardships of imprisonment. In NSW it is common practice in sentence appeals to the Court of Criminal Appeal to lodge affidavits detailing the conditions of custody and any achievements made by the prisoner. This has not gone as far as recognising the probability that a prisoner will not get parole as a reason to reduce the non-parole period; however, a number of Victorian cases indicate that the court will consider evidence of hardship in custody in appeals against severity of sentence (Edney and Bagaric 2007, p. 308). As discussed in Chapter 2, in NSW the finding of "special circumstances" required to allow the court to vary the ratio between the parole and the non-parole period is made in a very high proportion of cases. Statements such as "acceptable by a sentencing court" not only imply a normative construct of what is acceptable, but they also reveal that courts are willing to set those standards. Despite the separation of powers, courts may see themselves as the appropriate bodies to do so. As Edney and Bagaric put it:

> The comments of McHugh J are important because they indicate the continued operation of the law in the correctional context and the need for prisoners to be treated humanely in the serving of their custodial sentence (Edney and Bagaric 2007, p. 311).

Human rights perspectives on imprisonment, although largely ineffective in terms of individual prisoner litigation, provide some framework for judicial intervention. The impending ratification of the United Nations Optional Protocol to the Convention against Torture (OPCAT) by the Australian Government may provide an enhanced role for human rights litigation.

The role of the court in NSW in ensuring the sentence is carried out is limited, the suggestion in the Halliday Report in the UK that

> [a] system which encourages sentencers . . . to focus more on the outcomes and implications of their sentences could help improve results in terms of crime reduction and public confidence (Halliday et al. 2001, p. 46)

has been resoundingly ignored here as well as in the UK. Local manifestations of the worldwide trend towards restorative justice and therapeutic jurisprudence like the Drug Court and circle sentencing appear to have had little impact on mainstream criminal justice. While the "pilot program" nature of many of these initiatives along with highly restricted entry criteria will mean that these ideas will take some time to spread further, the mere existence of courts that routinely monitor progress and have direct access to information about the individual outcomes of the people who appear before them will inevitably have some effect on the habitus of criminal justice.

In the meantime, judicial officers may be sentencing on the basis of unsupported assumptions about the psychology of offenders. Are they also sentencing on the basis of unsupported assumptions of what the criminal justice system, specifically the prison and correctional system, can, or is willing to deliver? Is there any evidence that the period of fevered activity around sentencing really means anything in terms of the outcome in human terms? How does risk assessment affect the ability of inmates in prisons to access treatment or services? Has the focus on risk completely removed the individual from the criminal justice equation? Is this incompatible with the messages conveyed at sentencing about the obligations of the sentenced person? These questions inform the analysis of sentencing law and criminal justice policy in this book.

The Subjectivity of the Sentencers

What about judges' own subjective understandings of what they are doing? Studies of judicial officers' perceptions of sentencing find that judges resort to the at times "vague and meaningless" metaphor of "balance" (Mackenzie 2005, p. 163) to describe "the tightrope—like equilibrium which must be maintained in the courts between what can only be described as completely opposing interests" (MacKenzie 2005, p. 163). There is no doubt that the task of sentencing has become infinitely more complex in the sense that the legal rules governing the exercise of discretion are explicated and therefore need to be shown to have been considered. This is not to say that the task has not always been a complicated one, but the rise in public scrutiny of sentencing practices has given rise to an increased requirement for accountability and thus of careful reason giving. Attention to conforming to the various strictures imposed may preclude attention to the philosophical aspects of the task. In addition, the vexed question of the proper audience for sentencing may explain the universal failure to communicate with the subjects of the sentence, demonstrated by the comments of prisoners in the following. Tombs (2008) finds that the imaginative aspects of sentencing which are important particularly in the need to consider the subjective position of the offender are impaired by an overly technical concentration on form and guidelines (Tombs 2008, p. 108).

In studying the effect of constraints such as sentencing guidelines on the "story telling" that judges perform in order to make sense of their task, the following discussion of the particular situation in NSW proceeds from the outline of changes in policy and legislation in the last chapter to illustrate the climate of increased constraint and scrutiny of sentencing decisions. The discussion of the aims of sentencing which follows draws attention to some of the changes in focus and in particular to the implicit obligations of the offender contained therein.

3.2 Sentencing in NSW

As in many other jurisdictions in Australia and in other common law jurisdictions, codification of the aims of sentencing forms part of a push towards greater transparency and accountability in sentencing (Johnson 2003, p. 42). As the aims are derived from conflicting theories about the reasons for punishment (utilitarianism as opposed to retributivism), they are expressed in broad philosophical terms with an absence of guidance as to how these disparate and vague outcomes can be achieved. Some have arguably introduced a different flavour into the sentencing process, hinted at by judges but not yet fully examined in case law.

In the past 10 years, sentencing in NSW has developed into a complex area of law. Legislative change has been rapid, with a codification of common law principles, mandatory minimum sentences, guideline judgments etc. As Potas and Donnelly have pointed out, the 2002 amending Act "has been the most radical and controversial piece of sentencing legislation since the Sentencing Act 1989" (Keane, Potas and Donnelly 2004, p. 1). The concept of individualised justice has been ostensibly preserved in case law, as has the common law understanding of the principles of sentencing. The development in many jurisdictions of attempts to confine and direct judicial autonomy in the name of consistency has led to a widespread use of statistical data by the judiciary. Political and popular media attention to some of the perceived inadequacies of judicial discretion and individualised justice has led to the recognition that sentencing must be able to be justified and explained to the general public. Although avoiding some of the excesses of this trend (grid sentencing for example), NSW now has a comprehensive statistical information system, used widely throughout the judiciary and the legal profession (Warner 2006, p. 247).

The creation of sentencing councils in Victoria and NSW, with Victoria having a statutory responsibility to ascertain public opinion, has led to some focus on the primary aims of sentencing. Research is conducted regularly on the attitudes of the general public, and a focus on education and dissemination of information about sentencing is becoming apparent, for example, in the recent introduction of community forums by the Sentencing Council of NSW. Guideline judgments have been promulgated to further encourage consistency and accountability. While there has been a large amount of critical and reformist scholarship and research in Australia on sentencing (Warner 2006, p. 250), as far as case law in NSW is concerned, there is a sense that, over a period of such rapid change, practitioners and the judiciary have had their hands full, interpreting such problematic concepts as aggravating and mitigating factors (Loukas 2008, p. 10) and trying to determine the "mid-range of seriousness" in standard non-parole period matters (Loukas 2008, p. 16).

Tombs sees a similar idea of judicial accountability in Scotland as "institutionalised within the context of punitive populism and useful for the closer monitoring of the actions of the judiciary" (Tombs 2008, p. 88). The doctrine of intuitive or instinctive synthesis which has received support from the High Court has been viewed as impeding this trend towards greater accountability and transparency (Bagaric 2000). In their joint judgment in *Wong v The Queen; Leung v The Queen,*[4] Gaudron, Gummow and Hayne JJ, in the course of deliberating on the validity of guideline sentencing, added their support for the instinctive synthesis approach. Intuition

[4] *Wong v The Queen; Leung v The Queen*, [2001] HCA 64.

may refer to "implicit knowledge or a learned emotional response" and is "so entrenched that it operates subconsciously" (Potas and Traynor 2002, p. 4.2). This approach implies that, despite the myriad of limitations on the exercise of their discretion, an internal, not rational, even emotional process is occurring when judges sentence. If something is "intuitive" or "instinctive" it is beyond the intellect. Tombs uses the term "imaginative sentencing" to describe the way judges in Scotland formerly approached the task; she views the use of statistics and guidelines as leading to an untoward emphasis on procedural accountability at the expense of judicial discretion, leading to "imaginary" rather than "imaginative" sentencing (Tombs 2008, p. 88). Tata's view is that enhanced calls for accountability lead to an ex post facto approach to giving reasons in sentencing, which reflect the socially constructed nature of sentencing rather than the reasoning process of the judge (Tata 2007, p. 419).

The shortcomings of the portrayal of sentencing as a mysterious process are apparent in the light of calls for consistency and transparency in judicial decision-making. Regardless of how it is described and structured the act of punishing, of inflicting pain on another is essentially an act of violence. The legal and rational justifications for it do not remove the element of subjectivity, of one person intentionally causing suffereing to another. Does the way sentencing is approached in NSW, when viewed retrospectively through the prism of a sentence served, represent the same type of doublethink identified by Tombs? A great deal of time and energy is spent calculating the right number of years and the reasons for this calculation. At sentence the judge, having considered extensive subjective material as well as having intimate knowledge of the facts of the case, hands down an appropriate sentence. This sentence is not only a tariff, but also involves the progress of an individual through a part of the criminal justice system purporting to fulfil a number of societal functions. In serious matters, the judge often makes detailed comments about the type of rehabilitation appropriate to the offender on the basis of input from probation and parole pre-sentence reports, along with psychological and psychiatric assessments.

Apart from the actual denunciatory quality of this stage of sentencing, the offender is clearly meant to take heed of any recommendations of the judge. Sentencing remarks are therefore important in directing the offender towards the steps they should make to make reparation, where possible, and effect whatever changes in themselves or their situation which would make a repetition of offending less likely. The question is whether the paucity of discussion in NSW of what these phrases really mean in practice as a sentence is carried out could mean that the sentence becomes about other things. In the light of this tendency to "imaginary sentencing" by judges (Tombs 2008), another question is whether the availability of risk assessment instruments, due to the comfort given by their quasi-scientific nature and the strong reliance by CSNSW and the Parole Authority, will presage their adoption by sentencing courts.

3.3 The Aims of Sentencing in NSW

The aims of sentencing are not easily reconcilable, despite the use of the "balancing" metaphor, and the influential analogy in *Veen v The Queen (No 2)* to "signposts pointing in opposite directions" (at 476).[5] While having a ring of truth about it, this statement does not add to an understanding of the way the contradictory approaches must relate to each other. In our purportedly individualistic sentencing model, it is understandable that the judiciary would want to retain discretion to emphasise certain factors.

Courts have largely undertaken the development of principle, somewhat reluctantly, as a response to legislative action. The creation of legislation is itself a product of social context. David Brown has pointed out that the enactment of the sentencing legislation in 2001, against the advice of the Law Reform Commission, was part of the "law and order" political auction prior to the state election rather than recognition of the need to clarify the law in relation to sentencing (D. Brown 2002, p. 65). Recognising the truth of Brown's statement, however, does not preclude a recognition that, however inadvertently, the legislature, in the inclusion of such aims as making the offender accountable and recognising harm done to victims and community, has reflected the influence of recent restorative justice currents of thought in the legal and political

[5] *Veen v The Queen (No 2)* (1988)164 CLR 465.

community (Fernandez 2003). This is not to say that judges formerly did not consider these matters: only that, in giving them legislative expression on the same footing as more traditionally accepted aims, the emphasis may have changed. Perhaps there is even more of a need now that these matters have been incorporated into the legislation to theorise and operationalise the aims to make explicit the processes and procedures of the criminal justice system.

The aims of sentencing in NSW are set out in s3A of the *Crimes (Sentencing Procedure)* Act, NSW (1999) (CSA):

1. to ensure that the offender is adequately punished for the offence,
2. to prevent crime by deterring the offender and other persons from committing similar offences,
3. to protect the community from the offender,
4. to promote the rehabilitation of the offender,
5. to make the offender accountable for his or her actions,
6. to denounce the conduct of the offender,
7. to recognise the harm done to the victim of the crime and the community.

All the matters which are relevant to the setting of the head sentence are relevant to the setting of the non-parole period, although they will have different weight: (*Bugmy v The Queen*).[6] Howie J equated "sentencing" with "punishment" when he referred to "the purposes of punishment set out in s3A of the *Crimes (Sentencing Procedure) Act*" (*A/G's Application under* s37).[7] Any attempt to distinguish the aims of sentencing from the aims of the criminal justice system (as does Ashworth 2010, p. 67) leads to an inevitable absence of philosophical guidance and a descent into acceptance of the bureaucratic outcome measures of agencies as adequate. It is logically unsupportable to view sentencing as merely "one part of the system" when it is charged with the considerable burden of

[6] *Bugmy v The Queen* (1990) 169 CLR 525.

[7] *Attorney General's Application under s37 of the Crimes (Sentencing Procedure) Act 1999 (No 2 of 2002)* (2003)137 A Crim R 196.

carrying out these aims in a practical and observable way. Arguably, and in contrast to the claims of Ashworth, the principles enunciated around sentencing offenders provide the framework for at least all that goes after it, the ongoing "sentencing" of the offender which continues beyond the courtroom. Without such consistent philosophical guidance, criminal justice organisations become vulnerable to conflicting directions and confused philosophies (Sotiri 2003) and to the presence of imaginary penalities, as discussed by Carlen (2008).

Punishment

Punishment is expressed as one of the aims of sentencing in s3A. The confusion between punishment as the catch-all phrase to sum up all the different emotional reactions to crime and punishment as a philosophical entity informing legally rational decision-making, which must be explicable and justifiable, is exemplified in the circular statement by Howie J, Grove J, Barr J in *R v Scott*[8]—"one of the purposes of punishment is to ensure that the offender is adequately punished." As logically unsatisfying as this statement is, as an end in itself punishment does not then need any other justification, although it functions as the mechanism by which other aims (most importantly, denunciation and deterrence) are ostensibly played out in practice. As the most retributivist element in the aims of sentencing, the concept of *lex talionis,* while unhelpful in deciding the quantum or nature of punishment in many cases, provides the overriding moral justification for the deliberate infliction of harm occasioned by punishment (Finkelstein 2004, p. 212). Moral arguments about the framework within which harm can be legally inflicted upon an individual by the state inform the analysis in this area. Quantifying suffering, which criminal courts are required to do in relation to all parties, is an inexact process and it is difficult to argue that logical and deductive strategies in sentencing are any more likely to come up with the "right" sentence in terms of the degree of suffering which needs to be inflicted, than a reliance on the subjective "gut feeling" of an experienced judge. The reason for this is that such "rightness" is a highly relative concept

[8] *R v Scott* [2005] NSWCCA 152.

which has to finely calibrate nuances of hierarchies of harm according to a shifting, contradictory agenda of community (and political) concern, translated into legislation in NSW which lists "aggravating" and "mitigating" features [s23A *Crimes (Sentencing Procedure) Act* NSW 1999].

Undue concentration on the philosophical underpinnings of punishment arguably detracts from the reality of the consequences of the infliction of pain. Abstracting the reasons and reasoning from the process and outcomes allows a stance which obviates the necessity to acknowledge the visceral nature of suffering of the human body and mind. "Rightness" of the sentence is therefore constructed on the basis of self-referential legal processes that contain no feedback loop to assess the actual effect of punishment on the individual involved. This is not to argue for a further severing of philosophy from practice but for a more nuanced view derived from experience rather than speculation.

The "pains of imprisonment" (Sykes 1958/1999), which represent the most obvious punitive aspect of imprisonment in NSW today, are to an extent self-evident to the point that official statements often make no mention of them. "The NSW Department of Corrective Services makes no mention of 'punishment' in its official discourse" (Sotiri 2003, p. 39). The truism that people are sent to prison "as" not "for" punishment tends to obscure some of these pains and lends credibility to the pervading perception that prison is a neutral experience if actual physical punishment is not handed out. Sotiri's documenting of the positioning of CSNSW NSW, in its own rhetoric, as different from the previous brutal administration, illustrates this tendency.

Discussions of proportionality are most often found when discussing this aim. The inclusion of the term "adequately punished" may be seen to indicate that an assessment of proportionality is paramount and that this depends largely on an assessment of the relative objective seriousness of the crime, only after which can the other factors that may include subjective features be assessed (*R v Dodd*).[9] Viewed in this way, proportionality is all about objective assessment and the placing of the offence in a rationally derived scale of ascending seriousness. The focus is therefore

[9] *R v Dodd* (1991) 57 A Crim R 349.

on avoiding subjectivity and arriving at a logically derived punishment which has meaning when compared to other crimes of similar gravity.

This denial of subjectivity arguably pushes the sentencer to disregard the other side of proportionality: that the punishment is not too severe.

In this regard, it should be noted that parsimony is no longer to be regarded as a sentencing principle in NSW (*Blundell v R*),[10] as such a proposition is "inconsistent with the notion of a range of sentences, and the discretions properly open to sentencing judges" (Simpson J in *Blundell v R* at [47]). Parsimony had previously been considered as a principle which limited the sentence to the minimum possible consistent with the public interest (*Webb v O'Sullivan*).[11] It is arguable that the absence of such constraint can only lead to the imposition of longer sentences.

Prevention of Crime by Deterrence

The problematic nature of reliance on deterrence, specific and general, as an outcome of sentencing has been well documented (Von Hirsch and Ashworth 1998; McGuire 2005). The assertion that there is a common sense link between the presence of criminal sanctions and the reluctance of most of the community to commit crimes has been restated many times in case law. The laments of criminologists that an evidence-based legal system should take note of the evidence that imprisonment provides a cost ineffective model of deterrence are perhaps the most cogent example of the disjunction between theory, evidence and practice in criminal justice. The omnipresence of this doctrine is reflected in case law, and in particular categories of offences. Sometimes it appears that judges are trying to convince themselves that it works; "the courts must assume, although the evidence is wanting, that the sentences they impose have the effect of deterring at least some people from committing crime"(King CJ in *Yardley v Betts*).[12] Is this another example of "imaginary penalty" as Carlen (2008) describes it?

---

[10] *Blundell v R* (1991) 57 A Crim R 349.

[11] *Webb v O'Sullivan* [1952] SASR 65 at 66 per Napier CJ.

[12] *Yardley v Betts* (1979)1 A Crim R 329.

Deterrence assumes an effective communication and effective understanding of the message being sent (Speigelman J in *R v Wong and Leung*). The subjective requirement is that the potential offender both receives the message that the behaviour will be sanctioned in a certain way and understands it. Individual deterrence is often ineffective, as evidenced by high rates of recidivism and, as it pre-supposes some kind of premeditation, is irrelevant in the majority of crimes which are impulsive or opportunistic (McGuire 2005, p. 450). Further, the conflation of deterrence with punishment acts to further disadvantage the already disadvantaged and provides an excuse for further punishment. To increase a sentence beyond the individual culpability of the offender for the purpose of sending a message to potential offenders appears unjustified in all but very few cases, that is, repeat offenders and those who have considered all of the potential consequences and offended anyway (McGuire 2005, p. 458, *Veen No 2 v R*). Bagaric (2000) points to evidence that the link between "marginal deterrence" and the incidence of crime is weak and that it may in some cases increase crime (Bagaric 2000, p. 37). It certainly seems clear that marginal deterrence, that is the deterrent effect of increasing a penalty, is ineffective and all but the most general effects of the existence of the criminal justice system in its entirety as a deterrent to crime are difficult to support with evidence (Robinson and Darley 2003, 951).

Deterrence is often spoken of as if it bears no relationship to the acts and processes, which ostensibly provide the effect of deterrence. It is in the processes of carrying out the physical actions connected to the other aims and purposes that deterrence is meant to be achieved: not only imprisonment or other limitation on personal freedoms, denunciation, but also rehabilitation. The subtle ascendance of modalities of psychological and psychiatric treatment brings some of the activities of criminal justice experts under this aim by virtue of their claims to be able to identify and "treat" risk, thus deterring individual offenders from crime. High rates of recidivism render such claims questionable even if programmes were delivered in ideal circumstances, which prison most definitely is not.

Cognitive behavioural modalities pre-suppose reasoning rational subjects who are able to calculate the benefits to themselves of dealing with their risk factors and desisting from offending. As Maruna and others have shown, desistance is a far more complex process and relates far more to the types of social supports available to the individual than any internal, transformative psychological process whether induced by way of therapy or not (Maruna 2001). This is not to say that individually transformative experiences such as embracing religious observance or meditation associated with Buddhist principles do not assist the individual to cope with the pains of imprisonment and adjustment to the world beyond on release. In any case, the "what works" approach, adopted wholeheartedly by corrections authorities, renders those modalities which, to paraphrase a popular saying around CSNSW, "makes crims feel good about themselves while planning their next armed rob" redundant unless they can be shown to have direct connection to those needs which have been transformed into individual risk factors.

Anthony has pointed out the unique role played by deterrence in relation to the sentencing of indigenous offenders in Australia, pointing to developments in NSW law following the decision by Wood J in *Fernando*[13] (Anthony 2008). The courts, in moving away from the use of the eight *Fernando* principles to place the actions of indigenous offenders in the context of the disadvantage suffered by the Aboriginal community as a whole, took the view that in NSW, the majority of offenders had moved away so far from traditional ways that they were "not indigenous enough" to have these considerations applied (Anthony 2008, p. 14). Anthony further argues that the prevailing view of Aboriginal communities as "morally corrupt" has led to a move towards the expression of deterrence as a major factor in sentencing indigenous offenders. In relating the unique role of crime control to the post-colonial setting as a continuing manifestation of a paternalistic, punitive pattern of relationships (Anthony 2008, p. 23), it becomes clearer that the position of indigenous people in relation to post-modern versions of control does not indicate a shift in focus, but a continuing pattern in which *Fernando* was an uncharacteristic and short-lived model. In "diminishing the role of community context in sentencing" (Anthony 2008, p. 25) NSW and NT courts have been part of an overall return to an assimilationist model in relation to indigenous communities and a failure to recognise the structural disadvantages suffered as a result

[13] *R v Fernando* (1992)76 A Crim R 58.

of colonisation (Cunneen 2001, p. 25). The recent High Court decision in *Bugmy,* while rejecting the Court of Criminal Appeal's contention that the relevance of this disadvantage decreases over time, may be seen as providing only limited support to the full recognition of indigenous disadvantage.[14]

Protection of the Community

The way that imprisonment provides protection to the community arguably goes beyond the incarceration of certain dangerous individuals for finite periods of time. Life sentences are still in the very small minority and the majority of sentences are for short periods. Protecting the community by imprisoning the small numbers of individuals, who have shown by their behaviour their inability or unwillingness to conform, allows the appearance of dealing with social problems without the need for attention to the complexity of human behaviour. The symbolic benefits for imprisonment in fulfilling this aim are manifold. Constructions of the community as a homogenous entity which needs protection from random individuals who, by virtue of their individual pathology are unable to comply with the requirements of citizenship, serves to legitimate strategies of containment and exclusion. People are saved from confronting the rifts and conflicts of diverse post-industrialised societies by virtue of the secretive and hidden prison. Politicians (such as former NSW premier Bob Carr) are able to point to high incarceration rates as proof that the community is being protected. In this way, protection of the community becomes the possible justification for a range of intrusions into the traditional basis for the common law criminal justice system (e.g. bail, parole).

Post-sentence detention exemplifies the rise in importance of risk-based strategies of containment. These are legitimised by and arise from public concern about community protection. Often community protection is privileged over the rights of individuals, most importantly the presumption of innocence. The ascendance of the view that the protection of the community is paramount to the extent that important individual human rights are willingly subverted can lead to the warehousing of prisoners.

[14] *Bugmy v The Queen* (2013) HCA 37.

In the context of increasing concerns about the futility of rehabilitation inside prisons and the huge increase in prisoner numbers, services are already severely limited. The terrible irony for those who protest that the prison is no place to rehabilitate anyone is that this argument is used to support the removal of those meagre services that may serve to partly mitigate the effects of imprisonment, for example the removal of psychologists from NSW prisons.

Rehabilitation

As one of the aims of sentencing in NSW, rehabilitation has acquired a legal meaning which is in constant daily use throughout the criminal justice system. Its aetiology, however, lies with the human sciences which have carved out and created specialist roles within a system that relies on this concept. As with many non-legal concepts drafted into service by legal functionalism and subject to inevitable reductionism, "rehabilitation" in the context of sentencing has become a creature of necessity, most often represented by a treatment program which can be included in the menu of the sentence. Chapter 7 considers this relationship in greater depth.

Apart from explicit mention in s3A, the *Crimes Legislation Amendment (Criminal Justice Interventions)* Act 2002, now Part 9 of the *Criminal Procedure Act* (1986), NSW provides statutory recognition that rehabilitation programmes may serve to protect the community. The objective in s173 (a) "to reduce the likelihood of future offending by facilitating participation in intervention programs" indicates that successful rehabilitation of offenders contributes to the maintenance of a safe peaceful and just society (Warner 2003). In other words, as well as being an aim of sentencing in its own right, rehabilitation contributes to another of the aims of sentencing, perhaps the most important, protection of the community. Some commentators have viewed the placement of "rehabilitation" as 4th in the list after punishment, deterrence and protection of the community as somehow diminishing its importance. A contrary argument can be made that rehabilitation extends into and provides the action necessary for the achievement of many, if not all, of the other aims.

The disavowal by therapeutic justice proponents of the old concepts of "rehabilitation" (Hutchinson 2006, p. 451) may contribute to the peculiar disjuncture between the newer practices within, for example drug courts, and the practice of the mainstream courts. While some of the reforms to procedures concerning victims have brought some recognition of restorative justice principles, in most serious mainstream criminal justice matters in NSW, such considerations are marginal at best.

Despite the influence of the "nothing works" school of thought, rehabilitation has survived the emphasis on punitive measures prevalent since the mid-1980s in NSW, to be enshrined in s3A, albeit in a different form due to the variety of coercive, cognitive skills-based courses which have emerged in correctional systems. Rehabilitation has undergone a transformation. Program access in NSW is officially linked to risk assessment and increasingly resources (e.g. psychologists) are being moved outside the prison. Programmes aimed at "reducing recidivism" in measurable ways are privileged over access to resources such as education or work release. Chapter 8 continues the discussion in the context of official policy and the responses of the prisoners interviewed.

In determining the non-parole period, regard must be had to the rehabilitative prospects of the prisoner (*R v Lian).*[15] In fact, as enunciated in the majority judgment in *Bugmy* (1990), the weight given to other factors such as "propensity to commit violent crime, the likelihood of re-offending and the need to protect the community depends upon a judge's assessment of the prospects of rehabilitation". Rehabilitation, then, is not only a factor in its own right, but has an effect on the weight given to other factors. In deciding the weight to be given to rehabilitation and the type of rehabilitation appropriate to the case, the court relies heavily on the assessment of psychological and psychiatric experts. This expertise is often expressed in the form of reliance on risk assessment instruments, although it must be said that experts prominent in the area are aware that clinical judgment "remains an important element in assessment of risk"

[15] *R v Lian* (1990) 47 A Crim R 444.

(*A/g of NSW v Tillman*).[16] How this can occur when risk assessment occurs totally on the basis of written material (as in *Featherstone v R*) is unclear.[17]

A further perspective on the importance of rehabilitation is: "A prisoner's prospect of rehabilitation will be important both by way of mitigation and because the community benefits from the reformation of one of its members" (*R v Bugmy*). Thus, while on the face of it, rehabilitation is:

> [t]he most humane justification for sentencing... despite the humane exterior of rehabilitation they are anything but caring, since they are not concerned with the offenders needs but are simply a means of improving our lot by reducing recidivism (Edney and Bagaric 2007, p. 69).

Edney and Bagaric point out that rehabilitation is primarily concerned with changing the values of offenders, assuming that can be achieved. The expectation that someone who is suffering the pains of imprisonment will adopt the value/stance of their gaolers is a basic impediment to the achievement of attitude/value change.

Given the presence of rehabilitation in the aims of sentencing, it is clear that, despite misgivings as to what it means and how it is achieved, judges "must assume" that their sentences contain this element in the vast majority of cases. The weight given depends on other factors, but, whether explicitly referred to in judgments or not, it is an integral part of every sentence. The debate in the penological community centred on the "nothing works" school of thought has had a devastating impact on CSNSW in NSW, but appears to have passed by the courts. Despite assumptions that rehabilitation is the soft and cuddly face of punishment, some rehabilitation programmes are so onerous as to place in question this assumption (Von Hirsch and Maher 1992). The potential for the extension of social control by the use of programs which may infringe the principle of proportionality has also been a point of

---

[16] Attorney General for the State of New South Wales v Tillman [2007] NSWSC 605.

[17] *Featherstone v R* (2008) NSW CCA71. A risk assessment was completed on the basis of material in the offender's file and no clinical interview was undertaken.

contention with some theorists, although evidence of this actually occurring in NSW is absent (D. Brown 2005, p. 27).

It appears that the "rehabilitative ideal" had only just begun having an influence on the criminal justice system in NSW when political factors (the most salient of which was the election of the Greiner Government and the enactment of the new sentencing regime thereafter) halted the process of reform begun by the Nagle Royal Commission and ushered in the era of law and order auctions. The "new orthodoxy" which "asserts that rehabilitative objectives are unattainable" (Allen in Von Hirsch and Ashworth 1998, p. 190) took somewhat longer to reach Australia, but as Sotiri (2003) points out, has left a vacuum in CSNSW which has been filled by a risk-based managerial approach where involvement in programmes is directly related to the administration of risk assessment techniques. This is not to say that the implementation of this agenda has been uniform, as the recent Performance Audit of Prisoner Rehabilitation demonstrates (NSW Auditor General 2006). The implementation of many of the essential elements of departmental policy such as case management—which has been given lip service for at least a decade—is at a rudimentary stage. Decades of constant change has left a culture within CSNSW, which can only be characterised as avoidant of criticism, a moving target, where change has become a constant to the point that an inmate can be prevented from doing a programme because it will be offered at a later stage of the sentence, only to find that the goalposts have change and the programme is required to be completed at the beginning of the sentence.

De Graaff, examining the requirement in NSW under the *Crimes (Administration of Sentences Act) s135 (2)* that the Parole Authority must take into regard a number of factors, including (i) the attitudes expressed by the offender and (ii) the offender's willingness to participate in rehabilitation programmes, points out the lack of accountability, particularly in relation to the provision of education. If inmates are required to demonstrate a positive attitude towards involvement in rehabilitative programming then the concomitant responsibility to provide them must be acknowledged. Leaving such important matters to the discretion of individual managers, risks the relegation of education to a secondary role (De Graaff 2005). Much easier is the provision of large, centralised offence-specific programmes, arguably also much more useful for calming punitive sentiments than the localised provision in each prison of an integrated educational system. Further discussion of the relegation of education to a subordinate position in relation to offence-specific programmes will take place in Chap. 8.

There has been a change in emphasis in the UK from rehabilitation to coercive control, despite the centrality of rehabilitation to "the parole image" (Lynch 2000, p. 58). Lynch notes that:

> [t]hose things that would normally fall under the rehabilitation part of the job of parole officers (addressing identified needs and obstacles faced by the parolee) are often turned in to problems of bad attitude... clients are encouraged to employ self-help (or self responsibilisation) strategies to transform themselves into normative citizens" (Lynch 2000, p. 58).

Accountability

The way this aim of sentencing is expressed indicates that it may be a new addition to the traditional aims of sentencing, or at least a new emphasis. The question of how this is to be achieved again raises the question of subjectivity. Arguably, the achievement of this aim requires an internal process on the part of the offender, manifested in some practical evidence of accountability. Does this accountability involve an ongoing process? When does it stop, and how can it be measured when the effects of making someone accountable are amorphous and difficult to describe if not quantify? As a manifestation of the trend towards individualisation and responsibilisation (Halsey 2008), this aim can be seen as another example of a direction to offenders to undergo some kind of ongoing process extending outside of the courtroom.

In discussing judicial accountability, Tata (2002, p. 417) points to two dimensions of accountability: "One (formal) view is of accountability as entailing an obligation to give account of activities within one's ambit of responsibility", implying the need for some kind of understandable narrative in which those affected by the crime can make some sense of it, and:

> [*a*]*ccountability*, in which the giving of the account is acknowledged as being affected by what has to be accounted for, who makes the demand . . . who is the intended audience and the spatial, social, cultural and communications format affecting the capacity to make an account (Tata 2002, p. 417).

The imperative to be able to "give a good narrative account of yourself" occurs throughout the various stages of the criminal justice system. Findings of guilt and innocence rely on a choice between competing narratives. The ability to "give good narrative" is another aspect of our criminal justice system which disadvantages people already overrepresented in the criminal justice system, such as poor and indigenous people (Eades 2008). Throughout the criminal justice process, from questioning by police through account giving in court, to interviews by psychologists and parole officers, offenders are required to give an account of their activities and life history in a way that is understandable to the variety of criminal justice functionaries they encounter (Hall and Rossmanith 2015 forthcoming). Once again, in the requirement that internal processes be demonstrated in a socially comprehensible way, differences in cultural, educational and language abilities can distort the way actions are perceived and the inability to demonstrate acceptance of accountability is punished.

Part of the rhetoric of the requirement for ongoing accountability is seen in the development of restitution-based criminal injuries compensation schemes, where the state pays the victim and then proceeds to recover the money from offenders (Part 2, Division 8 of the *Victims Support and Rehabilitation Act* 1996 (NSW)). In this way, prisoners who have finished their sentences and have often lost the means to repay debt given the low wages paid in prison and the diminution of earning opportunities following imprisonment, leave prison with significant debt. The punitive aspects of policies of offender reparation are obvious. The subtle differences needed in the conception and administration of such reparation schemes in order to fulfil the aim of "making the offender accountable" by true reparation to the victim, understood as such by both victim and offender, appear to be beyond the criminal justice system as currently constituted.

Conventional jurisprudence has little to offer an analysis of how this particular aim can be carried out in practice. Accountability implies an ongoing process of helping to make sense of what has happened, including supplying the victim with important information to assist them in constructing an acceptable narrative of what has happened to them. Restorative justice has only just begun to deconstruct the meaning of this aim in terms of the practices and procedures of offender/victim "mediation", let alone how it can be undertaken within conventional criminal justice procedures. In NSW it tends to be tacked on at the end of the process.[18] CSNSW has a small restorative justice unit which conducts a limited number of offender/victim mediations, usually towards the end of offender's prison sentence.

Denunciation

Denunciation has been identified as the element in criminal punishment that separates it from a mere penalty (Feinberg in Duff and Garland 1994, p. 75). The expression of condemnation, along with unpleasant consequences, provides the essential nature of a criminal penalty. The traditional view of sentencing is that denunciation happens in the courtroom, the judge solemnly pronouncing society's condemnation of the conduct of the offender. The unpleasant treatment itself expresses condemnation. "Denunciation (is seen). . . . as a kind of fusing of resentment and reprobation" (Feinberg in Duff and Garland 1994, p. 76).

Does denunciation become an ongoing process in imprisonment and afterwards due to the disadvantage experienced by former prisoners? Although a distinction is made in the language of the statute—it is "conduct" we are denouncing, not the individual—it is sometimes difficult to see the difference in practice. Halsey (2008, p. 230) points out that the comments from judges with the most impact (negative) on the young men he interviewed were those where respect was not demonstrated. Denunciation rituals pervade the trial process and make sentencing a public performance in which the offender takes on a symbolic role (Tait 2002). At the traditional sentence the offender is lectured by the judge and is the object of the words of the judge (see discussion of sentence comments later). There is little involvement expressively of anyone else, although the

[18] An exception is the conferencing provisions of the juvenile justice legislation in NSW.

role of the victim's family in a public courtroom in reflecting and representing the dignity of the victim by their silent presence may have been underestimated.

Recent attempts to involve victims in sentencing reflect recognition of the importance of symbolic involvement, and arguably, another "imaginary penality" (Carlen 2008), as it is widely accepted that judges must sentence offenders no differently on the basis of the social position of the victim (see later discussion on attention to the harm done to the victim). Should the ongoing "denunciation" experienced by the offender during and after the trial and sentencing process and throughout their life, be subject to the principles of proportionality? Newer versions of criminal justice processing for differing severity of offences, the absence of the traditional legal controls on expression of feelings by victims observed in some criminal justice for example, circle sentencing and conferencing, raise issues of proportionality such as levels of "shaming" appropriate for specific offences.

Is denunciation the same as "shaming"? Tait privileges the less-controlled environment of the French murder trial, where the defendant tells the story with fewer controls and the family of the victim is able to confront and ask the defendant questions. In some cases indigenous customary law in Australia provides the same opportunity for direct confrontation, the enacting of the pain and loss felt by relatives by wailing and verbally confronting the offender with the damage done (although this is by no means common to all indigenous customary law).[19] As Tait points out, in our system it is the judicial officer alone who engages in the denunciatory performance (Tait 2002, p. 477). The trial and sentence as symbolism relies on the use of culturally relevant and appropriate processes and symbols "as a public performance invoking state power to exact or forgo vengeance" (Tait 2002, p. 470). "Ritual was given a bad name, as a superfluous and obsolete set of practices designed to confuse and mystify ordinary people" (Tait 2002, p. 471). Tait argues for an acknowledgement of the power of ritual to "temper demand for revenge or restore the social order without needing to

[19] As Cunneen (2001:97) points out in the 'aboriginal domain' in which customary law operates, there may be a "lack of distinction between public/private" and a range of different sanctions used.

inflict further suffering", further arguing that it is "the performance of justice" which increases public awareness and support for criminal justice measures (Tait 2002, p. 473).

Similarly, Freiberg urges an acknowledgment of the importance of the symbolic in crime control policy, (Freiberg 2002, p. 265) in order to stem the tide of retributive justice. Marinos argues that:

> Conceptions of punishment and equivalency must include two neglected features of the literature—the nature of the offence *and* the offender. These qualitative dimensions of punishment need to be addressed in addition to the purposes and functions of individual punishments within criminal justice literature and sentencing legislation . . . creating expressive denunciatory sanctions can be useful for the purposes of decreasing the use of imprisonment within a relatively structured sentencing system" (Marinos 2005, p. 444, 451).

Denunciation, the expressive element in sentencing, has therefore been viewed as a popular panacea to the more extreme retributive elements which have developed in our criminal justice system. It is necessary to deconstruct this assumption. Are Freiberg and others, in their assumption that punitiveness can be headed off by symbolism, suggesting some deep atavistic need to see "one who does me wrong" suffer? If so, is it not somewhat naïve to assume that this need could be satisfied by the performance of ritual, however powerful?

Is it necessary for the object of the denunciation to acknowledge and accept the expression of denunciation? Does the denouncer need to experience this? How do they know that the person is subjectively being denounced? These questions clearly raise complex questions of subjectivity and psychology, and are rarely examined. If in fact more expressive sanctions do reduce punitiveness and rates of imprisonment, more attention must be paid to the subjective experiences of those performing and being subjected to the denunciation (McGowen 2000). Highlighting the importance of subjective states to the emerging restorative justice paradigm, Braithwaite and Mugford (in Laster and O'Malley 1996, p. 32) view the conventional courtroom as "(tending) to degradation rather than reintegration because the production line technocracy and discourse of legalism makes it easy for the offender to sustain psychological barriers against shame".

The emergence of the technocratic risk-averse approach to criminal justice, along with a revival of rational choice theory, must not be seen as exclusive, and as Laster and O'Malley (1996, p. 31) point out: "It appears that technocratic and emotional tendencies cannot be thought of simply as exclusive and hostile alternatives as they appear to relate to each other in quite a variable fashion."

Recognise Harm Done to Victim (and Community)

Clearly a new addition to the explicated aims of sentencing, this bald statement begs the question of how this is to be done. Piecemeal reforms to procedure in sexual assault trials and the submission of victim impact statements, underpin attempts to insert the victim in the dialogue between defence and prosecution which characterises our criminal justice system. While victim impact statements have been able to be tendered in limited cases since 1987, a raft of victim-related legislation (*Victims Support and Rehabilitation Act 1996* and the *Victims Rights Act 1996)* reflected in s26-30 of the *Crimes (Sentencing Procedure) Act 1999* (Johns 2002a, p. 14) has brought increased attention to the victim. The new act allows for restitution action to be taken in the same way (Part V, *Victims' Rights and Support Act 2013).*

The role of the victim impact statement is problematic for the judiciary, recognising the political need for such measures but demonstrating understandable discomfort with the way it has been inserted into the criminal justice process and the lack of guidance provided by the legislature as to how this information should be used. The words "can be received" give no guidance as to how the information is to be used and the confusing language "must not be used unless the judge thinks appropriate" places a prohibition not helped by the broad discretion granted afterwards. Understandably, "judges have largely been unwilling to do more than receive victim impact statements" particularly where the offence involved the death of the victim (Johns 2002a, p. 17)[20] except where relevant as

[20] Although Kirchenghast (2008) suggests that NSW is more restrictive than other jurisdictions and that victim impact statements may help "define victim interests as part of the broader public

factual material going to the seriousness of the offence. The resulting disappointment and confusion particularly for relatives in murder cases, of having expectations raised was pointed out by Hunt J in the case of *Previtera*[21] (Booth 2012).

This aim requires a subject. Who is recognising the harm done to the victim? The sentence and the process of reaching it is a public recognition by the court that harm has been done. Punishment is meted out in acknowledgement of the need to inflict pain to assist in that public recognition. Is it only by way of setting an appropriate tariff that this recognition is to be achieved, of ensuring that the punishment fits the crime? This bald view of "just deserts" can lead to disproportionate results. Does the offender also need to recognise and, more importantly, display that recognition in some way as part of the process? Again, a requirement that the offender undergoes a subjective process of "recognition" and offers some demonstration of this, underpins this aim. Clearly related to the concept of "remorse" and as riven with problems of identification in the individual, true recognition of harm caused is clearly part of the rehabilitative project and underlies many of the treatment modalities, from sex offender treatment to 12-step drug rehabilitation programmes (see later discussion of remorse).

The conflation of harm to the victim with harm done to the community adds an extra dimension to the prescription for action underpinned by this aim. Broader recognition of harm beyond that to the individual victim often takes the form of particular censure of common or particularly socially invidious crimes, and can easily be affected by community concerns deepened by widespread media coverage over, for example, child sex offences. This can lead to a distortion of the emphasis of the sentence away from the particular circumstances of the offence and the offender to a more abstract position of viewing the "community as victim", thereby aggravating the seriousness of the offence. While understandable in relation to underreported and poorly dealt with crimes such

interest" (Kirchenghast, 2008: 630), suggesting that s 3(g) of the *Crimes(Administration of Sentences Act)* supports this.

[21] *R v Previtera* (1997) 94 A Crim R 76.

as sexual assault and domestic violence offences, distortions in perceptions of harm can lead to undesirable outcomes, for example, juvenile sex offenders of whatever seriousness or dangerousness placed on sex offender registers for life.

3.4 Risk and NSW Courts

Having analysed the aims of sentencing in the light of the subjective expectations contained therein, the impact of decisions of future dangerousness and risk by the courts in NSW is now considered. The importance of risk has been emphasised in the last chapter as an increasingly dominant paradigm in correctional practice which, as will be examined in Chap. 7, has arguably transformed the way "rehabilitation" is conceived and practiced in NSW prisons.

The question arises as to whether, and if so, how this influential discourse is playing out in the sentencing practice of the judicial officers of NSW. While courts have always made such determinations as part of their sentencing practice, the mode and substance of these decisions may reflect the impact of new technologies of assessment and treatment. The use of risk assessments developed by psychologists and widely used elsewhere in the criminal justice system is beginning to become evident in sentencing, although judges may not be ready to completely cede this area to the experts and there is often considerable discussion about the need to contextualise such assessments with other evidence such as clinical assessment.

Nevertheless, the increasing reliance on actuarial methods of risk assessment to ground some of the most prominent features of modern correctionalism and penal policy, such as "what works" (discussed in Chap. 8) and, more recently "justice reinvestment"[22] demonstrates their ubiquitous nature. As discussed in Chap. 2, preventive detention legislation aimed at serious sex offenders further legitimises the use of

[22] Justice reinvestment relies on careful targeting of resources – much of the literature (eg Clement M, Schwarzfeld M, Thompson M (2011) relies on risk assessment and evidence of "what works" in order to argue for a reinvestment from prisons to community resources.

actuarial risk assessment and arguably presages an enhanced role in the future in general sentencing matters.

Historically, notions of dangerousness were transformed by the introduction of a "systematic way of dealing with hazards and insecurities and introduced by modernity itself" (Beck in Pratt 1998, p. 1). In a self-sustaining way, fears about repeat offenders have resulted in an undermining of "traditional" legal protections and a commensurate perpetuation and deepening of these fears. "Dangerousness" as a descriptive term for this future manifestation (of behaviour) is a legal construct (Yannoulidis 2002, p. 158). The term is a guideline that presumes clinical expertise. In the present context, recourse to "dangerousness" as a means of justifying preventive detention is legitimated by its objectification in terms of "disease". "Dangerousness is a subjective concept, which is attributed to individuals taking account of calculable actuarial risk and the subjective fear which they invoke" (Yannoulidis 2002, p. 155). In order to accommodate the law's concern with ascriptions of responsibility, the metaphoric use of the notion of "disease" finds expression as a reified construct that is "dangerousness". By moving between different levels of analysis, the law exploits the contradictory and vague nature of the concept and gives expression to overriding social, cultural and political demands.

The tendency is for legislation and policy dealing with preventive detention to be "counter law" and designed to "circumvent legal barriers" (Hebenton and Seddon 2009, p. 347) in the sense that the "problem" (in this case of public perceptions of safety from dangerous offenders) has been constructed as being located in the application of traditional legal principles. Viewed in this way, extra-legal measures can be seen as a rejection of principle and tradition and recognition of the need to take extraordinary measures to deal with certain populations. Further evidence of the "extra" or "counter" legal nature of some of the measures taken is demonstrated by the case of *GTR*[23] where principles regarding juvenile offenders were contravened by preventive sex offender legislation.

[23] *Director of Public Prosecutions v GTR* [2007]WASC 318.

Risky Subjects—Sex Offenders

During the 1980s, concern about the treatment of women and children transformed into an increase in focus on sex offenders. "The impulse of (this) preventive logic can be seen in its strongest form in this area of dangerous sexual and violent offenders" (Hebenton and Seddon 2009, p. 344). This diverse and non-unitary category of offender became the most common subject in discussions about risk. "Responses have been strongly influenced by the image of paedophiles as recidivist offenders who are stubbornly resistant to attempts to reform them" (Kemshall and McGuire 2001, p. 241), although evidence regarding propensity to re-offend indicates that this group is at low risk. The singular focus on sex offenders has resulted in a variety of practical outcomes for them during and after incarceration when viewed through the lens of risk and dangerousness, which may not follow for other equally violent offenders. The sex offenders interviewed for this book were an easily identifiable group: they all knew their "risk levels" and were aware that the completion of cognitive behavioural programmes would be essential for their release on parole.

Preventive Detention of Sex Offenders in NSW—Advance Guard for Risk-Technology-Reliant Judges?

As Mark Brown (2008b) points out, preventive detention legislation raises the issue of "the response to the problem of imprisonment when it is framed within the new discourse not of punishment but of security". For Mark Brown the debate over who should be punished and why has been eclipsed by "a new field of hygienist social defence: the monitoring and internment of 'suspect' citizens". Applying a lesser standard of proof to the internment of suspect citizens involves:

> a court shifting back and forth between criminal and civil standards and precepts in order to establish an entirely new field of legality that makes possible the governmental objectives of quarantine and exclusion (Mark Brown 2008b, p. 9).

As the results are punitive in that they invariably involve incarceration, the use of shifting standards of proof is especially problematic.

The focus on sex offenders in NSW as subjects of preventive detention legislation allows for an enhanced role for expert psychological/psychiatric evidence regarding risk and dangerousness.[24] Here, risk assessment and the medical model of psychiatric practice appear to coexist comfortably, although it is clear that at least some courts are aware of some of the biases intrinsic to risk assessment . . . "It may well be that Mr Radford's level of risk is much greater—his general presentation and commendable work efforts may create an overly optimistic impression of his general level of risk" (*Brett Stuart Radford v Parole Board).*[25] Buddin J commented regarding risk assessment: "The instrument is only as good as the quality of the information available in making an assessment. Generally speaking, it is lack of information that leads to lower scores." Kirby J in his dissenting judgment in *Fardon*[26] said, "[e]xperts in law, psychology and criminology have long recognized the unreliability of predictions of criminal dangerousness." Nevertheless, the High Court has upheld the validity of such instruments.

In *Tillman v Attorney General for the State of NSW,*[27] Bell J held that the words "satisfied to a high degree of probability" in 17(2) and (3) of the Act means "more than likely". Although the provisions of s17 (3) do not employ the terms "risk" or "risk management", it is clear that "the section is aimed at an assessment by the court as to the risk of the offender committing a further serious sex offence" (Hall J cited by Mason P, Giles JA & Hodgson JA in *Cornwall v Attorney General of NSW).*[28]

The case of *NSW v Fisk*[29] indicates that for some offenders, programme completion does not reduce perceptions of risk. Indeed, successful completion appeared to have been viewed as evidence of Mr Fisk's

[24] The legislation requires the court to consider evidence from two psychologists or psychiatrists.

[25] *(2002) NSWCCA 70 (12 March 202).*

[26] (2003)223 CLR 575.

[27] (2007) NSWSC 605.

[28] (2007) NSW CA 374.

[29] [2009] NSWSC 778.

manipulative abilities. One of the most interesting aspects of the case law around preventive detention in NSW is the dialogue between the experts, the Department and the court, often as to who will shoulder the financial burden of providing the services which is according to the evidence better provided outside prison (for example, *NSW v Wilde).*[30]

Doyle and Ogloff point out the fallacious basis of much of Australia's preventive detention legislation, emphasising the reliance of the law on unsupported assumptions about human behaviour. They point out that evidence of sex offender recidivism (which is very low) was overlooked in the "hasty" enactment of this legislation and argue "the evidence suggests that the legislation will not meet its aims in any meaningful and sustainable way" (Doyle and Ogloff 2009, p. 183). The problems inherent in the "translation of clinical risk to legal risk" mean that in NSW what the legislation requires, a conditional risk assessment or one which assesses risk as a function of variable living conditions, is unable to be provided by the instruments currently used (Hart in Doyle and Ogloff 2009, p. 197). Indeed, determinations of "dangerousness" reliant on the expert evidence of psychiatrists may be an invalid exercise of judicial power and not supported constitutionally (Ruschena 2003, p. 122).

Another fertile area, which may be revitalised by the recent decision of the United Nations Human Rights Committee in *Tillman*, is the human rights implications of the post-sentence detention regimes present in many Australian jurisdictions including NSW. The stretch to authorising preventive detention on the basis of predictions of risk has been viewed by commentators who support the lone voice of Kirby J in *Fardon*, concerned as to incursions into individual human rights posed by such legislation. The recent decision of the United Nations Human Rights Committee in *Tillman*[31] places the issue of preventive detention as double punishment squarely back before the state government. The Committee's somewhat trite observation that "imprisonment is penal in character" (p. 10) gives lie to the representation of the legislation in NSW, that the preventive detention scheme is primarily rehabilitative. The reliance on psychological

[30] 2008 [NSWSC] 1211.

[31] (UNHRC 2010).

risk assessment instruments to determine such matters raises questions as to their efficacy, as does the reliance on mandatory or coercive cognitive behavioural programs to reduce "risk". Mark Brown points out the "fundamentally punitive nature" of the post-sentence detention measures (M. Brown 2008b, p. 12) and the danger of privileging community fears and anxieties over the liberty rights of individuals.

Concomitant with this focus, post 9/11, new security categories relating to "terrorist" prisoners reflect an increasing willingness to suspend individual rights for those considered especially risky (McSherry 2005).[32] The rhetoric of "balancing" security concerns with concerns about personal liberty often results in the dominance of security concerns and the perpetuation of a type of "zero sum game" in which individual rights are seen as always in conflict with the need for security (Bronitt in Gani and Mathew 2008, p. 68). A similar "zero sum" discourse can be detected in relation to recent concerns relating to victims.

Cementing Them in Their Cells—Risk as a Cipher for Punishment and Denunciation

Is it misguided to look to the form of governance for assistance as to its significance as a "penal marker" or evidence of a different way of doing things? Is it not as instructive to take a bottom-up approach and look to the effect of policies and legislation on individuals subject to criminal justice interventions? Viewed in this way, such measures as the retrospective legitimatisation of judicial comments expressing the view that the prisoner should never be released represents a legitimate object of study, as the result is the application of continuing incarceration on the basis of a prediction of future behaviour.[33] Or is it really a continuing denunciation of extreme violence and recognition that a purely punitive approach is the only politically acceptable one with certain serious violent offenders? "These

[32] AA prisoners are said to pose a "special risk to national security" Cl 22 *Crimes (Administration of Sentences) Regulation 2001*.

[33] Lucia Zedner touched on this in a recent account of the wide ranging study of Preventive Detention currently underway at Oxford University (Zedner, 2012 UNSW Scientia Lecture).

changes mean that Baker and other never-to-be-released prisoners can only ever be released if they are on their deathbeds or so incapacitated that they would pose no threat" (Ackland 2005). This comment seems to indicate that they would only be released when they posed no risk of re-offending whatsoever. Certainly the punitive and retributive nature of these policies is undoubtable; however, the presence of risk thinking is also strongly demonstrated. Perhaps risk is here a subsidiary concern to the need to continue to punish offenders convicted of particularly heinous crimes. Is risk, then a kind of cipher for ongoing denunciation and retribution, a way of manipulating science to justify treatment which otherwise may be viewed as disproportionate and unjust?

Adams J, in a dissenting judgment in *Knight,*[34] expressed scepticism about psychiatric evidence in evaluating the applicant's dangerousness and took the view that the applicant's previous acts of violence in no way approached the extreme nature of that perpetrated on the victim. His Honour doubted the reliability of predictions of future dangerousness: at p. 65 the ground of appeal that it was not open to the sentencing judge to find that the applicant's dangerousness meant that she should never be released was upheld.

Lawyers may be reluctant to engage in debate about the measurement of future dangerousness due primarily to the "representation of risk as a scientific measurement" (Murphy and Whitty 2007, p. 802) and thus "non-legal knowledge" (2007, p. 804). As a result, the concept of risk as applied in a legal context is relatively undeveloped. It may also be, as Brown has asserted, that individualistic conceptions of justice conflict with actuarial notions of risk (M. Brown 2000, p. 104).

The development of technologies of risk management centred on conceptions of dangerousness has strengthened the reliance on expert evidence from psychologists and psychiatrists. The use of predictions of dangerousness to authorise indefinite detention takes acceptance of psychiatric and psychological evidence to a new level as the reliance of the courts on such opinions is mandated in legislation. Section 15(4) of the *(Crimes (Serious Sex offenders) Act,* NSW requires the court to appoint either two

---

[34] [2006] NSWCCA 292.

psychologists, two psychiatrists, or one of each: s 17(b), (c) and (d) involve psychological or psychiatric testimony as matters to be taken into account when determining the application.

Sentencing and Risk—Freiberg's "Guerrilla Judges"

As Pratt predicted, a hybrid model of "psy—knowledge" retains credibility in the courts of Australia—augmented by an increasing reliance on actuarial methods (Pratt 1998, p. 176). Freiberg states, "[t]he courts still prefer human diagnosis and judgment to clinical diagnosis or statistics" although "they will not ignore the latter completely" (Freiberg 2000, p. 65). In the everyday sentencing practice of the courts of NSW, the plethora of new legislation, amendments and important case law has increased the intensity of the sentencing process for the legal profession and the judiciary alike. It is arguable that the willingness of the legislature to allow such a pivotal role to expert psychological and psychiatric evidence in the preventive detention legislation is due to the continuing acceptance by courts of the validity of this evidence in general sentence matters. Conversely, it may be that the reliance on actuarial methods of risk assessment in preventive detention matters may influence the court in general sentencing matters.[35] The doctrine of instinctive synthesis may be, as Brown suggests, indicative of an approach to "categorical risk". It also results in a degree of opacity when attempting to calculate the weight given to various types of evidence on sentence.

Nevertheless, as the High Court in *Fardon* found, sentencing courts are accustomed to making findings of future dangerousness when considering such basic and entrenched sentencing aims as "protection of the community". Freiberg sees the more extreme versions of control of judicial discretion as evidence of the increasing contempt and mistrust of traditional legal processes demonstrated by the general population in dealing with the more visceral fears of modern life. Freiberg characterises the reaction of the judiciary towards extreme types of governance techniques such as mandatory

[35] The fact that these orders are made by the Supreme Court may serve to limit this tendency.

sentencing and indeterminate sentencing as "challenging the paradigms within which the courts have operated". He highlights the importance of the common law in "limit(ing) the scope of the legislation" (Freiberg 2000, p. 59). While courts must "be respectful of the will of the parliament, they are not subservient to it" and "some can be described as 'guerrilla tactics' (though certainly not by the judges) others amount to open confrontation" (Freiberg 2000, p. 59). As Freiberg points out, most of the challenges have been on the basis of infringement of the principle of proportionality.

This "dialogue" between the courts and the legislature also involves a number of "sub-dialogues" within the criminal justice system, whereby the wishes of the legislature as interpreted by the police and courts on sentence are really put into practice—in policing practices, correctional staff practice, clinical psychology and psychiatric diagnosis and practice. All of these are in play to a heightened degree when courts are deciding about future dangerousness.

In particular, the "psy—professions" now occupy an increasingly privileged place in judicial practice due to preventive detention legislation. Little critical scholarship has been directed to the acceptance by courts of psychiatric and psychological testimony in NSW. It would be understandable if the judiciary, under threat from all sides, were to accept empirically based scientific evidence purportedly involving the ability to demonstrate and measure the critical factors highly relevant to sentencing practice. It appears, however, that reliance on medical model psychiatry supplemented by actuarial psychology for sexual offences and extreme or recidivist violent offenders continues to characterise the NSW courts in their everyday sentencing practice.

Mark Brown sees the two discourses (psychiatric knowing and actuarial justice) as philosophically opposed and coexisting as part of a range of disparate practices which are subsumed together in criminal justice processes (M. Brown 2000). There is no doubt that reliance on psychological and psychiatric evidence in the legal arena, in the face of ample evidence of its limitations, is common. Whether one accepts this conflict as another example of the existence of contradictory and often conflicting currents in criminal justice, or as insufficient to explain the widespread adoption of actuarial judgments forming the subtext of much criminal justice decision making, the ubiquity of this kind of evidence is clear. While the types of knowledge professed by the two coexisting professions may be philosophically distinct, in practice the language may be blending and conflating. Further discussion of the impact of psychiatric and psychological discourse on imprisonment will take place in Chap. 7.

Sentencing and Risk—Case Law

In *R v Schlenert*,[36] Barr J exclaimed, "What actuarial risk assessment has to do with the chances that a person might commit a sexual offence I do not understand." More recent cases, mostly involving sexual offences, demonstrate a more sophisticated albeit sceptical understanding of the language of risk assessment. "As noted this assessment is based on actuarial measures. It says nothing about whether *this* applicant is likely to reoffend" (*Featherstone v R).*[37]

Many of the NSW sentencing cases involving substantial consideration of conceptions of future dangerousness and risk are the murder cases where life sentences are in consideration. While NSW courts continue to express doubts as to the ability of anyone, courts or experts, to predict future behaviour, inevitably the matter arises. The most important sentencing principle in relation to risk and dangerousness is proportionality, assessments of future dangerousness, it is recognised, should not result in disproportionate sentences.

In *R v SLD*,[38] on the basis of psychiatric reports, the court found that the applicant "must be judged as posing a significant level of future dangerousness and to be at *substantial risk* of re-offending in both violent and sexual ways". At the same time, the judge directed himself that he had to sentence "in the light of what is presently known" and that the experts were not "certain of what the future holds" (at 9). The sentencing process is also unable to ignore possible criminal behaviour by the prisoner in the future and the consequent

[36] [2008] NSWCCA 481.

[37] *Featherstone v R* (2008) NSW CCA71.

[38] *R v SLD* [2002] NSWSC 758.

risk to society: (*Veen v The Queen [No 2]*. In order to comply with one of the aims of sentencing, the protection of society, the court must consider future risk.

R v Robinson[39] and *Lyons v The Queen*[40] both emphasised that certainty was not required to establish a "likelihood of re-offending". Rather, what was involved in "giving weight in sentencing to protection of society against future re-offending must involve an assessment of both degree of likelihood and gravity of consequences" (*R v Robinson* at 34). Accordingly, a court is able to be "... satisfied beyond reasonable doubt that the test of dangerousness has been met (where) there exists a certain potential for harm" (*Lyons v The Queen* at 35).

Often, as one would expect from the focus on repeat offenders in criminal justice policy and politics in the recent past in NSW, the fact that the offence was a repetition of an earlier offence (as in *Veen No 2*) appears to be the deciding factor in determining that the offence is so serious, the offender so dangerous that only a life sentence will suffice. In the case of *Veen*, the repetition of the offence warranted substantial components of retribution and deterrence, but also "the knowledge of the offender himself of his "dangerous propensity for violence in certain circumstances appears to have been a factor in this consideration" (at 142). Thus the knowledge of the offender as to the types of circumstances which pre-disposed him to act violently and his willingness to place himself in those circumstances appeared to have exacerbated the seriousness of the offence beyond his status as a repeat offender.

As discussed in the previous chapter, the preventive detention regime in NSW elevates and legitimates consideration of risk. For serious violent offenders and almost all sex offenders, risk assessment is central to their correctional management. All inmates in the NSW correctional system are meant to be assessed in accordance with the "what works" philosophy of rehabilitation, that programs should be aimed at those offenders posing a high risk of recidivism. While not as ubiquitous in general sentencing, the attractiveness of this quasi-scientific method to

[39] *R v Robinson* [2002] NSWCCA 359.

[40] *Lyons v The Queen* [1987] 2 SCR 309.

judicial officers under increasing pressure to quantify and justify decisions may indicate an enhanced role in sentencing in the future.

3.5 Conclusion

In NSW the placing of the aims of sentencing in legislation (if not codification) has not been an entirely direct transfer of accepted common law principles, at least in the emphasis given and the language used. It is the last three aims that have added a different flavour to our sentencing legislation. Although some mention has been made in case law of the possibility that "protection of the community" and "making the offender accountable" have introduced new elements in sentencing [Spigelman J in *Attorney General's Application under s37 of the Crimes (Sentencing Procedure) Act 1999 (No 2 of 2002)*], there is a surprising absence of discussion about this except in relation to victim impact statements. Questions remain as to how the sentenced person is to carry out his/her part in the sentence if the meaning and practical import of such aims is not made understandable. To whom is the offender accountable? How is that to be demonstrated? When obligations arise in legislation there is a basic requirement for them to be clearly articulated and understandable. As the next chapter will demonstrate, sentencing often fails at the most basic level to adequately communicate to the recipient of the sentence even the most basic information.

In analysing the law relating to sentencing in NSW, themes involving subjectivity and the expectations for action particularly on the part of the offender are suggested. Undergoing the sentence, the offender will be subject to a variety of processes and procedures, often based on decisions made in the courtroom as to the correct narrative of the offence and the obligations of the prisoner. The additional layer in the "hall of mirrors" for the prisoner is the ongoing reliance of the authorities on measurements of risk to establish the way the sentence will be served, access to programs and eventual release. While still clamouring for a place at the table in the courts, risk has subsumed all others in the field of corrections, where a distorted and limited form of rehabilitation has resulted.

The discussion of the heightened role given to assessments of risk and dangerousness by the legislature of NSW and the way that judges have reacted—cautiously but optimistically—is by no means meant to demonstrate the wholesale acceptance of risk assessment by the courts. It is suggested, however, that the *Serious Sex Offenders Act* may be a kind of "advance guard" for the use of these instruments in general sentencing matters. The influential and pervasive use of actuarial measures of risk is considered in the context of the courts of NSW as a supra-level influence on general sentencing practice. While not supplanting reliance on more traditional psychiatric evidence, risk assessment is undoubtedly as attractive to courts as it is to other sectors of the criminal justice system required to justify their decisions. The role of risk in influencing the sentencing practice of judges is a fertile area for investigation. It appears that considerations of risk of re-offending may be, in the courts as in corrections in NSW, focussed more keenly on sex offenders and recidivist violent offenders. The question is whether courts will expand their reliance on actuarial risk assessment into more general sentencing matters.

The need for any analysis of sentencing to acknowledge the multi-layered and multi-process nature of the exercise has been emphasised because the carrying out of the sentence is as important as the preceding steps of investigation, police processing and legal process. The following chapter will explore the subjectivity of the sentenced person experiencing the in-court phase of the sentence.

4

Experiencing Sentencing

4.1 Introduction

> As a "one shot" actor, the accused lacks the "recipe" knowledge (pragmatic organizational knowledge and access to other power resources that would allow him to fight back) . . . even at a minimal level comparable to inmates of total institutions (Ericson and Baranek 1982, p. 3).

The previous chapter examined the law of sentencing in NSW with an emphasis on the implications of the aims of sentencing for the sentenced person. The existence of subjective requirements, or, in other words, expectations that the sentenced person undergoes or experiences certain internal states, feelings or states of mind which are integral to the operationalisation of the sentence, was related to the aims of sentencing. This chapter will examine some of these aspects from the viewpoint of the sentenced person. To begin with, the very basic question of what the sentenced person heard affects their ability to participate in the process of sentencing at even the most minimal level. Reasons for judgment and remarks on sentence crystallise the sentence and are expected to constitute communication with the sentenced person (among others). Remorse will

M. Hall, *The Lived Sentence*, Palgrave Studies in Prisons and Penology, DOI 10.1007/978-3-319-45038-4_4

be examined as a foundational although largely unexamined subjective expectation which runs through the sentencing process and which is crucial to some to the aims of sentencing, such as rehabilitation and recognition of harm done to the victim.

The position of the accused in the criminal process is as rarely examined today as it was in 1982, when Ericson and Baranek claimed that defendants are more like "dependants." The absence of opportunities to "challenge representations of reality" (Ericson and Baranek 1982, p. 23) means that the accused, and even more so, the convicted and sentenced person, must accept the official narrative, not only of the offence, but also of their personal characteristics and life history. The structural disadvantage of the sentenced person, whose fate, on some accounts, has been sealed long before the courtroom process merely legitimates and validates official (police) constructions of reality and militates against meaningful participation (Bottoms and McLean in Ericson and Baranek 1982, p. 23).

David Indemauer's work shows that offenders often have a very different understanding of the reasons for their predicament. His assertion that "our system of justice relies on a number of psychological functions to function properly . . . the sentencing process . . . attempts to communicate to offenders that they have done wrong," but many view themselves as the victims (Indemauer 1994, p. 140). The importance placed by the criminal justice system on expressions of remorse by the offender supports the first assertion (Indemauer 1994, p. 140). The way offenders experience the sentencing process, whether the assumptions made about the way the different actors understand the situation is shared or different according to their position in the process, is a vital question, considering the importance placed on the understanding of the offender of what is now required of them in order to fulfil the expectations of the aims of sentencing. With imprisonment, punishment is self-evident, but what of deterrence, rehabilitation, accountability, attention to the harm done to the victim? All these imply some degree of participation by the offender, even some kind of a process, if only in the form of acknowledgement or understanding by the offender. The recognition of the addition of two new aims, which have the flavour of restorative justice about them (Fernandez 2003), adds to the urgency in identifying how these aims are operationalised in the serving of the sentence and what implications this has for the person serving the sentence.

Findlay and Henham, in proposing a model for international criminal justice, advise that

> recognizing the moral and cultural relativity of concepts such as "justice" and "fairness" requires a contextual appreciation of the subjectivity of trial participants' experiences in terms of these measures . . . The deconstruction of participant experience in a trial so contextualised offers a phenomenological account of process and its ideological significance (Findlay and Henham 2011, p. 7).

Indemauer takes issue with a purely legalistic approach to sentencing; he defends the involvement of psychology in uncovering and explicating the views of the sentenced (Indemauer 1996, p. 63). Another aspect of the problems of expecting a subjective response to the sentence by offenders is the conflicting nature of the aims of sentencing. The difficulties faced by courts in balancing (if this is an appropriate analogy) these aims are magnified in the difficulties experienced by prisoners in understanding what is required of them, when the aims sometimes appear to cancel each other out or at least make the performance of the operationalised aims very difficult indeed, for example, feeling punished and denounced may well be incompatible with feeling rehabilitated and able to make restitution. The discussion of remorse in this chapter is presented as a prominent example of these difficulties.

The actual sentencing process in court is exemplified by the handing down of the sentence and so the sentencing comments/remarks of the judge are taken as the starting point of the examination of subjectivity in sentencing. Despite this, it is acknowledged that the sentencing process, in common with the entire criminal justice process, is largely shaped and determined by pre-trial processes, most particularly the investigation by police which shapes the type and content of the evidence presented at the trial or in the case of pleas of guilty, in the statement of facts agreed to by the parties. The limitations of this study preclude examination of these matters, although the oft-mentioned disagreement of the prisoners interviewed with the accepted version of the offence clearly relates to such factors.

4.2 Reasons for Judgment and Remarks on Sentence

Remarks on sentence should be given orally rather than in writing and should be formulated so that they can be understood by the offender. Reference to authority should be kept to a minimum: (*Curtis v R*).[1] The sentencing process is a powerful public expression and confirmation of the norms and boundaries of society. Kirby J in *Ryan v The Queen*[2] said, "A sentence should also *communicate* society's condemnation of the particular offender's conduct. The sentence represents a symbolic, collective statement that the offender's conduct should be punished for encroaching on our society's basic code of values . . . " (emphasis added). There is thus no doubt that the expression of this condemnation, while received by a wider audience, is, in a very particular way, directed at the offender and requires his or her participation in the process to become meaningful. Even denunciation, which sits comfortably within a punitive framework, implies some level of communication with the offender and some evidence of recognition from the offender that their behaviour infringes important social values.

While the fact that the remarks must be formulated so as to be understood by the offender indicates that he or she is the primary audience, the question of the proper audience of sentencing comments is more complex than this. The existence of the appeal process constrains and shapes the way the reasons for the sentence are presented (Mackenzie 2004, p. 250). In addition, Mackenzie's study of Queensland judges showed that judges felt that their remarks were just as importantly directed at the victim or their family and to the

---

[1] *Curtis v R* [2007] NSWCCA 11.

[2] *Ryan v The Queen (2001) CLR 267.*

community generally, in an attempt to communicate the reason for the decisions. She also appears to subscribe to the view that proper communication of sentencing decisions may assist in moderating calls for increased punitiveness borne out by research which shows that if people are informed they are less likely to be punitive (e.g., Lovegrove 2007). The difficulty in crafting a sentence, or the verbal expression of the sentence presented at the sentencing hearing which addresses all relevant parties seems obvious but is largely ignored. The sentence must contain not only meaningful instructions to the offender as to how they can fulfil the obligations which they have engendered by their conduct and at the same time satisfy the community's perceived need for denunciation and the victim's need for recognition of the harm caused.

Tata (2002, p. 410) points out that the expectation to give reasons does not mean "that the decision itself is a simple revelation of the decision process nor does it mean that the process becomes more logically reasoned." The view of sentencing as something performed solely by judges as an exercise of logical reasoning is challenged (Tata 2002, p. 417). The explanation of sentencing decisions is socially constructed and constrained by the expectations of the audience to which the comments are directed (Tata 2002, p. 420). Given the recognition that sentencing comments are directed to multiple audiences, it is to be expected that some conflict would be perceived between the need to deliver individualised justice which is understandable to lay members of the audience as well as providing the consistency required by the law. Tata views this tension as causing judges to have a "shifting and social situationally specific identity" (Tata 2002, p. 419).

4.3 Prisoners and Sentence Comments/ Remarks

> This is the judge—Errrr Errrrr, Errrrrrrr. . . . I had to ask the lawyer. What happened? What did I get? (Dave).

The proposition that sentencing comments be understandable to the person being sentenced is, as discussed earlier, a fundamental requirement.

A complicating factor is clearly the multiple audiences to which these comments are directed; the complex nature of sentencing law in NSW may privilege the Appeal Court as the preferred audience. Another salient factor may be the perceived need for judges to demonstrate that they are "tough on crime," thus privileging the victim's lobby and other law and order pressure groups as the representatives of the community to which sentence comments are directed.

The fact that these comments are commonly used by the Parole Authority as a type of "checklist" to assess the prisoner's readiness for release highlights the importance of ensuring that they have been actually understood by the recipient of the sentence, as he or she will ultimately be assessed as to their compliance with them. In addition, many of the aims of sentencing require the engagement of the court with the convicted person, a communicative theory of criminal justice requiring, not unreasonably, effective communication about the elements and the reasons for sentencing. Overwhelmingly, the participants in this project reported that they were either focused on the numbers, did not understand what the judge was saying, or the comments were so negative that they did not accept them (Hochstetler et al. 2010).

> Um there were a lot of words used that I didn't understand- there were so many numbers thrown at me at the time and that was basically it (Chris).

Only a Number?

> I actually didn't hear what he said . . . because at the time my mind was going on the length of the sentence I was going to get as well (Frank).

Many prisoners reported that, understandably, they were only listening for the number of years they were going to have to serve. Many reported that the judge focused solely on the number of years, the complexity of sentencing particularly for multiple offences perhaps contributing to this tendency.

> "Just a 5 with a three." Interviewer: "That's it, no other words apart from that?" Prisoner: "No" (Mark)

> "He just say sentence 20 years that's it" (Xu).

The severity and high-profile nature of Xu's offence makes it unlikely that comments were not made; this man's understanding of English was still extremely poor after 15 plus years' incarceration. He was accompanied by another prisoner who was clearly acting as a carer for him, showing concern for his well-being. Other prisoners reported this caring relationship within ethnic groups. The effect of the ageing of the prison population raises many issues for correctional authorities and prisoners, chronic ill health plaguing many older long-term prisoners.

On the impact of going to court and being sentenced

> "I don't know, it's not doing anything, you know, I suppose because I've been through it so many times" (Dennis, medium security, city prison).

Having been a long-term heroin addict, this prisoner had been incarcerated for most of his adult life, the effect seemingly reduced by its mere familiarity. He represented the sizeable group of prisoners whose age and health problem precludes involvement in many rehabilitative programmes.

In No State to Listen

> No, I couldn't hear nothing. I'm 50% deaf in both ears (Jack).

The prevalence of mental illness, intellectual disability, brain injury and lack of educational achievement among prisoners in NSW should alert the courts to the need to ensure that sentences and legal proceedings generally are understandable to defendants. This responsibility invariably falls onto the shoulders of overworked Legal Aid solicitors, or private practitioners paid by Legal Aid who are likely to perceive that Legal Aid rates are so poor that the time taken to go down to the cells or out to the prison to explain to the prisoner what has happened is not worth the trouble.

> It took me awhile to sort of work it out—he didn't say much about programs, my short term memory's not great. Generally I don't remember my sentencing (Tom).

> I'd been taking Rowies (Rohypnol) so I virtually forget everything that was said to me . . . I don't remember the judges remarks (John).

In addition to the difficulties caused by language, education and disability, a large number of prisoners are likely to be suffering from the effects of long-term drug use or withdrawal at the time of sentence. This illustrates the importance of supplying the prisoner with information at a time when some stability may be expected, for example, at the time of classification.

Sentencing is clearly a stressful and difficult event for prisoners. Even those prisoners who pleaded guilty and were fully expecting a custodial penalty, report feeling distressed and confused. The highly technical nature of modern sentencing law and practice in NSW means that even educated literate prisoners often found it difficult to understand what was going on.

Strangers in a Strange Land

> My English not good—I didn't really understand what he (the judge) said. The interpreter—he's. . . . not good at all (Chan).

Non-English-speaking prisoners are clearly disadvantaged by their inability to understand the proceedings. Many were suspicious and critical of the court-appointed interpreters, pointing to the need for individual interpreters to be appointed, particularly in complex serious matters. The lack of evaluation of the performance of interpreters from the defendant's point of view is consistent with an overall absence of accountability and evaluation of the performance of the legal actors in the criminal justice system. Complaints made by prisoners as to the adequacy of legal representation are invariably attributed to bitterness as to the outcome rather than valid concerns.

I can't remember . . . I couldn't speak English. . . . I was not clear what they were talking about. Pretty much all the things my solicitor was dealing with it. But I don't remember how, he was speaking really fast (Xu).

Condemning the Person, Not the Act

> Interviewer: "Did you hear the judge say anything to you about what you needed to do to rehabilitate yourself?" Prisoner: "Nothing. . . . . Nothing at all. He goes in and says. . . . Cause I was only a kid . . . . 19. . . . . 'You have no chance of rehabilitation.' He was rude on the day of sentencing he was, like 15 minutes, late and he just stumbles up and then he didn't say nothing, just started reading out the facts out of what happened that day and then um the sentence and then he just walked out" (Van).

This young prisoner, contrary to the prediction of the judge, has taken impressive steps to rehabilitate himself, and still speaks of feeling extremely distressed at the judge's highly negative comments about him. He reports that he had the "sleeping judge," a judicial officer who subsequently retired before action could be taken against him for sleeping through numerous trials and sentence matters. This factor has clearly had an impact on the attitude of this prisoner to the administration of justice and the fairness of the way in which he was treated. Even though the sentence may have been fair, the circumstances in which it was handed down have had a long-term impact and have arguably affected this prisoner's ability to accept the official record and thus participate in rehabilitation. While it appears that the victim in one case before this judge was contacted and spoken to by the then Attorney General, no effort was made to contact prisoners convicted and sentenced by this judge or explain to them the actions taken or the consequences to their particular situations.

> (Asked what he would say to someone in his position) "I know you're just a kid. I don't know what really happened that night. I can only assume by the evidence. Um you're going to get this amount of time, you have to

> serve it no matter what but you have to show us that . . . you will have to rehabilitate . . . .you know what I mean, stuff like that" (Van).

While it is understandable that sentence comments will contain comments critical of the behaviour of the prisoner, many commented on the negativity with which the court regarded them and, as may be expected, rejected this negative view of themselves as people, even when they accepted culpability for the offence/s (Hochstetler et al. 2010, p. 49).

> "He (the judge) said that I'm a cold blooded murderer." Interviewer: "And you're not?" Prisoner: "He didn't die" (Mario).

This prisoner continually missed the point in questions about himself; he gave an account of being chosen at an early age to, in his words:

> " . . . look after the family for outside trouble, that sort of thing" (Mario).

His fundamental disagreement with the accepted narrative of his crime precluded him from expressing any feelings of culpability or remorse. In his case, the judge merely confirmed his own personal narrative as someone who was destined to be a cold-blooded killer.

> Interviewer: "So when he came to sentence you what did he say about your prospects of rehabilitation?" Prisoner: "Nothing at all. . . . Oh, he criticised me . . . just sort of blah blah heinous crime . . . not heinous . . . heeeeeeeinous, you know" (Tommy).

While mocking the manner of speech of the judge, this prisoner, who maintained his innocence, was clearly disturbed by the lack of attention given to his subjective circumstances. As a perceived drug dealer, but not a drug user, he was also suffering from the inability of the correctional system to come up with an appropriate programme for him; he was continually referred to drug and alcohol workers who are often at a loss as to what to do with this category of offender. The assumption that, because of the type of offence, there is no rehabilitative component unless the person is a drug addict, often makes the long sentences served by so-called drug "traffickers" only about incapacitation and punishment.

The Turning Point—The Power of Positive Comments

One former prisoner (the only former prisoner interviewed for this project) identified the positive comments made by the judge on sentence as the turning point for him in his rehabilitation, pointing to the importance of judicial officers taking very great care in what is said on sentence. At times, their words appear to have the effect of providing the sentenced person with a positive narrative with which to view themselves.

> He said, "at first glance of the criminal antecedents it would appear that he is a violent criminal. This is not the case. . . . " Without him, before that, I was sort of . . . I'd made the changes but I'd still resolved myself that that was my life . . . then that all changed with that sentence, I went back, started doing my studies (Francis).

Getting Sentence Comments

One very proactive prisoner obtained his sentence comments from the court, after several attempts, claiming that those held by the Department of CSNSW were highly edited versions.

> In my case the sentence comments I think were something like ten pages. . . . And in my report that goes to the commissioner it's only two paragraphs. Now, I don't believe that the Commissioner or any person reasonably instructed can formulate a view better than a judge based on two paragraphs (William).

Another prisoner had made a number of attempts to obtain the comments but despite the fact that he was in a rehab programme and believed that a copy of the comments were held by the programme he had hit a wall. . . .

> What I can't understand is that when I go to CUBIT to do my course they say "Oh I've just been reading through your judges remarks. . . . ." And they're at an advantage to work against you not with you when you're really trying to refresh your memory and work out what happened and I'm saying "I don't remember that but if you're saying this is what the judge said it must have happened because I can't remember" (John).

It must be noted that, although in theory prisoners can write to the court and obtain copies of court documents, there are a number of problems with this. Apart from the problems with mail which is heavily censored, many prisoners, particularly those sentenced for particular offences (child sexual assault in particular) would not want documents relating to their offence in their cells. The lack of privacy means that cellmates and others are highly likely to have access with potentially damaging results. It is therefore often preferable that professional staff obtain the documents and allow prisoners to access them in confidential circumstances.

The difficulties experienced by prisoners in obtaining copies of sentence comments seems counterproductive, given the need for them to understand the reason for their sentence and to engage themselves in carrying out the directions of the judge. These difficulties were reflected in the experience of this researcher. While the original aims of the project included obtaining sentence comments for each prisoner interviewed, the lack of any centralised system meant that liaison with each individual prison was necessary and the difficulties experienced were so great that this aim was eventually abandoned. Instead, it was decided that the most valuable activity was to document these difficulties and attempt to ascertain the process by which CSNSW itself obtains sentence comments. Even this reduced aim became extremely difficult, with different answers given depending on the prison of classification and the classification of the prisoner. It seems that there is no definite protocol with the courts as far as the procurement of such documents and they seem to be obtained on an ad hoc case-by-case basis.

Further discussion of the "information vacuum" that prisoners find themselves in takes place in Chap. 6.

4.4 Remorse in Criminal Justice

The nexus between the expectations of subjective transformation and the necessity of appropriate demonstration can be found in the element of remorse. Out of place, under-interrogated and largely taken for granted, the concept, whether in practice of much use to defendants given the utilitarian approach to sentencing taken in NSW, is still a continuous thread that links the sentence in the courtroom with the sentence as served.

> You know, I do want to apologise to the family, you know and it'll make me feel better (Frank).

While expressing remorse, this prisoner conceived of the opportunity to apologise as a way of "getting it out of his head" and allowing him to move on with life, but which would also help the family of the victim. While regret for their actions was commonly expressed by the prisoners in this study, it was often expressed in this way, including the devastating effect on their own lives. Whether this type of remorse is sufficient to satisfy the requirement that remorse be about the victim rather than the effect on themselves and their families is questionable. Is it unreasonable to expect those being punished to be able to conceptualise, experience and demonstrate (perform) regret and remorse in any kind of pure form?

As the first manifestation of the subjectivity of the sentenced in the criminal justice process, it is argued that remorse is a foundational and largely un-interrogated aspect of criminal justice. Remorse is considered so important so as to ground a possible reduction in sentence, or conversely, the absence of which can significantly aggravate not only the sentence as handed down by the court but also the sentence as served and delay release on parole. The subjective nature of the concept of remorse brings it squarely within the interests of this project, and although participants were not asked directly about it, it was raised often enough to confirm its importance.

The corresponding notion of apology was viewed as impossible to attain due to restrictions on offenders contacting victims. The comments of the prisoners support Weisman's assertion that the importance of apology is insufficiently emphasised in criminal justice processing, the distancing between victim and offender serving to prevent the notion from even arising. This work adopts the definition proposed by Weisman that "the work of remorse is to call attention to the feelings that accompany the words . . . " and, although not unproblematic, the contention that because of the "possibility that expressions of self condemnation will be more strategic than authentic," remorse is preferred by the criminal justice system (Weisman 2009, p. 51). The "performative" aspects of the criminal justice system, as examined by Leader (2007, 2008), and remorse in particular (Rossmanith 2009, 2015) are fertile grounds for performance ethnographers, who analyse the performative aspects of the court process. The difficulties for defendants in ascertaining what is required of them then are magnified when their ability to perform the acts of, for example, remorse, is also under scrutiny.

> No, I'm not sorry No, (spoken very softly) kill most things that crawl on this continent, no different from a rabbit, break its neck . . . (Brett).

While chilling to read, this comment by a prisoner, who is at the lowest classification of any of the prisoners interviewed and had a trusted and relatively well-paid job, occurred in the context of a long discussion about remorse. He was rational about his choice to use violence in the situation and was prepared to accept the consequences. He argued at some length that the "system" was not tough enough, in particular for young drug-using prisoners (see the chapter on prisoner experience). His considerable interpersonal skills and his possession of high-level trade skills appeared to have allowed him to avoid some of the negative consequences of a lack of remorse, although he was yet to reach the stage in his sentence where the approach of the Earliest Possible Release Date (EPRD) attracts the gaze of parole and the Parole Authority.

Weisman argues that "attributions of remorse are used in legal discourse to distinguish those whose character is perceived as different from their wrongful act (the remorseful) from those whose character is perceived as not different from the wrongful act (the remorseless) (Weisman 2009, p. 47). In other words, the remorseful self must separate and

distinguish itself from the self that commits the wrong (Weisman 2009, p. 50). Weisman further points out that this focus on the "inner life" of the transgressor "informs us.... about how someone who committed the wrong should feel about their own actions", and, in addition, "what form these feelings should take" (Weisman 2009, p. 48). The tremendous effect of remorse on the likelihood of jurors sentencing the offender to capital punishment in the USA places it at the forefront of those penal phenomena that should be understood in order to prevent injustice, but it is argued that the detrimental effect of having been judged to show no remorse can also be ongoing and severe here in NSW.

Remorse is an ever-present construct throughout the processes of criminal justice; early pleas of guilty are characterised as demonstrating remorse, the translation of which into the "discount" of the tariff involves a finely calibrated scale. "The presence of remorse can operate to reduce significantly the severity of the punishment meted out to the accused" (Edney and Bagaric 2007, p. 174). It has also been suggested, however, that the importance of remorse may be diminishing in favour of more utilitarian benefits such as efficiency and assistance to authorities.

The "difficulties in distinguishing real from feigned remorse" (Edney and Bagaric 2007, p. 175) lead some to advocate its abandonment as a sentencing consideration "unless demonstrable empirical data indicates that rehabilitation is an attainable sentencing objective" (Edney and Bagaric 2007, p. 179) as "there is no justifiable doctrinal basis for according a sentencing discount to offenders who evince regret for what they have done" (Edney and Bagaric 2007, p. 179).

> Well, I didn't actually think (I was) doing anything wrong until 1990..... a guy said if anyone touched my kids I'd kill em, and I said "Yeah—if anyone touched my kids"—Hang on, whoa hang on... I did that and that's what I'm, in gaol for. Interviewer "So it took a long time for it to really sink in?" Prisoner: Yeah—it was like an abnormality thing, well from a teenager right through, you think well it was a normal situation, just normal, though, it was normal.... (Leslie).

The fact that an appreciation of the wrongfulness of their actions can take some time to manifest is exemplified by this interview. This child sex offender disclosed in the last moments of the interview that he had been voluntarily castrated.

> It wasn't only for me –it was um if there was any potential for further victims and I didn't want any of those.....well I'm a grandfather now- ...and I'm going to make sure that they're safe (Leslie).

His comments also indicated that, despite his remorse and his determination not to have any further victims, he felt that castration and the removal of any potential for sexual arousal was the only way he could be absolutely sure he wouldn't return to what had been a lifelong pattern of behaviour. His appreciation of the harm to others caused by his behaviour took a lifetime, like many sex offenders; despite being identified as "high risk"[3], he was now an elderly man with a range of health problems. As a successfully "treated" sex offender, his characterisation of the dramatic change in attitude towards his offending not only "like an abnormality" but also "it was normal, well from a teenager right through..." reflects his own experience as well as the type of fundamental change in attitude and understanding necessary to undo such deeply embedded behaviour.

Remorse also acts as an important marker for risk (M. Brown 2000, p. 105), the remorseful prisoner is "redefining the self as more enlightened and thus as a responsible and non-risky person" (Kilty 2010, p. 165). The emphasis on remorse in assessing future risk becomes heightened with the availability of post-sentence detention, where assessments as to future risk often rely on the completion of offence-specific programmes. Whether common-sense assessments of heightened risk due to the absence of remorse are material in decision making around parole or extended detention is largely unknown. Parole decisions are unreviewed, there being no effective right of appeal and, in relation to post-sentence detention, psychiatric reports are not on the public record.

[3] While actuarial measures do not predict re-offending in individuals, the use of this language in the penal and criminal justice context reflects the reality of the individuals thus characterised.

I didn't get me remorse. (Jason)

Understandably, given the way remorse is characterised in legal discourse, this prisoner conceived remorse as a reason for sentence discount, while further exploration of what he meant may have uncovered a deeper meaning, it is clear that for many, including lawyers, remorse is an instrumental concept, something that gets a discount but needs no further explanation.

In NSW, the high-profile cases of *MSK* and *MAK*[4] specify the way that remorse or contrition is to be addressed in sentencing. In these cases, the court said that the discount for a plea of guilty is to be given for the utilitarian value of the plea and that remorse is to be taken into account separately as a mitigating factor under s23A (3) of the *Crimes (Sentencing Procedure) Act 1999*. In *Stricke*[5], the discount for the plea of guilty included an allowance for contrition. In *Kite*[6], the court reiterated the inappropriateness of quantifying exactly how much the sentence has been discounted due to the presence of remorse or contrition. The judge in this case expressed the discount as being both for the utilitarian value of the plea and for the presence of remorse. The Court of Criminal Appeal, while agreeing on the inadvisability of quantifying the discount for remorse, found, however, that the prisoner was deserving of a further reduction in sentence due to his remorse and prospects of rehabilitation.

While always an important mitigating factor, courts have been free to use their discretion in assessing the presence or absence of remorse in individual cases. Now, however, the insertion of s23A (3) into the Act requires some evidence to be provided as to the remorse or contrition of the defendant (the coexistence of these two factors indicating judicial acceptance of the notion). Some lawyers have predicted that this will require the calling of the convicted person to give evidence on sentence, a practice not often followed in the lower courts and which leaves them open to the possibility of cross examination by the prosecution not only

[4] *R v M.A.K., R v M.S.K.* [2006] NSWCCA 381.

[5] [2007] NSWCCA.

[6] [2009] NSWCCA 12.

on the validity of their claims of remorse but also on other matters traditionally dealt with in the discretion of the judicial officer (although see *R v Butters*[7] where the court found that the section did not give rise to an obligation to give evidence). There are clearly disadvantages to a convicted person in NSW attempting to claim remorse without giving the judge an opportunity to assess demeanour, that is, without giving evidence (*R v Pfitzner).*[8]

The importance of remorse in sentencing in NSW is arguably heightened by the inclusion of "new" aims in sentencing that refer to restorative justice aims. While judicial comment by the NSW judiciary on these new aims is scarce, it may be appropriate to refer to a Canadian decision which addresses similar additions to the aims of sentencing (Fernandez 2003). In the case of *Gladue,*[9] the court, in construing similar provisions in the Canadian act said, "Central to the process is the need for offenders to take responsibility for their actions." While "taking responsibility" is not the same as demonstrating remorse, in the traditional sense of displaying emotion, it is argued that the expectation would arise that an offender, in taking responsibility or being accountable, would express feelings of contrition and remorse as part of the "focus on the human beings affected by the crime." This view is supported by the suggestion that adjournments be sought in sentencing matters to allow the offender to make some reparation for the crime (Fernandez 2003, p. 12).

Clearly, a connection between remorse and the attainment of rehabilitation (if cessation of offending is defined as rehabilitation) is assumed here. There is limited evidence of this, which may be a surprise to parole officers, Serious Offenders Review Council (SORC) and the Parole Authority who often work under the assumption that this is so. The willingness to undergo a process of "self transformation" such as that promised by rehabilitation programmes is one of the requirements for remorse (Weisman 2009). Rather than counter indicative of rehabilitation however, the presence of

[7] [2010] NSWCCA 1.

[8] [2010] NSWCCA 314.

[9] [1999] 1 SCR 688.

justification and excuses for the offence, which may preclude the court finding that remorse exists, may indicate a pro-social attitude to the offence more conducive to rehabilitation (Maruna and Mann 2006).

> Interviewer: "So you accept that you did something wrong?" Prisoner: "Yeah, the way I grew up was different and that's nobody's fault. When I was 9 years old they put a fuckin' gun in my hands and told me to shoot the trees. You are going to be the protector, you know of the family" (Mario).

This prisoner's insistence that his violent childhood made his actions inevitable, far from endearing him to treatment agents within the prison, had led to the conclusion that he failed to take responsibility and, on his account, had precluded his involvement in treatment programmes. His characterisation of himself as a victim clearly placed him outside of the dominant paradigm of remorse. Prisoners are rarely allowed to be victims, the role seemingly at odds with their convicted status.[10]

The Inconvenience of Innocence

The other components of remorse postulated by Weisman—admission of responsibility (Weisman 2009, p. 52) and showing one's true feelings (Weisman 2009, p. 56) are clearly not available to those who maintain their innocence. This dilemma will continue throughout the serving of the sentence unless they recant and confess prior to the EPRD. The possibility of intensification of the punitive nature of the sentence by confessing after maintaining innocence may be a powerful disincentive to do this, in other words, the perception that the prisoner has attempted to get away with the offence and then recanted upon realising the practical disadvantages attached may result in a mistrust of the person worse than continuing to maintain innocence.

[10] Reflected in s24(4) *Victims(Support and Rehabilitation) Act* 1996 which precludes prisoners from claiming compensation for injuries incurred in prison, subject to ss(5), which allows payment in "special circumstances."

It is a truism that prisoners will continue to protest their innocence in the face of overwhelming evidence. This was not encountered in this research and the one prisoner who did claim innocence was enmeshed in constant legal proceedings trying to prove it. Many indicated that the account of the offence accepted by the court was not the whole story, but on the whole, the participants in this study were accepting of their culpability. However, the imposition on the prisoner of the constructed narrative accepted by the court can lead to a wholesale rejection of anything the prison and correctional system has to offer.

> Look, I made a mistake and I know I must pay for that. When they grabbed me I said "I did it. I won't tell you why, but I did it. Alright?" I didn't stuff anyone around. But I don't have any faith in the law system, the justice system. . . . I've seen too much filth. Too much filth (Mario).

The reluctance of this prisoner to give an explanation for his actions places him in an invidious situation even though he had admitted responsibility. The lack of a psycho- social narrative precludes the type of sorting, classification and treatment ordinarily viewed as the proper course of action in prison and places the prisoner at great disadvantage compared to those who give an acceptable narrative. While accepting that his stubbornness had cost him an easy sentence, like many prisoners, he clung to his privacy in at least one area of his life. He exemplifies the somewhat perverse and self-defeating resistance displayed by several prisoners in this research. A further discussion of this type of resistance takes place in Chap. 5 in the context of the managerial apparatus of the prison.

While therapeutic agents within the system continue to look for ways of working with people, such as deniers programmes and allowing admissions of historical offences, the fundamental distrust that the system has of those who protest their innocence in the face of official proof in the form of a conviction reflects the paramount nature of considerations of remorse in the discourse of redemption (see earlier discussion of remorse). The prisoner who continues to deny responsibility cannot express remorse or demonstrate rehabilitation, thus undermining a fundamental requirement of the emotive or expressive functions of criminal justice.

Indeed, for those prisoners nearing the end of their sentence, maintaining innocence is a risky business. While programme acceptance formerly relied on acceptance of responsibility, the implementation of "denier's programs" reflects the awareness of the Department that there is a significant minority of prisoners who will continue to protest their innocence, despite the very significant incentives not to do so. Still, for those prisoners who refuse to accept responsibility for the offence(s) for which they have been convicted, there is a very good chance that they will not be released at their EPRD and may do their entire parole period in custody. The overarching and overwhelming paradigm of denial requires strict adherence to the official narrative, despite the existence of denier's programmes.[11]

In a 5th amendment case before the US Supreme Court, the notion that coercion affects an individual's constitutional right not to incriminate him or herself was disavowed. The court held that "the state's interests in rehabilitation and effective prison administration outweighed the individual prisoner's right to silence" (Johansen 2008). While the primacy of the public interest over the individual rights of the offender is clear, part of the reason for this decision was the belief that denial is anti-therapeutic, that offenders must sometimes be forced to take responsibility for their actions. The US Supreme Court appears to echo the hands-off position taken by Australian courts in deferring to the expertise of prison administrators. Johansen explicitly rejects the notion of successful compulsory rehabilitation where the precondition is acceptance of guilt.

The Parole Authority and Innocence

The difficulty of analysing a body which does not have a set of legal precedents or publicly available policies leads to the necessity of gleaning

[11] The deniers programme run by CSNSW NSW requires "categorical denial." According to the coordinator of the sex offenders programmes, there has been little demand for the programme which, at the time of the interview, had only run once. This does not accord with anecdotal evidence from legal officers dealing with prisoners.

whatever information can be inferred by experienced practitioners. The Parole Authority in NSW does not entertain pleas of innocence in any way. While not formally using a prisoner's refusal to admit the offence as a reason to refuse parole, there are many ways that the legislation governing parole and the way it is interpreted by the NSW Parole Authority can perform precisely this function.

A refusal to admit culpability has up until recently precluded involvement in cognitive behavioural programmes, which may be perceived by the Parole Authority to reduce risk, in addition to protestations of innocence engender and entrench oppositional interactional experiences with prison authorities which mitigates against reduction in classification and progression through the system. While therapeutic agents within the system continue to look for ways of working with people, such as allowing admissions of historical offences which the prisoner does admit to and deniers programmes, the fundamental distrust which the system has of those who protest their innocence in the face of official proof in the form of a conviction reflects the paramount nature of considerations of remorse in the pursuit of redemption (see earlier discussion of remorse). The prisoner who continues to deny responsibility cannot express remorse or demonstrate rehabilitation in an acceptable way, thus undermining a fundamental requirement of the emotive or expressive functions of criminal justice. The long-term result of maintaining innocence can be a perception on the part of prison staff that the prisoner is at the very least a nuisance. Ultimately, this may result in an assessment of future dangerousness, which may not accord with other characteristics of the individual.

The Elephant in the Room: The Relationship Between "Truth" and Redemption and the Unbearable Unfairness of the Privileged Narrative

The highly contested and constructed device of the legal narrative inadequately captures the nuances, complexities and subjectivities of human behaviour. Once "the offence" has been captured, constrained and defined, from the construction of the police narrative (McConville 1991) followed by the court process, what is produced is a set of "facts" which are thereafter set in concrete and follow the prisoner throughout the criminal justice process. There is even less room for nuance and complexity in the managerial correctionalism of the modern prison. Any explanation or divergence from this narrative which the prisoner will seek to maintain is viewed as self-serving or evidencing a lack of remorse and denial, essentially a challenge to the lawful process of sentencing and correction. The prisoner is "on the bottom of the 'hierarchy of credibility'" (Ericson and Baranek 1982, p. 21).

The captured, static narrative of the offence must be fully adhered to by the prisoner in order to facilitate interactions with correctional workers and eventual release on parole. Correctional workers must emphasise this by getting the prisoner to accept responsibility by acknowledging the harmful effects of their actions. This often involves forcing adherence to this manufactured narrative rather than encouraging a spirit of true repentance. Blind insistence that this manufactured narrative represents "the truth" often prevents the prisoner from acknowledging their part in the wrongdoing as they fixate upon the unfairness of the privileging of the official account over their subjective story. While undoubtedly an element of denial may exist in some offenders, the paradigm amongst correctional workers is a dominant one and thus every prisoner is expected to manifest it. An alternative and much more productive paradigm may be an acknowledgement of the constructed nature of the legal narrative. The possibility that alternative explanations may exist and an acknowledgement of subjective truth may be a more therapeutic attitude to take. The insistence that the legal narrative represents some kind of objective truth may be viewed as another example of Carlen's "imaginary penalties" (Carlen 2008), in many cases an extremely counterproductive and unjust one at that. Maruna and Mann urge a reconsideration of this perspective on offender denial in order to facilitate a more therapeutic approach (Maruna and Mann 2006).

Martel sees remorse (or "confession")[12] as a particular discursive transaction "an obligatory passage point or an oral corroboration indispensable to complete the written demonstration (i.e., psychological and

[12] While the religious connotations are undeniable, no attempt will be made to theorise about this aspect of remorse.

parole reports) of an offender's successful integration of the 'Truth' about her and her crime" (Martel 2010, p. 426). As the central event that substantially provides the rationale for the sentence which ensues, the offence[13] is central to all that follows. The importance of the recognition of the narrative of the offence as a legal artefact, rather than affording it the status of some abstract notion of "truth," is central in understanding the difficulties experienced by many sentenced people in accepting this official version, even where they may feel culpable and responsible.

Police facts in particular are versions of events, often factually inaccurate, constructed to present the narrative most favourable to a finding of guilt. The reliance on the official record as "truth" does not allow for prisoners to have their versions at all. The perpetuation of psychological theories of "denial," particularly in relation to sexual offenders, has permeated all dealings with prisoners and underpins the rejection of any kind of nuance to their understanding of what has happened. This is not to deny that the inability or unwillingness to accept responsibility for actions may be a factor in rehabilitation, although it is doubtful whether any evidence exists to connect re-offending with denial (Maruna and Mann 2006; Yates 2009; Hall and Rossmanith 2015 forthcoming).

As the "elephant in the room" that underpins most of the dealings prisoners have with prison staff, the details of the offence, often in the form of truncated, inadequate accounts, are solidified and incorporated into the psychologically based assessment procedure. Prisoners become accustomed to giving narratives that suit the practices and procedures of the prison and its staff. No direct questions were asked about the offence/s in the prisoner interviews and a varied amount of detail was given. One prisoner spent the whole interview giving his account (a good reason for not asking this question directly!), and there appeared to be few for whom the official record adequately reflected their truth about what happened. Towards the

[13] Or, more accurately the account of it which has been accepted, as a legal artefact as the preferred narrative by a jury or judicial officer, or to which the defendant is prepared to agree by entering a plea of guilty.

end of their sentence however, prisoners mostly learn that (outward) acceptance of the official record is a prerequisite for release at the EPRD.

The problematic role of remorse in sentencing prefaces the examination of remorse as an ongoing theme in the lived sentence. The performance of rehabilitation requires the acceptance of the official narrative of the offence and the appropriate demonstration of remorse throughout the sentence.

4.5 Conclusion

If we begin with the premise that obligations are to be placed upon prisoners during the sentencing process, then it follows that these obligations should be clearly communicated to them. Prisoners are often unable to understand or even hear the words of the judge, which in any case may be more likely to be directed to the Court of Criminal Appeal than to them. The power of the ceremonial aspects of the sentencing process invokes a feeling of passivity and non-involvement by the sentenced person. The sentence is something being imposed upon them rather than a communication of values and moral principles.

To further require sentenced people to feel and demonstrate "remorse" which, it has been argued, relies upon strict acceptance of the official narrative of both the offence and their personal characteristics, is often a bridge too far and leads to a kind of oppositional defiance which may not be necessarily reflective of their true feelings about the offence. The discussion of remorse in this chapter has focused on the legal aspects of its use in sentencing in NSW. It will be argued that the requirement that prisoners feel and perform remorse persists throughout the sentence and is highly relevant to correctional determinations of risk and rehabilitation and, subsequently, readiness for release on parole.

The importance of an examination of the context of the experience of prisoners serving the sentence is further emphasised in the next chapter with a focus on some of the everyday, routine incidents, which make up the lived sentence. These incidents, coupled with the miscommunication (or non-communication) of the sentencing process described in this chapter, can adversely affect the ability of the prisoner to engage with and carry out the expectations contained within the sentence.

5

Managerialism, Discipline and the "Responsible Prisoner"

5.1 Introduction

To this point, the focus of this book has been to identify the context in which sentencing takes place. The socio-political context and the aims of sentencing have been analysed to draw out the way that obligations arise when these aims are operationalised. The aim of this chapter is to foreground the processes and systems, which operate in a largely hidden and unacknowledged way to mediate, modify and, in some cases, nullify the aims of sentencing. A proper examination of criminal justice processes, which are largely taken for granted by the actors within, necessitates a reflexive and critical stance. It is important to identify and analyse these embedded and highly naturalised acts and beliefs. The next three chapters use the words of prisoners to drive the argument that the minutiae of prison life is worth examining, not merely as a socially useful exercise but as a vital part of ensuring legitimacy.

The managerial apparatus of the prison has been taken as the starting point to contextualise the words of prisoners. Highlighting the way the mundane processes and procedures of the prison come to be the sentence, to constitute the daily meaning of the sentence, brings into focus

M. Hall, *The Lived Sentence*, Palgrave Studies in Prisons and Penology, DOI 10.1007/978-3-319-45038-4_5

the way that the legal sentence fails to consider or adequately conceptualise what the prisoner is meant to do. Chapter 2 places the sentencing and imprisonment process in historical context, charting the rise in populist punitiveness as well as other complementary and contradictory currents in criminal justice in NSW. This chapter focuses on the internal, managerial processes of the prison through the lens of an examination of managerialism and the responses of prisoners. The importance of this to the fundamental questions underpinning this book is, first, in respecting the methodological commitment to highlight the concerns of prisoners in their living of the sentence and, second, to examine the processes which contribute or detract from the fulfilment of the obligations of the sentence In addition, in examining the way that the sentence as a performed legal artefact in court relates to the sentence as lived experience in prison, it is necessary to contextualise these processes as part of the overall philosophy and functioning of the criminal justice system and will inform an examination of the subjective understandings of prisoners of the processes of sorting and management undertaken as part of the "sentence as served."

5.2 Managerialism and the Department of CSNSW NSW

The Department of CSNSW, having been a prominent part of a highly politicised process of reform after Nagle and the subsequent managerialist, purportedly economically conservative but radically punitive Greiner/Yabsley regime, has emerged as a secretive, organisationally focused body throughout the past decade (see Chap. 2). The need to limit the exposure of politically damaging events such as escapes and industrial disputes and the concomitant dominance of custodial-based senior managers has led to a privileging of security concerns over the development of humane and rehabilitative programmes such as education and work release. Recent efforts to reform programmes and reflect evidence-based approaches to the types of programmes and services within the prison have not resulted in a resurgence of the rehabilitative ideal within NSW prisons. Rather, the type of programmes and services offered have been severely limited, especially to short-term prisoners, an inevitable result of a reliance on the "what works" argument, but also to those without a "programmable" problem. In keeping with other areas of the NSW public service since the 1980s, a trend towards a managerialist, process-focused organisational culture is evident. In Queensland, as in NSW, the political effect of individual cases on policy formation is evident: "to our interviewees the primary cause of the changes in MSU policy from an interest in rehabilitation to a more managerial position was the change in political environment caused by the events surrounding the escape of Brendan Abbot on 4 November 1997" (Douglas and Touchie 2006, p. 76).

Garland explains the rise of managerialism as filling the gap left when a more "social" approach lost credibility (Garland 2001, p. 188). Freiberg also gives the impact of the "nothing works" argument prominence in the rise of the managerialist ethos in Victorian criminal justice, where the imposition of strict performance measures led to an overall more punitive approach (Freiberg 2005, p. 30). While it is true that the "demise of rehabilitation" provided fertile ground for the flourishing of managerialism in NSW, the widespread adoption of a more neoliberal style of governance also saw radical changes throughout the entire NSW public sector.[1] In NSW, the election of the Greiner Liberal Government in the late 1980s marked not only a radical change to sentencing but also an increasing focus on "value for money", which continues in the rhetoric (if not the practice) of CSNSW to this day.

The way that the ideology of managerialism, with its focus on matters such as efficiency, has impacted on the criminal justice system in Australia is under-interrogated, the practices and policies having become naturalised and, in the Bourdieuan sense, part of the habitus of those who work within it. Freiberg notes that this ethos has dramatically affected the way courts now see their work (Freiberg 2005, p. 23).

[1] The introduction of accrual accounting, for example, an expensive process recommended by the 'big six' accounting firms, which has resulted in no appreciable improvement in efficient spending of public money (Christenson 2009)

In addition, in corrections "for frontline staff the environment and expectations were dramatically altered" (Freiberg 2005, p. 30).

The ongoing push towards the "commodification" of public sector services (McCulloch and McNeil 2007), that is, the view that public sector services can and should be delivered in the same way as in the private sector, repels any critique by the implicit assumption that it will always result in positive improvements. While privatisation and contracting out of services provides the ultimate expression of this process, the effect within the public sector internally has also been profound. The potential for this conception of "service delivery" to "clients" (Donahue and Moore 2009, p. 326) to undermine positive rehabilitation initiatives has as its obverse the potential to invoke notions of reciprocity or rights. That is, the "consumer" or the "client" has the right to expect the services to be provided. Of course, in the criminal justice system, the "client" may not be the prisoner but judges, or perhaps the wider community (McCulloch and McNeil 2007, p. 231). Even so, it is still arguable that this conception of the criminal justice system invokes obligations which can be meaningfully evaluated. One of the underlying questions in this book is whether this kind of evaluation can be performed by a full enunciation of the expectations contained in the aims of sentencing. Implications of reciprocity in this approach and the existence of parallel obligations (for the Department, to provide the means by which the sentence can be carried out) indicate that each party's performance in carrying out these aims should be fully evaluated.

The adoption of private sector values by the NSW public sector is a largely untold story, however, through the lens of CSNSW, which adopted this ethos enthusiastically, it can be said that this approach, culminating in privatisation, is central to the way imprisonment is now conceived. Although the official commitment to a managerialist approach is clear in the official statements of the CSNSW, performance, especially fiscal, often fails to live up to this paradigm. The paradoxical and contradictory nature of the excessive costs of imprisonment and the impetus for a managerial approach may partly explain this (Garland 2001, p. 188). Garland sees the "clash between the institutional logic of cost effectiveness and the sovereign state gestures of the war on crime (as) a clash of irreconcilable principles" (Garland 2001, p. 191).

For CSNSW faced with a rapidly increasing prison population and a punitive orientation towards criminal justice, managerialism is a way of placating political and populist entities as well as a way out of the philosophical morass of imprisonment. "Managerialism frequently operates as the umbrella under which all manner of ideology can rest without scrutiny" (Sotiri 2003, p. 305). Expenditure on the construction of new prisons has not been matched by expenditure on the development of healthy systems of operation for these new establishments (evidenced by the high number of prisoner complaints about basic services from, for example, Wellington (Office of the NSW Ombudsman 2008, p. 123)). Arguments about value for money may affect the internal workings and budget allocations for prisons but has failed to prevent the steady expansion of prison building in NSW.

Clearly, other factors such as the expressive aspects of sentencing and criminal justice generally may have had an equally important influence on criminal justice policy in NSW (Freiberg 2005, p. 30). One of the major arguments of this book is the importance of subjective expectations of the sentenced person arising from sentencing aims. Arising from this recognition is the need to attend to the actual subjective states of those imprisoned. The expectation that the guilty feel and be able to express appropriately, remorse and responsibility must be part of this "expressive" dimension. Therefore, while Freiberg's argument is persuasive, there is a need to further interrogate and explain what he means by "expressive" and how this actually works to maintain the paradox of imprisonment.

Overall, the official adoption of the ethos of managerialism may be most important for CSNSW in a symbolic or cultural sense. The capacity of managerialism to foster other complementary discourses, such as the emphasis on responsibilisation of the prisoner (discussed later in this chapter), arising from an ideological preference for explanations of crime focusing on individual choice rather than structural factors such as disadvantage and poverty, has been part of its strength in corrections in NSW (Sotiri 2003, p. 368). Although clearly brimming with ideological and philosophical tenets, managerialism also sells itself as a kind of practical philosophy devoid of moral or emotive content, very attractive for a department dealing with the complex, contradictory and volatile nature of criminal justice. While fostering other highly ideological approaches such as individualism, the managerialist ethos allows for the adoption of the pretence of a value free, evidence-based ethos.

The managerialism evidenced in the official statements of this Department is unique to its context and focused ideologically rather than in practice. Nevertheless, the creation of processes and data which can be used to fulfil managerial imperatives is a powerful part of the equation. An allied and complementary discourse is provided by the rhetoric of scientific objectivity and a professed reliance on "evidence-based practice", which has been operationalised recently by a restructure involving moving psychologists from prisons to the community and a radical restructure of programming towards offence-specific cognitive skills programmes (see Chap. 7). Despite high numbers of prisoners on remand and serving short sentences, the Department appears to be trialling a programme which absolves them of any case planning or management beyond very basic processing for sentences of less than 18 months (APP I/V CSNSW 3)[2] on the grounds that the evidence suggests that not only is programming a waste of time on practical and administrative grounds, but the research also suggests that it may actually harm "low-risk" prisoners. The "scientific" basis of the argument makes it perfectly suited to the prevailing ethos, but the short-term result is a diminishment of already stretched services and assistance to prisoners inside NSW gaols.

The coexistence of different rationales for action in criminal justice policy or, more specifically, the relationship (or lack thereof) between the legal act of sentencing and the subsequent carrying out of the sentence is one of the major interests of this book. In proposing a model for studying imprisonment, Alder and Longhurst (1994) distinguish between "ends" and "means" discourse. In their typology, discussion of the aims of sentencing (see Chap. 4) is categorised as "ends"

[2] The Australian Prison Project conducted interviews with various correctional and legal staff. This book was written as part of this project although direct use of project interviews was limited. (See Australian Prisons Project forthcoming). The coding used to identify these interviews in this book may not correspond to that used by the APP:

discourse, while managerialism is a "means" discourse. While these concepts provide useful modalities for thinking about the field, examination of the intersections of these different ways of thinking provides the most illuminating and complete view. In addition, the ideological and philosophical implications and the embedded nature of practice and discourse may be overlooked if too strict typologies are employed. The work of Alder and Longhurst is important nevertheless for their reliance on a detailed knowledge of the working of the Scottish prison system, focusing on the impact of organisational practices on the prison "careers" of long-term prisoners (Alder and Longhurst 1994).

5.3 Prison as Management of Bodies

The following discussion of some of the main incidents of imprisonment as expressed by the prisoners is loosely based on the organisation of the Department of Corrective Services Classification Manual and the temporal progression of the prisoner into custody, beginning with reception and classification. Other themes, such as movements, resistance and compliance, arise from the interview material and follow the prisoner through the sentence. These incidents of imprisonment combine to form the milieu that the prisoner must negotiate.

Some of the themes reflect other important studies of prisoner life (in particular, Liebling 2004; Crewe 2009; Drake 2012), although it is important to note differences in emphasis unique to the NSW context – for example, movements may have a different quality and importance due to the comparatively vast distances between prisons and between prisons and court, and therefore may take on a heightened disciplinary meaning. In the absence of a comprehensive study of NSW or even Australian prison life, it is only through glimpses of the experience of prisoners that the differences and similarities can be examined.

The "thousand little cuts" of imprisonment are the daily torment of many prisoners. Crewe (2009) speaks of the growth of "soft power" in prisons, insidious and all encompassing, while at the same time less physically abusive than previous regimes. The psycho-dimensions of this exercise of power will be further examined in Chap. 7. The questions posed in this book concern the barriers to fulfilment of the sentence, in particular, rehabilitation, and therefore the interview extracts and the analysis focuses on this overall theme, rather than attempting to give a comprehensive examination of the texture and quality of prison life.

Processes of Sorting and Classification

> Once they're inside, they're in "the mechanism" ... I keep telling new people when they come in that they're in Wonderland and they're Alice . . . The White Rabbit is them (prison officers and prison administration) and we're Alice! (Mick).

The metaphor of Alice in Wonderland, coupled with the image of a "mechanism," illustrates institutional, mechanical processing of bodies in a social environment as capricious, bizarre and contradictory as the world into which Alice fell. As this chapter will argue, like Alice, prisoners are also made responsible for their predicament in ways which, given their lack of agency, seem unfair and contribute to their sense of alienation from the world they have entered. At the end of the custodial part of the sentence, their performance is judged against a kind of ideal-type progression through the prison system without reference to their capacity to either understand or negotiate the complexity of the systems with which they are confronted.

When the prisoner is taken from the court after being sentenced to imprisonment, a series of processes occur, which take the focus from the formal ceremonial habitus of the law to the administrative, pragmatic world of "corrections." Foucault's conception of the nature of carceral power encompasses these mundane processes. "Throughout the penal procedure and the implementation of the sentence there swarms a whole series of subsidiary authorities . . . and all fragment the legal power to punish" (Foucault 1977, p. 21 in Grey and Salole 2006, p. 661). The recognition of the disciplinary nature of managerial correctional processes is to foreground otherwise unexceptional processes, which become the norm but which also contribute to the way the sentence is operationalised in a real and concrete way.

The Bourdieuan conceptions of "habitus" and "field" provide a useful conceptual framework for an examination of the way that the practices and discourses of an organisation inform and shape its practice. The concept of "field" as "the "rules of the game" that are the contexts for social interactions" or as "a metaphor for the metaphorical space in which we can identify institutions, agents, discourses, practices and values" (Webb et al 2002, p. 86) provides the means to delineate and explain the different parts of the criminal justice process. While the fields of the courts and the prison system overlap, there is a gulf between them which can be explained with reference to the individual, personal dispositions of the people within the organisations, in Bourdieuan terms, their "habitus."

Habitus refers to the individual's "feel for the game", or the set of bodily dispositions and mental structures through which we interpret and respond to the social world, based on our past experiences (Bourdieu 1990). The maintenance of the habitus relies on the unconscious adoption of practices as if they are "common sense, natural or inevitable" (Webb et al. 2002, p. 38) and thus this conception lends itself very well to the study of practices within institutions such as prisons. In addition, Bourdieu's work, in its insistence on a rapprochement between a materialist and a symbolic analysis, is consistent with the need in studying imprisonment to attend to the "instrumental role of penality as a vector of power" as well as the "expressive and integrative capacity" of systems of punishment (Wacquant 2009, p. xvi).

Leader's examination of the criminal trial in NSW illustrates the way in which the processes of law become a seemingly natural and inevitable part of the institution of criminal justice. She speaks of

> The transformation of the adversarial criminal jury trial from a particular mode of cultural production that is a manifestation of a *field*, to a process that is apparently cohesive, universal and unquestioned, not only by the layperson, but also by most of the legal agents who work within it (Leader 2007, p. 3).

The processes and procedures involved in imprisonment itself lend themselves to this lens, as a set of socially constructed and maintained practices which are largely taken for granted by the actors themselves and "misrecognised" (Bourdieu 1990) through responsibilisation, as choices made by the subject, the prisoner, in negotiating the "field" of the prison. As Bourgois points out "policy debates and interventions often mystify large scale structural power vectors and unwittingly assign blame to the powerless for their individual failures and moral character deficiencies" (Bourgois 2009, p. 297). This phenomenon is magnified by the very fact of imprisonment, as the disempowerment of the subject is arguably a central part of the punitive, denunciatory aspect of imprisonment.

"Bound and Gagged"

While at certain times the prisoner will be required to demonstrate appropriately required subjective states, in the main, the processes of managerial corrections do not require the active participation of the prisoner, they are assessed, sorted, screened and classified; they have little agency in what happens to them and little recourse regarding review of decisions. The "bound and gagged" nature of the defendant throughout the criminal trial (Leader 2007, p. 9) is continued throughout the incarceration process. Towards the end of the sentence, the wheels of accountability again grind into action, reviewing and assessing their progress. The way that the prisoner negotiates the managerial habitus of the prison largely determines his or her progress through the sentence and impacts on eligibility for release on parole.

> But the attitude is, you are not people, you are things to be moved from A to B, and whatever we can do to make that unpleasant, we will do (Mark).

This quote epitomises the realisation by the prisoner that the system has now stopped focusing on him as an individual. The unwavering gaze of the criminal trial and sentencing court, while denunciatory and punitive, at the same time holds the promise of individual attention to personal deficits – the criminal justice system as "gatekeeper" to health and welfare services. This focus gives way to the depersonalising sorting and processing of "corrections" where categories – by offence, by classification, by ethnicity (see Chap. 6) – overwhelm and obscure any individuality and uniqueness.

For many prisoners, this is the most bewildering realisation of all, that, despite the minute dissection of their faults at sentence, nothing will now be done to help them remedy the situation (see further discussion in Chap. 7). "Unpleasant" is also a "soft power" (Crewe 2009) word. Not brutal or harsh, such power at a distance is exercised in a morally vacant, casually cruel manner.

The "self-referential" systems integral to the processing of prisoners (Aas 2005, p. 87) quickly become an end in themselves; the need to develop processes and systems privileges numerical knowledge over narrative knowledge: what Aas calls "how information lost its body" (Aas 2005, p. 51). The disembodiment of the prisoner is reflected in the allocation of a "Min" number by which they will be referred thereafter. Depersonalising processes are reflected in the way staff discuss inmates: "There are inmates, receptions, recidivists, remands, returns, turn-arounds, and lifers" which "act(s) to reinforce the dehumanising processes characterising many other aspects of prison life" (Sotiri 2003, p. 307).

Prisoners often report feeling mortified, humiliated and embarrassed by many of the minor processing incidents which are part of the everyday life of the prison – for example, one prisoner pointed out that staff had made a point of giving him a pink fastener for the overalls worn by prisoners for visits – a not-so-subtle reference to his sexual orientation. This prisoner took what was a clumsy attempt at humour with good grace, but was clearly discomforted given his previous experiences of victimisation due to his homosexuality (see Chap. 6). The demeaning nature of many of the processes involved in "reception" can be characterised as "mortification undergone by the prisoner as a part of "prisonisation" (Goffman 1961, Clemmer 1940, Goulding 2007, p. 40).

However mundane they appear, these "correctional incidents" can have a huge impact on the outcome for the individual prisoner as far as the content of the sentence is concerned and ultimately their access to their earliest possible release date. When considering barriers to the fulfilment of the aims of the sentence, attention must be paid to the way in which prisoners are sorted, processed and contained and the meaning these processes hold for the prisoner and the sentence. Before examining the impact of some these processes, it is necessary to outline the specific context in which they occur in NSW.

Risky, Secretive Systems

"There are also programmes and procedures which, far from working to foster desistance in offending, literally assemble the conditions for recidivism and repeat incarceration" (Halsey 2008, p. 1212). Halsey's concept of "risky systems" which he applies to post release processes and systems can be extrapolated backwards to the processes and systems set up inside prisons. These are ostensibly value-free elements merely there for the management of prisoners providing a rationale for the operation of prisons and a way to make sense of the waves of human beings thrown at it each day. They also operate in a moral vacuum where any failure is placed at the door of the prisoner, thus absolving the Department from responsibility and depriving it of the opportunity for improvement. Coupled with the political undesirability of adverse comment, the result is a non-reflective culture where dysfunctional systems are allowed to flourish.

"Routinization masks the casual injustices and sometimes tragic consequences which modes of control can have for dispossessed outsider groups" (Armstrong and McAra 2006, p. 12). The casual cruelty of managerialism is evident in NSW, for example, in the way that family relationships are torn apart by location in remote facilities with no public transport. Lengthy delays for approval to attend funerals, dismal and oppressive visiting areas for children, all add up to a culture that is hostile to the maintenance of family relationships, despite official statements as to their import. The various processes or correctional incidents that a prisoner is likely to encounter throughout a sentence are largely taken for granted, in terms of their effect on the carrying out of the sentence as a socially related process with consequences for both the prisoner and the community.

The Information Vacuum

No, no, they don't explain a damn thing to you (Leslie).

A number of prisoners had made considerable efforts to obtain information about their position in relation to their progression through classification, psychological assessment or eligibility for programmes. The only prisoners to have copies of any of this were those with above average literacy skills, a privileged position or job within the prison, and considerable perseverance. Information is not given out lightly and Freedom of Information rules are applied strictly. Recent investments in technology systems are said to have improved the ability of the Department to coordinate and access information about the prisoner. Very little information is made available to prisoners, however, without a Freedom of Information application. Rarely, if ever, did prisoners in this study say that they had received feedback and assistance in processing the information from any assessments performed on them, and they appear to exist in an information vacuum until approaching their "Earliest Possible Release Date" or EPRD, in Departmental jargon. The NSW Ombudsman commented, "we put significant resources into providing information to inmates (and other complainants) that they should have been given by CSNSW, GEO, or Justice Health in the first place" (Office of the NSW Ombudsman 2010, p. 93). Thus, the rhetoric of individual choice and responsibility is a one-way street; rarely did prisoners in this study feel as if they were given enough information to make realistic choices. The choices were all made for them.

As a form of power, information is highly restricted in NSW prisons. The security focus of the modern prison, exemplified by the wide gathering of intelligence, means that information is a valuable commodity. Unfortunately, this mitigates against the prisoner understanding what he needs to do to fulfil the expectations of the sentence, as information about the content of the sentence, the assessments carried out on the individual and the way the system plans to manage them, is vital to the recruitment of the individual into his own redemption. Whether part of the neo-paternalistic "soft power" proposed by Crewe (2009) or, as may be more likely in NSW, a continuation of the old power in the guise of the new, prisoners spoke of the lack of information about their situation as a significant barrier to acceptance of the sentence and subsequent engagement in positive rehabilitative activity.

"Soft Power"

In common with Wellingsborough, NSW prisons have seen a significant diminution of direct physical violence by prison staff to secure compliance. "Soft power" (Crewe 2009) certainly exists in NSW prisons but is combined with a continuation of traditional attitudes among correctional staff, although the paucity of studies in Australia on prison officers makes such statements largely reliant on the accounts of prisoners.

On the whole, Crewe's analysis describes accurately the current situation in NSW prisons:

> Physical brutality in prison is far less common than it was two decades ago, but the misuse of soft power can have consequences that are just as profound. (Crewe 2011, p. 465)

One of the most insidious but elusive aspects of the exercise of soft power is the hold that correctional authorities have over information about the prisoner. Even where directly relevant to the ability of the prisoner to negotiate the everyday expectations of the sentence, information is tightly guarded and rarely given freely. In the security-focused prison, information about prisoners is valued for intelligence purposes only, and the same secrecy is applied across the board.

The connection between "knowing where you stand" being given a reason or given feedback as to decisions was strongly emphasised by prisoners as crucial to managing their imprisonment. Issues of procedural fairness are rarely raised or dealt with formally within the Department and are arguably a huge source of discontent among prisoners. The Ombudsman commented in this regard that "people should be told why decisions have been made especially if those decisions are detrimental to them" (Office of the NSW Ombudsman 2010, p. 94).

> And then just a straight answer, just say "Maybe I need this", if you say "yeah maybe I'll look into it", then I have to go all right then, there's a bit of hope there . . . You never get a reason (Van).

Again, the concentration by the prisoners in this study on the often capricious, unpredictable decisions of prison staff, made in secrecy and without procedural fairness, accords with Crewe's analysis, and dovetails with the earlier point made in Chap. 3 that legitimacy relies on acceptance by the prisoner of the strictures of the sentence and the conditions in which it is carried out. (Crewe 2009; Sparks and Bottoms 1996)

Access to information about the prisoner, including court transcripts and sentencing comments, is a contentious and difficult issue. Despite heavy investment in computerisation of inmate records, privacy and confidentiality issues are yet to be settled regarding access to detailed material about prisoners. Sentence comments, for example, while arguably an integral part of the sentence management process given the resources spent producing them and their importance at EPRD, appear to be requested in a piecemeal and inconsistent manner, except for Serious Offenders Review Council (SORC) inmates and prisoners already in treatment programmes (who nevertheless had difficulty obtaining them).

5.4 Processes of Sorting, Classification and Management

As part of what is called, somewhat euphemistically, "reception", the regulations to the *Crimes (Administration of Sentences)* Act 1999 provide that, as soon as practicable, personal information is to be recorded on a form comprising 23 questions. A medical examination is also performed. The prisoner must at this point also surrender all personal property. The information collected by the Department about the prisoner goes into a myriad of different files (up to 16) (CSNSW 2008, p. 121).

The Rules

At reception, prisoners are also told about rules relating to discipline and conduct. A complicating factor for prisoners as well as those who visit them is that, despite a depressing similarity in atmosphere, each prison in NSW has its own distinct way of operationalising "the rules". Indeed, significant differences between prison officers were also identified by interviewees, illustrating the high level of discretion possessed by individual officers (see later discussion of discipline in this chapter).

As Crewe points out, "discretion can function for or against legitimacy"; however, the lack of consistency in decision making was identified by many prisoners as a problem (Crewe 2009 Ch. 4, p. 14).

> Every day is a different set of rules. As soon as I walk out of my cell I look down the stairs to see who's in charge of the shift cause I want to know which rules I've gotta go by (Chris).

The shifting, ever-changing nature of the parameters of institutional behaviour intensifies the "Alice in Wonderland" aspects of imprisonment and advantage those prisoners with social skills which allow them to make the adjustments necessary to living with the daily uncertainty of what will be allowed and what will not.

Liebling et al characterise as a "paradox" the fact that "prisoners value consistency", while it may suit the administration to have a mix of different staff, divergences over even what may be considered minor issues on the outside can be vitally important in prison (Liebling et al. 1999, p. 90). This variation has been seen as problematic to the notion that managerialism predominates, that is, one would expect a system which favoured a managerialist perspective to foster uniform treatment of offenders (Vuolo and Kruttschnitt 2008, p. 311). It can be argued, however, that in addition to providing evidence of the "governmentality gap" so often commented on in the implementation of criminal justice policy, this variation in the exercise of discretion is consistent with the role of other low-level criminal justice functionaries such as police, where a high level of individual discretion (albeit somewhat more accountable than that exercised by prison officers) is an important feature of the organisational and legal culture. Certainly in NSW, each prison has its own unique organisational culture; however, a powerful trend has been an increasing centralisation of power into the hands of the Commissioner in some important areas (see later discussion of special categories of prisoners).

The literature on order maintenance in prisons demonstrates the importance of negotiated aspects of prison order, "authorities manipulate order through informal systems of power sharing with prisoners" (Carrabine 2005, p. 898; Crewe 2009). Certainly, prison officers were seen to share power with some prisoners, this perspective was common among those (including CSNSW) who engage in the "good old days" discourse (see Chap. 6). A precondition for such power sharing is the exercise of high levels of discretion at very low levels of the organisation. It is evident to those dealing with CSNSW that on a number of levels variations in practices between institutions can be great, indeed even between wings of the same institution. For example, Tony Vinson's comments about Goulburn gaol on the Four Corners programme in 2005 indicate the idiosyncratic culture of some institutions. "It had staff over several generations who had worked at the gaol . . . so their concept of what a prison should be . . . was set in stone" (Masters 2005). Alder and Longhurst made similar findings in their study of Scottish prisons; local differences often overrode attempts to impose consistent rules and practices (Alder and Longhurst 1994). Differences between privately run and CSNSW institutions will be discussed in the next section.

Unofficial Processes of Sorting

> They have to put funnelling sections through the gaol. You see one at um Long Bay X wing and Bathurst X wing, that's where all the other "hard arse longies" go . . . the ones that beat on their chest. Now, here's different: you funnel in your normals which want to get on with things and have no hassles (Mick).

The way that prisoners categorise each other and themselves reflects their internalisation of some of the categorisation undertaken in the sorting process. The placement of prisoners into different prisons is often perceived by prisoners to have a certain logic and rationale. Some prisons are seen as more appropriate for "normals", that is, not "spinners" (those with a mental illness or unpredictable behaviour). Long-termers, having become accustomed to institutional rules and processes are often resentful of those, often short-termers, who one prisoner called "weekend warriors" for whom the maintenance of a tough rebellious persona, while laughable to older, wiser inmates, is a common coping strategy. Many of the older more settled prisoners agreed with the logic and rationale of this kind of sorting.

> Now you've got to keep in mind a lot of the situations that we inmates find ourselves in has been engineered by the officers . . . They've worked out, okay, fine; look if you divide them you'll conquer them (Dave).

The recognition that correctional authorities work against the creation of prisoner solidarity by encouraging the formation of groups that are perceived to have affiliations with some other groups and grievances with others pervaded some of the interviews. These unofficial processes of sorting lend themselves to use in an atmosphere of public concern about the formation of gangs in prison. The use of intelligence and prison informers to base placement decisions adds another layer of secrecy and control over the process (Drake 2012). The fact that the processes and decisions as well as the evidence grounding them is generally not available to the prisoner creates further feelings of disempowerment and suspicion when outwardly arbitrary, sometimes even perverse, decisions are made without explanation.

Other types of unofficial sorting used by CSNSW vary from the openly racially based system at Goulburn (called "ethnic clustering" or "yarding")[3] (see Chap. 6) to less obvious placement of older, wiser prisoners in metro prisons away from the "hard arse longies." Elderly prisoners or those with chronic health problems may be kept at Long Bay because of the need for proximity to medical treatment. Other placement involves avoiding potentially catastrophic confrontations between prisoners with some kind of history, which may lead to conflict.

[3] MP Michael Richardson Member for the Hills cited a report by Laurence Goodstone to the Commissioner of Corrective Services "Essentially, he is saying that ethnic clustering makes managers lazy, it increases group tension and it creates a siege mentality amongst some staff." (NSW Parliament Legislative Assembly Urgent Motions 26/9/2002)

Classification

In anthropological terms, systems of classification are "completely social" (Alder and Longhurst 1994, p. 51), that is, deriving from "and indeed properties of the social systems in which they are used" (Douglas in Alder and Longhurst 1994, p. 51). Although considered as a managerial process in this chapter, classification systems in prisons predate the modern managerialist phenomenon. Historically, classification in NSW prisons as elsewhere reflected distinctions between "habitual" criminals and those who were redeemable. Modern classification systems are based mainly on security considerations. The Department in NSW says that it is guided by the principle of "lowest possible classification"; however, this begs the question of the criteria used to assess suitability. Certain categories of prisoner are scrutinised much more than others, and for some categories (e.g., E classification, deportees) their status provides an instant barrier to the application of this principle.

As per clause 32, prisoners of different "classes" – convicted, unconvicted, civil, are to be kept separately (although, in practice, this is often not the case, particularly with women). The Commissioner also has the power to direct that other groups be kept separately; and female prisoners must be kept separately.[4] The classification categories have recently been expanded to include a higher security classification: 7 for men – AA (national security) A1, A2 (both maximum security, B (medium) and C1, C2 and C3 (minimum), 5 for women. In addition any prisoner who has previously escaped (including police custody or as a juvenile) (without necessarily having been convicted of an escape offence) is classified E1 or E2. The classification manual is 371 pages long, reflecting the amount of attention paid to these matters. (Compare this to the Case Management Manual which comprises 11 pages.) A urine sample free of illicit drugs must be provided for each inmate to progress from a B to a C "classo" (s19.2.2.1 (i) CSNSW Operations Procedures Manual).

[4] Although the recent tendency to hold small groups of women in wings of male prisons is a cause for some concern, due to difficulties in access to programs and services.

While delegation is used in relation to the classification of the vast majority of prisoners, the Manual states:

> It is important to bear in mind that the legislation reserves to the Commissioner those decision-making powers which relate to the case plan, classification and placement of inmates in the following categories: serious offender, public interest inmate (when seeking progression to C3/Cat 1), escapee (when seeking progression to a minimum security classification), extreme & high security inmate and an inmate charged with or convicted of terrorist offence(s). In making certain decisions on such inmates the Commissioner first seeks advice from the Serious Offenders Review Council or sub committees of the Council" (CSNSW Operations Procedures Manual).

In a small jurisdiction such as NSW, violent crime is relatively rare and each case is reported extensively in the media. In some cases, mere association with certain groups despite the irrelevance of the association to the crime prevents prisoners from progressing through the system.

> I've copped hell from the officers ever since (a media report). That's why I ain't getting classo, because of the media (Mario).

This young offender (mid-twenties) was related to a high-profile alleged member of a particularly reviled outlaw motorcycle gang. He was not a member himself, but had been mentioned in media reporting, leading to serious problems in the way correctional staff treated him. Media attention to high-profile crimes provides an important driver to the adoption of highly risk-averse strategies within the Department in relation to all of the correctional processing undertaken on certain offenders. The highly politicised nature of criminal justice in NSW places pressure on correctional authorities to ensure that offenders imprisoned for such crimes are treated in a sufficiently punitive manner.

> "Public interest" inmates can be any inmate designated by the Commissioner, including, but not limited to those serving a sentence of more than 5 years for a drug offence, more than 3 years for an offence involving actual or potential bodily harm, more than 3 years for

fraudulent behaviour, more than 3 years for a driving offence causing death or GBH (CSNSW Operations Procedure Manual 18.1.14).

There is a common perception that the Commissioner keeps an unusual level of control over decisions relating to classification and that even though SORC may recommend a reduction in classification the Commissioner often refuses it (in 2008 the Board made 1715 recommendations and the commissioner approved 1580 (SORC Annual Report 2008)). The importance of these regimes and processes of governance to the way the sentence is worked out is particularly clear in the case of sex offenders and categories of violent offender where progression through security classifications is directly linked to completion of offence-specific programmes. For serious offenders as defined in s3 of the *Crimes (Administration of Sentences)* Act 1999 (NSW) (including those serving a sentence for murder or where the EPRD is 12 years or more), there is a rigid policy of progression (C1 not before 4 years from EPRD, C2 – 2 years, C3 – 1 year). Victims (and the state) can make submissions, which must be considered by SORC before allowing any unescorted leave. Serious offenders have a strictly staged reduction in security classification contingent on the approval of SORC and ultimately the Commissioner who must also consider any submission made by a victim.

Escapes and the Discourse of Security

The obsession with security and preventing escapes, at least partly due to the unwelcome public attention which such events attract, leads to a disproportionate focus on previous escapes or attempts to escape, as a barrier to progression. Drake finds the obsession with security part of a broader trend towards securitisation (Drake 2012). In a similar fashion, the security focus of CSNSW means that any escape, whether as a juvenile or from police custody, may be used as a means to override all other aspects of the sentence, leaving the focus on punishment and incapacitation. The resulting failure to progress through the system means that the prisoner has diminished access to programmes, to work and consequently has little preparation for release.

> "Always just an E, all the way through." Interviewer: "So, released from maximum security each time?" Prisoner: "Yeah, they say "here's a dole cheque, on your way . . . " Interviewer: "How many times has that happened?" Prisoner: "Be about . . . 10 . . . 10 times now" (Kevin).

E classification inmates have a notoriously difficult time having their classification reduced. The fact that control of these processes in relation to inmates deemed especially risky resides and is exercised at the very highest level with SORC, and ultimately the Commissioner, has arguably restricted progression and thereby rehabilitation for this category of inmate. The fact that no conviction needs to have been recorded for a prisoner to be categorised in this way leaves considerable room for injustice. As a group for whom risk has been elevated to the primary parameter for processing and classification, E classification prisoners arguably represent, along with sex offenders, the embodiment of the risk paradigm as applied in the correctional context. Access to progression in classification and thereby to programmes and services is thus restricted, leaving the prisoner in a kind of circular limbo: where reduction of risk is tied to programme completion, but access to programmes is contingent on reduction in classification, which is tied to risk.

> Interviewer: "Are there any . . . gaols where you as an E classo prisoner can do programs?" Prisoner: "Lithgow's the only one" (Kevin).

It appears that services and programmes are often severely restricted for this category of inmate, including access to Drug Court and the Drug Treatment Correctional Centre, with a record of escape precluding consideration for access to reduction in security and viewed as evidencing unreliability. While it is difficult to gauge the number of indigenous and other overrepresented groups in this category, the fact that escapes from police custody are included may indicate a higher prevalence of these over-policed groups in this category. Potential deportees are another group for whom progression through classification is more restricted (see Chap. 5).

There is no right of appeal from a decision as to classification, although, strictly speaking, the prisoner could file a summons in the Supreme Court on the basis that the Commissioner, in exercising his discretion, has made an error of law. Unsurprisingly, this expensive and difficult option is rarely, if ever, taken.

The Holy Grail – Reduction in Classo, Access to External Leave

> I was supposed to be a C classo three years ago. Even the judge, Judge Levine – he says "you're way behind, we gotta try to push you forward" But the Commissioner never signed off on my classo. They've been recommending me a B classo since 10 years ago (Antony).

Classification affects access to almost every service and programme in prison. For example, to become eligible for participation in sex offender rehabilitation, a prisoner must have reduced his classification to a C. The opening of programmes at Parklea, which can accommodate other prisoners, is a pragmatic recognition of the difficulties inherent in this, especially for prisoners such as escapees and high-profile prisoners, for whom reduction in classification is more difficult.[5] In the idealised version of a sentence as a linear process of decreasing classification, with external leave and work release as a precondition for release for longer-term prisoners, classification assumes a pre-eminent place in the life of the prisoner. Statistics on work release illustrate the rarity of this ideal; in 2010, there were 127 prisoners on work release, 86 of those from Silverwater Correctional Centre (CSNSW 2010).

Diagnosis

It is difficult to generalise about the role of the clinical diagnosis in the sorting process as even prisoners found not guilty by virtue of mental illness are often kept in mainstream prisons in NSW. Their special position by law is not really reflected in the way they are processed in the prison environment. An increasing awareness of the need to screen

[5] It appears that these programs have now been discontinued and again only C category prisoners can access sex offender and violent offender programs.

for suicide has resulted in some improvements for prisoners with mental illness, as have such unsung but valuable programmes such as mental health nurses in some Local Courts, and the improvement to the hospital at Long Bay. The ubiquity of mental health problems in prisoners is not really reflected in the processes and procedures. Diagnosis is mentioned here to reflect the importance given to it by the prisoners when discussing the initial sorting and processing, which they were subjected to. However, it was more the lack of attention paid to these matters by prison authorities which came through in their interviews, the shock felt when, as mentioned earlier in the discussion of sentencing, after all the focus on identifying and documenting their failings and weaknesses, nothing would now be done to assist them to ameliorate them. Therefore, diagnosis in itself can become part of the pains of imprisonment and relevant to the ability of the prisoner to act on the expectations arising from sentencing.

> I was diagnosed by the Crown Psychiatrist as being so unstable that I should have been taken out of the prison system and put into an institution. But the Immigration Department refused that (William).

This prisoner, like many in this study, referred to feelings of depression and hopelessness early in his sentence. Another description of the post-sentencing state of mind was as if they were "in shock." Rarely is treatment offered except where major mental illness is present. One inmate reported that methadone was a common way to self-medicate, even without the existence of a prior narcotic addiction (see Chap. 6).

The information about prior diagnosis of a prisoner with a mental illness or intellectual disability may be available if the person has a history with CSNSW, but the fact that much of the early screening and classification is performed by prison officers may lead to imperfect recognition of prisoners with these conditions. The role of "diagnosis" in prisoner management is somewhat uneven, and may have little impact on their placement. In the era of offence-specific programming, such characteristics as mental illness and intellectual disability are only relevant insofar as they interfere with the delivery of generic programmes.

> I've got no real treatment for my mental disability . . . when I see the psych it's just . . . this medication or that one, change this, change that (Jack).

While people with diagnosed mental illness can be stabilised to some extent in custody, there is a strong reliance on medication. This young prisoner was desperate to engage in a therapeutic relationship. In common with many prisoners with a mental illness and coexistent drug problem (which must be the new paradigm, to speak of "dual diagnosis" as an occasional clinical aberration is to ignore its prevalence) he had fallen between the gaps of mental health and drug and alcohol services outside and inside the prison. As a sex offender, he was required to complete a medium-intensity sex offender programme, giving no time for him to get help for the problem he himself identified as key to his staying out of trouble, his mental illness and the need to manage it. This concentration on the offence rather than the person may be a feature of the new rehabilitation paradigm where completion of the appropriate programme is privileged over individualised assessment and treatment. In the case of this prisoner, his coexisting problems were pushed to one side.

Prisoners were often dismissive of such interventions. The stigma of mental illness prevalent in prisons may prevent some prisoners from acknowledging problems.

> I went from there to the ACMU (Acute Crisis Management Unit). Interviewer: Is that the Kevin Waller Unit? Prisoner: "No, it's next door to 'Wally's World' " (Mick).

The use of the term "Wally's World" to refer to the unit where prisoners at risk of suicide are kept was noted more than once. Prisoners used demeaning language to refer to others with mental health problems, one prisoner, who clearly had some issues himself, was contemptuous of "spinners." The problems caused by sharing a cell with someone experiencing mental health difficulties were mentioned often, and the opinion was expressed more than once that prison was no place for someone with these problems. Few were willing to accept that they themselves had psychiatric problems, perhaps reflecting no more than the prejudices of the general community about mental illness but also the reality of living in close quarters with a range of people with interpersonal difficulties.

Movements and the Transportation of Inmates – The "Tour of the State"

In common with other Australian jurisdictions, CSNSW must grapple with the reality of distance. Many prisons, including those constructed in the past 20 years, are located in country regions. Movements and transportation thus acquire prominence in the management of prisoners.

> I been to Silverwater, Long Bay Kempsey, MRRC, Parramatta, Lithgow in between, X wing and next door (Chris).

Each prisoner in this study recited a litany of prisons they had inhabited, with most of the movement occurring early in their sentence. A significant number had been at their current prison for a considerable period, but all had experienced considerable movement, sometimes for reasons understood by the prisoner such as court attendance and medical treatment. More often though, movements were considered to have a random, punitive flavour, although, as indicated earlier, prisoners are generally supportive of the need to control others by such processes as separation and segregation. The allocation and transportation of prisoners to different prisons is a complex process with significant implications for individual prisoners. As a purely managerial process, oversight is limited and recourse for prisoners is minimal despite the potentially large ramifications. The former minister, John Robertson, in answer to a question regarding transportation of inmates, stated that CSNSW has the equivalent of a full prison of inmates on the road on any given day (Robertson 2009).

Movements as a Disciplinary Tool

While it is expected that some movement of prisoners is inevitable; prisoners reported that movements are often used as disciplinary mechanisms. The line between using transfers of prisoners to safely contain a volatile and potentially conflicting prison population and overreliance as a technique of control may be thin. "Doing the bounce" may involve disconnection from services and family and increasing alienation often results.

> Then what happens then if somebody does get upset – bang, they get the tour of the state! They go from here to Wellington, to Bathurst and Lithgow and that's another little trick!(Jack).

This prisoner's use of the word "upset", rather than painting the transgressive prisoner as aggressive or difficult, indicates his understanding of the context in which many confrontations in prison occur, the prisoner's frustration at his powerlessness even (and often) in relation to minor matters.

> "Yeah, they just do the bounce with them . . . " (prisoners who misbehave) (Mick).

"Doing the bounce" is a particularly apt description for the often uncomfortable journey in the back of a prison van. The intertwined nature of industrial issues and management of prisons in NSW is again a concern following a decision by the Industrial Relations Commission in 2009 to cut the number of escorts required due to the availability of surveillance technology in vans. Expenditure on transportation by CSNSW NSW has dropped from $67,834,000 in 2004/2005 to $47,202,000 in 2008/2009 (Report on Government Services 2010, table 8A.25).

The following extract clearly illustrates the reality of prisoner transport, while also highlighting the difficulty of proper involvement in legal proceedings under such conditions, an issue enlivened by the *Benbrika* decision in Victoria, where onerous custodial conditions including transportation were found to be interfering with the defendants' right to a fair trial[6]

[6] *R v Benbrika & Ors* (Ruling No 20) [2008] VSC 80

> This is one day – they wake you up at 4.30 in the morning. 5 o'clock they come around and see that you're washed up having a cup of coffee or whatever. They take you down to the holding cell. You get changed, you might be there for half an hour, you might be down there for an hour and a half. They load you onto the van. Then the van takes you to Silverwater. Now you could go to another gaol, pick up another bloke and go to Silverwater. Silverwater becomes the central pick up and let down point. So you sit in Silverwater for an hour. So you are awake at 4.30, court starts at 10 o'clock and in 4.5 hours they've retrieved you from one gaol to another.... Then it's just waiting, waiting... Then you get to court and you wait in the cells. You go up, (they tell you) it's been adjourned. Then they put you back in the cell and the van comes at 4.30. They take you back to Silverwater and you wait until 8.30-9 until you get the van back to the Bay... If you're on a six week trial that happens every day... It gives the DPP, the prosecution a huge ace up their sleeve because after about the third day the bloke is going to be pissed off, tired, weary and he's going to miss things (Tommy).

Movements are a cause of great concern for prisoners. The often arbitrary and abrupt transfer to another prison can cause considerable disruption in their progression through the correctional system, as well as dislocation from family, access to programmes and services and education. In addition, each prison has its own culture and habitus which may take some time to navigate. The numbers of complaints about "transfers" may not be representative of the actual numbers due to the way the Office of the Ombudsman classifies complaints: in the 2007/2008 Annual Report, the Office stated that it was so concerned about the numbers of prisoners who complained about the impact of transfers on prisoners' ability to access or complete educational programmes that they began an "own motion" enquiry (NSW Ombudsman 2008, p. 123).

The transportation of prisoners has recently been highlighted as a problem for prison agencies across Australia. The death of Mark Holcroft, a minimum security inmate serving a short sentence (Australian Broadcasting Commission 2010), suggests that transportation of prisoners to remote prisons causes huge problems for individual prisoners, including restricted access to medication and basic hygiene on the journey. The widespread use of audio-visual technology has to some extent reduced the need to transport prisoners to courts (see earlier discussion of the other implications of the use of audio-visual in criminal justice); however, the large number of movements of prisoners as a managerial tool is a cause of concern. While location of prisoners near to family and support networks is often used as a rationale to construct prisons in regional areas of NSW, there is little evidence that once the prisons are built local people occupy them. It is far more likely that families must then make the trek to remote country towns with limited transport and accommodation options. Since the RCIADC, the duty of care owed by the Department towards inmates in its care has been clear and the issues involved in transportation and movements of inmates often involve breaches of basic human rights. Prisoners are well aware of the "duty a care", although as one prisoner said, "it doesn't mean they do care, though."

The former Commissioner of Corrective Services made no apologies for the use of movements as a disciplinary tool.

> But the gang problem in gaol is under control, because we've got that capability of movement. Some of these young people that are coming off the street now, it's the first time in their life where . . . they've been made to do what someone else wants them to do. They have no say if we open their cell door at 11 o'clock at night and say, "You're moving from Lithgow to Goulburn, because you're going to get yourself into trouble if you stay here any longer" (Masters 2005).

Lockdowns

In many NSW prisons, for at least half to 1 day per week or fortnight, the prison is "locked down" to the outside world. Prisoners are locked in their cells, visits are unavailable, programme/education participation is impossible (although because lockdowns have been regularised in many gaols programmes are now structured to accommodate this). This also does not prevent an additional lockdown for any number of other reasons (usually staffing related) occurring on other days. As a management tool, lockdowns clearly enable savings on staffing to be made; however, they often provide a further barrier to prisoners accessing services and programmes. Excessive lockdowns are a well-known cause of prison tension and, in conjunction with overcrowded conditions, may contribute to violence between prisoners.

5.5 Discipline, Resistance, Compliance and Punishment

Any discussion of discipline and resistance in prison must take place within the context of an examination of power. As a total institution (Sykes 1958), the prison is inextricably bound by the ties of disciplinary power (Foucault 1977). The prison itself is emblematic of the exercise of power over prisoners and each interaction with prison staff is imbued with this potential. Of course, compliance is the norm; in the sense that most prisoners realise the futility of outward resistance. As Crewe says, "the prison is replete with symbolic reminders of institutional dominance and the futility of resistance." (Crewe 2009 Ch.4 p. 40) Nevertheless, resistance does occur although perhaps in less overt ways in response to the more "soft power"-oriented neoliberal prison (Crewe 2011).

> And we do bad things in here. Everyday something bad happens, someone who deserves it. That's part of gaol. You know, you've got heroes, you've got followers, people do anything for a shot (Chris).

There is a level of acceptance among prisoners and others about the existence of violence and threatened violence in gaol. While some of the prisoners in this study had not personally experienced it, the vast majority demonstrated awareness of the potential and reality of violence, whether because of the nature of the offence, their sexuality (John) or as a "trophy" for younger prisoners (Chris). Prisoner taxonomy is also demonstrated here – "heroes" and "followers" as well as a "just desserts" type of attitude – "someone who deserves it". This prisoner also highlights the prominence of drugs as the motivation for the "bad things". Further discussion of violence and a brief examination of some aspects of drug use take place in the next chapter in the context of interpersonal relationships.

Disciplinary matters are almost exclusively dealt with internally.

> In regards to a correctional centre offence, governors **may** choose to hear and determine the charge or **may** refer the matter to the Visiting Magistrate if they are satisfied that the offence is serious enough for referral (clause 4, s. 16: Inmate discipline, CSNSW Operations Procedures Manual).

In the vast majority of cases, the 'delegated officer' plays the part of police officer plus judge, jury and executioner, in that they decide on the charge, make a determination of guilt and innocence, decide on a sentence (although this must be approved by the Governor) and carry out the sentence. Interestingly, while penalties are listed in the Manual, no list of correctional centre offences is provided.

Offences relating to drugs and mobile phones are given particularly detailed treatment. Only governors can deal with mobile phone offences and penalties can be up to 6 months' withdrawal of privileges. In relation to failing to supply urine sample or supplying a dirty urine, withdrawal of privileges can apply for up to 6 months as opposed to 56 days for other offences as per s57 of the *Crimes (Administration of Sentences)* Act NSW 1999.

Sotiri's conclusion that the utilitarian discourse of CSNSW infantilises the prisoner by recourse to phrases such as 'good order' instead of punishment for infractions of rules reflects the change in the handling of prison discipline over the past 20 years (Sotiri 2003, p. 269). Goulding (2007, p. 68) notes the strategies of control used by prison officers include control over information and control over access to families (Goulding 2007, p. 69) (see Chap. 6). The loss of remissions as a management tool in NSW has led to withdrawal of 'privileges' becoming established as the alternative.

The internal disciplinary record of the prisoner is clearly a relevant consideration for most of the processing undergone by the prisoner, including the ultimate decision regarding parole. The consequences of correctional charges can be ongoing; the State Parole Authority takes such matters very seriously when considering parole and disciplinary matters can have a huge impact on decisions about classification and placement.

In New South Wales, a governor or delegated officer is granted wide discretion to decide whether a disciplinary infraction proceeds as a minor or major offence. This discretion adds another layer of control over the prisoner.

> If a wide, but uncertain, range of conduct may fall within the scope of such offences, the constant potential that disciplinary charges may be laid provides a formidable and continuing means of control over prisoners (Groves 2002, p. 27).

The breadth of the category of offences against 'good order' provides almost limitless scope for the punishment of undesirable behaviour (Groves 2002, p. 21). Liebling et al characterised two models of prison officer work: the "rule following or compliance model and the negotiation model actually delivered by most prison staff" (Liebling et al. 2001, p. 477). The conflict between the two models, one favoured by prison administrators and one actually practised by staff on the ground means that realistic training in prisoner management is difficult.

> One officer, he was pretty good, cause he knew what I was doing, I'm not that kind of person you know. He said "Just for a warning, I'll give you a one week lock in." But they have to put the paperwork in, you know (Xu).

Therefore, an enormous amount of discretion exists on two levels – whether behaviour can be characterised as an infraction and whether to deal with the matter internally by way of disciplinary charge or other sanction or, in some cases, through normal criminal justice processes. There has been a notable recent expansion in both the existence and the exercise of the discretion to deal with matters internally, reflected by the dramatic decrease of legal representation by the Prisoners Legal Service in internal disciplinary matters.

> You just put your hand up, cos you get found guilty anyway, so why delay the punishment for another couple of days, just get it over with (Chris).

This prisoner expressed a common view among interviewees in this study that internal disciplinary processes were a foregone conclusion; that is, once accused of an offence, prisoners were invariably convicted and punished without attention to the need for procedural justice. In support of this contention, the NSW Ombudsman commented in the 2008 Annual Report, "The inmate disciplinary system does not seem to provide an appropriate/reasonable safe level of procedural fairness." The lack of "clear and sufficient rules and procedures . . . hampers any later examination of the procedures followed or the reasonableness of the outcome" (Office of the NSW Ombudsman 2008, p. 99). Not only is this cause for concern for abstract notions of justice, such denial of natural justice has the effect of further alienating the prisoner. When assessments of behaviour in custody are so important in determining the release date of the prisoner, it would seem important to highlight the legitimacy of the process.

One prisoner, clearly well behaved and trusted, expressed the view that good behaviour was not necessarily rewarded, particularly where parole eligibility is concerned.

> Interviewer: "So there isn't a direct connection between doing the right thing and being treated well?" Prisoner "Yeah, because I've seen like some of my friends, they very good friends we've known each other for 3 or 4 years already. They've done 18–19 years and they've been doing what I've been doing and uh, they just couldn't get parole" (Yan).

The absence of a relationship between the type of offence and the relevance of custodial behaviour to the gaining of the 'holy grail' of progression through the system is evident in the case of sex offenders who are generally well behaved in custody but may be kept in considerably more restrictive conditions than other types of offenders because of fears of a public backlash.

> But then again, you have to look at the screws. What power have they got? If a bloke comes out and bops a screw what are you going to do? What punishment are you going to take his television off him and put him in segro for 6 months? That's all they can do. But then again that doesn't happen as frequently as it used to, even though they say there's a lot of assaults in gaol. It's usually prisoner on prisoner . . . there's always the potential of that. Always (Brian).

This prisoner had suffered through the particularly violent regime at Grafton in the early 1970s and so was somewhat contemptuous of the non (physically) violent nature of modern penal sanctions. He highlighted the changes in prisoner culture brought by increasing numbers of drug-addicted and mentally ill prisoners and expressed some degree of sympathy for prison officers for having to deal with more difficult prisoners with less access to direct physical means. This was despite his own personal experiences of violence under the pre-Nagle regime in NSW. This "diminishment of pure authority" (Crewe 2007, p. 12) brought about in part by improvements to conditions and structures of accountability leaves intact other structures of authority, such as the new psycho-power wielded by psychologists and prison officers through case management.

> I'm not raising hell now. I just sit back and a watch what goes on and roll with the punches and I don't think anyone knows me name out here. I've done the hard yards (Brian).

> Due to the design of the research, most of the prisoners interviewed had served a number of years of their sentence already. Most had, in the parlance of the prison officer, 'settled down' and were focused on dealing with the need to get out at their EPRD ('earliest possible release date') except for the sex offenders who were mostly remarkably accepting of the fact that they were unlikely to be released at their EPRD due to non-completion of programmes. Thus the level of overt resistance demonstrated by these men appeared to be minimal.

Liebling's statement: "the mission to eliminate residual resistance and secure a new mode of compliance has been the largely undocumented penal project of the past decade or so" (Liebling in Crewe 2007, p. 256) rings true for NSW, where themes of security and control have dominated (e.g., the obsession with escape rates). In NSW, with its brutal correctional history, physical punishment has largely been displaced post-Nagle by power operating "in ways that are insidious, intangible, opaque and highly effective" (Crewe 2007, p. 256). The project of self-governance, which accompanied the increase in managerial-type thinking, responsibilises the prisoner and creates an environment, which masks the exercise of institutional power. Again, Crewe's conception of "soft power" (Crewe 2011), while evident in the practice of CSNSW, coexists with elements of the old regime in NSW prisons

> Basically I'm on protection because if I'm not I might get killed by certain Corrective Services Officers (William).

This prisoner appeared to be genuinely fearful for his life, as he had been victimised by staff due to other reporting of his situation in a published work. He was insistent on his non-identification and the highly idiosyncratic circumstances of his offence make it necessary to change some of the details of his account. Kept in strict protection, he was waging a paper war with the Department as well as other agencies involved in his prosecution and conviction. Highly educated and intelligent, he was anomalous in the prison environment although adopting a well-known stance of oppositional behaviour. On an everyday level, resistance can be demonstrated by the smallest action. For this prisoner, it was demonstrated by constant engagement in legal proceedings and complaints against the Department. He had been successful in forcing the Department to provide him with certain resources and felt that his activities had put his life in danger.

A particularly common type of resistance was demonstrated by one prisoner (Kevin), who, while compliant and indeed a valued worker with high-level skills, planned to refuse to engage in a therapeutic programme, even with the high probability of parole refusal or at least delay. His frustration and anger at the refusal of the system to recognise the significant gains he had made was palpable. The need for him to gain work release to provide the material conditions, which he highlighted as vital for his successful reintegration, conflicted with the rigid application of policy. In this prisoner's case, exceedingly positive case notes and the support of the prison was insufficient to overcome SORC's concerns, and provides an example of the type of centralised control exercised over certain categories of prisoner.

Crewe (2007, p. 256, 2009, pp. 35–75) in offering a typology of prisoner adaptation to "mechanisms of penal power" describes the different types of compliant prisoner – committed, instrumental, detached and strategic. Elements of each were detected in many of the prisoners interviewed who mostly demonstrated an attitude of resigned compliance. As Crewe observes, "compliance did not generate stigma if it could be seen as self-serving rather than passive and acquiescent" (Crewe 2007, p. 273). As Carrabine points out, "the everyday resistances of prisoners . . . constitutes a continuum so that when a riot does happen this should not be regarded as an aberrant event" (Carrabine 2005, p. 907). For Carrabine, the question is not why riots happen in prisons but why do they not occur more frequently.

Punishment – Segro and Removal of Privileges

While in the modern prison outright brutality may be rare, prisoners still spoke of the effect as physically assaultive. Images of the prison as a "cage" from which the prisoner emerges "to attack the first thing it sees" reflect the ongoing negative impact on the community of the effect of imprisonment.

> Now if you lock an animal in the cage and you beat it with a stick, when you let that cage door open the animal's going to attack the first thing it sees. And that's basically what happens in gaol (Mario).

Although the truism repeated in Nagle, derived from Sir Alexander Paterson, an early UK prison reformer, that prison is as, not for punishment, is common in the discourse of those working in the system, it seems to have passed the prisoners by. The disavowal of imprisonment as punishment at all is evident from the language of the Department – the word simply does not exist in their recent official records. This arguably adds another dimension to the "Alice in Wonderland-like" situation of the modern prison – if prison is not for punishment then there is no legitimacy in prisoners feeling punished. The multiple dimensions of the interpersonal aspects of imprisonment (more than one prisoner spoke of prison staff metaphorically "beating them with a stick") must surely constitute "extra" punishment. As demonstrated in the discussion of movements, many prisoners interpreted the outwardly morally neutral processes of correctional managerialism as punishment.

In addition, the time-honoured use of segregation continues in the modern prison.

> Interviewer: "So do they still use segro as much?" Prisoner: "Here? Oh of course, for any reason whatsoever. You yell and you scream and call them arseholes and stuff like that. They only tolerate it for so long and they go bang, crash- segro" (Dave).

Segregation, while expressed to be for the good order of the prison, is clearly punitive. Sotiri makes the point that the 'good order' rationale is infantilising and inconsistent with other currents of responsibilisation dominant within CSNSW (Sotiri 2003). Removing prison punishments from the normal arena of criminal justice, the courts deprive prisoners of the protections of the presumption of innocence as well as the other procedural and evidentiary safeguards of the criminal trial. Prison management are judge, jury and executioner as well as informant, police and victim.

As a management tool within prison, punishment becomes about removing the things that prisoners value (Crewe 2009, p. 16). Improvements in physical conditions can allow staff to manipulate prisoners with the threat of removing the small but important things in a prisoner's environment. The world shrinks for prisoners and the existence of small comforts acquire a heightened importance. For example, small electronic cooking devices such as rice cookers and toastie makers are highly valued and withdrawal of these items can be used to control prisoner behaviour. Other sanctions feared by prisoners include withdrawal of visits, and lack of progression in classification.

If you be cheeky, they cut off your phone calls (Chris).

This is a more severe punishment than it sounds; in country prisons the telephone is often the only connection with the outside world (see Chap. 6). Just being "cheeky" implies that low-level dissent can have serious consequences for the prisoner. As one of Crewe's interviewees said, "the prison system will only give you stuff which they can take away from you" (Crewe 2009, p. 16). Thus, access to material benefits becomes a coercive mechanism in the absence of other tools such as remissions.

5.6 Special Regimes

At the same time that physical conditions in NSW prisons have generally improved, special categories of prisoner are kept in extreme conditions such as Supermax at Goulbourn. These regimes hold a meaning and importance to the maintenance of the carceral state in NSW beyond the numbers of prisoners contained therein. Their symbolic value serves to legitimise the imposition of extreme conditions of incarceration and serve as a handy disciplinary tool in the absence of positive incentives such as remissions. In this regard, Crewe points out "the need to evaluate modes of order across prison estates" (2009, p. 6), as the existence of harsher regimes in other parts of the prison system provides a powerful mode of control.

AA, -'Public Interest Inmates' Reg. Cl. 277(1) (e) (OPM 18.1.)

Keeping Crewe's point in mind, the creation of a special category AA (special risk to national security) may not have had an impact in terms of numbers, but it is arguable that the very existence of such a category legitimises the creation of conditions which may not comply with human rights standards and can create an atmosphere in which further incursions into prisoners human rights occur in other areas of the prison. A recent feature of the way prisoners convicted of serious violent offences are managed is the creation of special categories of inmates whose cases are of such interest as to require extreme care and caution in decision making.[7] Clearly, such factors as sentence length and risk assessment are one way of identifying this group (although it is questionable whether long sentences means greater risk of recidivism). The possibility of adverse political or media reaction is perceived to be the foremost consideration in relation to these groups. The Commissioner can designate an inmate high security or extreme high security if of the opinion that they constitute a danger to other people or are a threat to the good order of the gaol.

> "Even in Goulburn and that you know there wasn't any stabbings or nothing down there." Interviewer: "Really, do you think that's because there's a lot of security now?" Prisoner: "Yeah and also the fear of the Supermax" (Dennis).

The maintenance of regimes of extreme deprivation has useful consequences for discipline outside the containment of the individuals held within, as a powerful metaphor of control throughout the rest of the prison system. The use of the threat of extreme punishment as deterrence is common. Despite evidence that conditions are detrimental to mental health (Arrigo and Bullock 2008), the use of isolation persists.

> "Um, the isolation . . . is exhausting." Interviewer: "That's an interesting way to describe it . . . exhausting. 'Cause you're with yourself all the time?'" Prisoner: "You don't know what's going on around you so you're constantly battling with yourself trying to describe what it might be or might not be . . . but it's . . . exhausting, because I don't care how tough you are or how you want to portray yourself being a hard person, you still need that contact verbally or whatever . . . when you don't know what's going on around you and you've got no control, even more so, it is exhausting cause it's a constant battle to

[7] It must be acknowledged that the HRMU is merely the most recent manifestation in NSW of a long tradition of isolation of certain prisoners – other examples are Graftons's "intractable" section and Katingal.

> try and reassure yourself... But I think I have lost some feelings toward other people" (Chris.)

In trying to explain the effect of Supermax on him, this prisoner spoke of an internal battle with himself, a daily, exhausting struggle. Even as a 'hard man' in prison, a long-term prisoner with a serious record of violent offences, he expressed the anguish of having no contact whatsoever with the outside world and very limited contact with other prisoners. He expressed concern about the long-term effect of the loss of feelings for other people, particularly in relation to his children whom he had discouraged from visiting him. His vision of life on the outside was quite isolated and solitary, and he feared that he had lost his ability to communicate with "normal people."

While prisoners in Goulburn's HRMU had already been kept in segregation-type conditions without the normal review processes operating, this practice has now been institutionalised by the 2009 amendments to the *Crimes (Administration of Sentences)* Act 1999 NSW, s78a (5) which allows the Commissioner (retrospectively) to 'separate' inmates, without the use of a segregation direction, resulting in the effective segregation of certain groups of prisoners without the type of scrutiny and review required when a segregation direction is made (NSW Ombudsman 2010, p. 908)

Protective Custody

The truism in NSW is that there are so many prisoners on protection that it has become the new "main", protection now becoming the norm. This has necessitated the formation of different levels of protection, as one inmate said, "protection from the protection."

> You know in gaol when you're on protection people start passing on rumours and that, because I know what I did was bad definitely, no doubt about it. But it wasn't like that kind of crime, some crime that everybody hates (Xu).

The "crime that everybody hates" is clearly child sexual assault, as ever, these prisoners are at the bottom of any prison hierarchy. The assumption that prisoners are on protection because they are 'rock spiders' pervaded many of the interviews and caused a great deal of angst for those on protection whose crime was not related to child sexual assault.

Protective custody may not be a matter of choice for some prisoners, as the Commissioner may place a prisoner in protective custody pursuant to s11 for their own protection. A prisoner can also request placement in a protected area. There are different levels of 'protection', limited association or complete non-association. Very high numbers of prisoners are on protection (for sex offenders it is almost an automatic process) and entire prisons are now virtually protection prisons. "21% were held in isolation from all other inmates (non association) or some other inmates (limited association)" (SORC Annual Report 2004, p. 10).

> "They reintegrate a lot of the protection back into the main . . . (but) a lot of the time someone finds out and, you know and the blokes go again" (back on protection) (Dennis).

This prisoner, as a long-term drug user, had never been in protection and exhibited the usual distaste for the subjects of protection. Entering protection is a double-edged sword. Once a prisoner has been on protection, it is unlikely that they will ever go out into the 'main' (although 'mainstreaming' is attempted from time to time). The stigma attached to protection is still strong despite the large numbers and associated with reviled prisoners such as child sex offenders and informers (see next chapter on concerns of prisoners in programmes).

Protection often precludes a prisoner from being classified to a particular prison, undertake a particular programme or access education resources. Nowadays, paradoxically, the opposite situation sometimes prevails, that is, programmes are provided for protection prisoners but not for those in the "main." Interestingly, the conditions for non-association prisoners are often indistinguishable from those of prisoners placed on punitive segregation (although segregation is not meant to be punitive, being for the "good order of the prison," there are clearly strong punitive elements to solitary confinement).

5.7 Case Management, Throughcare and SORC

This section is concerned with the conflict between the official discourse of the Department and the experience of prisoners in relation to the overall management of their sentence. While the philosophy of case management and Throughcare pervades the official reporting of the Department, prisoners were almost universally scornful of their practical application. At the root of many problems is the obvious conflict between the disciplinary functions of CSNSW staff and the social work values exemplified in Throughcare and case management. Chapter 6 continues the discussion of relationships between staff and prisoners through the lens of relatedness.

Case Management and Throughcare

The slim volume that constitutes the case management manual, as opposed to that covering the more administrative and disciplinary aspects of the management of prisoners, gives little clue as to how prison officers and prisoners are to reconcile the contradictions inherent in the role.

> Here's one for you – I don't even know who my case officer is! And I've had two case officers in the past 2-3 months (Mick).

"As soon as practicable" a case plan is to be developed for each sentenced inmate and reviewed every 6 months. This plan is to consider a range of matters, including the sentencing remarks of the judge (clause 5-12). This implies that the sentencing remarks of the judge are to be available on the case file of each prisoner. As noted earlier, sentencing remarks are the "non-numerical" part of the sentence which represent, among other things, a communication with the offender and the community and which provides a kind of checklist for the Parole Authority when the prisoner reaches eligibility for parole.

Relationships between prison officers and prisoners (canvassed again briefly in the next chapter) are problematic for most prisoners who were unlikely to view them as sources of assistance.

> I don't really like talking to them . . . Because you don't know what they're saying (Mick).

The theme of trust between prisoner and prison officer is clearly relevant here. Prisoners know that information will not be treated confidentially and many are therefore reluctant to discuss personal information.

> "She who must be obeyed" was my case officer, a two striper. I overheard her, very early in the piece, go . . . " You maggots", I'm going to go up and talk to her about my innermost secrets, aren't I? (Leslie).

As well as demonstrating contempt and disgust for prisoners in her comments, the disciplinary nature of the relationship is emphasised by the reference to "she who must be obeyed." On two levels then, this prisoner clearly perceived the futility of taking case management seriously, particularly as a member of a particularly reviled offender group.

> Yeah, one minute they're trying to be your best friend and talk to you and counsel you the next minute they're bashing you or writing you up for some trivial little thing. Before it was us and them and that's how I preferred it (Mick).

The "old timer" attitude to staff/prisoner relationships was echoed in many of the interviews, particularly from those prisoners with long imprisonment histories. The preference for clear and well-guarded boundaries between prisoner and prison officer was also related to prisoners who need to "know where they stand" and be given clear and definite information about their imprisonment. "If Corrective Services is viewed as an implementer of punishment then throughcare is easily construed as an extension of *punishment* in the community rather than the extension of care" (Sotiri 2003, p. 321).

The difficulty in reconciling the rhetoric of case management and Throughcare with the reality of the holding of direct disciplinary power by the same functionaries is rarely addressed (Sotiri 2003, p. 379). Prisoners, however, are all too aware of the incongruity of the situation; "inmates were defined and define themselves as being in opposition to correctional officers and/or even the justice system itself" (Grunseit et al 2008, p. 7).

> Um they've got this thing called case management which is a load of shit. . . . Case management is when an officer sits down with you and he asks you if you have any welfare issues. . . . They want to know the ins and outs of a rat's arsehole . . . No, I don't tell them jackshit. I tell them what they think they need to hear (Jack).

Case management is derived from basic social work principles and purports to provide a holistic approach to the management of prisoners by expanding the role of the prison officer to a quasi-welfare role. Leaving aside the issue of the holding of direct disciplinary power by prison officers, it is unlikely that the level of training and the very basic support provided by the procedures manual would result in a workforce skilled in case management except on the most basic level. The 1999 research report prepared by ICAC indicates that, "it is at the point of service delivery, the case officer- inmate interface where case management stands or falls" (ICAC 1999, p. 64). Officers themselves felt ill equipped to carry out the requirements of case management, and there was abundant evidence that it was implemented only in the most minimal and administrative way.

> He came up to me – he was an Islander fella. He goes "I'm your case officer. Any problems? Nah?" that's it! (Mick).

Most of the comments from the prisoners in the study, all of whom had served at least 3 years, indicated that case management was, at best, given lip service by the majority of Corrective Services staff.

> "And that's with the case management . . . the friendlier the officers, the more relaxed an inmate fells with 'em." Interviewer: "So a lot of the time

its information gathering from the officers point of view?" Prisoner: "Yeah and they use it for sure" (Dennis).

This inmate saw case management as intelligence gathering for officers to get information with which they could better manipulate inmates, rather than a process which could help him. Sotiri points out that, in a Foucaultian way, "supervision in CSNSW frequently involves examination of all aspects of prisoner life." She notes that:

> reports by officers often involve psychological evaluations of the prisoners they are managing… easily clouded by the primary and frequently antagonistic relationship which exists between prisoner and officer" (Sotiri 2003, p. 379).

Again, Crewe's conception of "soft power" is apposite to explain the use of the "power of the pen" through the soft mechanism of case management. The fact that many prisoners see this for what it is but are forced to play the game adds to the "imaginary" aspects of imprisonment (Carlen 2008). By purporting to provide a system of caring, social work-oriented management, CSNSW can ignore the disciplinary meaning imbued in each interaction. It would be most interesting to see whether staff have the same attitude as prisoners, Carlen's experience in a NSW prison, upon which she based her conception of "imaginary penalities," indicates that it is most likely that staff privately acknowledge the shortcomings of case management but are forced to pretend that it works.

SORC

The Serious Offenders Review Council is an independent statutory authority, created by the *Crimes (Administration of Sentences) Act 1999* to advise on the security classification, placement and case management of inmates classed as Serious Offenders. The Council also advises the Parole Authority concerning the release of Serious Offenders and provides reports about these offenders to the Supreme Court and the

Minister for Justice. SORC is made up of judicial members, officers of Corrective Services and representatives of the community. The number of SORC inmates (broadly speaking, those prisoners with an EPRD of at least 12 years) constituted about 7 per cent of the total prison population in 2004 (SORC Annual Report 2004, p. 1) has risen from 662 in 2006 to 671 in 2007. The NSW Law Reform Commission in the 1996 report on Sentencing recommended a review of the functions of the Council to assess whether any duplication of services exists (NSWLRC 1996). In 2005 amendments to the *Crimes (Administration of Sentences)* Act inserted ss3 to s135, in effect preventing the Parole Authority from making a parole order against the recommendation of SORC. It is instructive that in the former Commissioner's words, "The system in NSW now has a Serious Offenders Review Committee in place *to ensure that the most serious offenders aren't moved through the classification system too quickly*" (emphasis added) (Woodham 2005, p. 59).

> I saw SORC a week ago for the third time in 15 years. Um I've got plans for when I get out, for work, education everything like that . . . The only two questions they asked me – were "do you consider yourself a dangerous person" and I pride myself on being fairly honest in most cases I said "In some circumstances yes, I am dangerous . . . ." The second question was "Are you are trustworthy person within the system?" "How can you answer that . . . ? I said no and I shot myself in the foot and now I'm knocked back for another 12 months." Interviewer: "Do you go back and be honest again with SORC?" Prisoner "Yeah of course I would. That's the only thing I've got left" (Chris – still an EHR prisoner after 15 years).

The contrary, self-defeating nature of this prisoner's behaviour only makes sense when viewed through the lens of resistance to unfettered power. Having been rendered powerless not only through incarceration but also through extended placement in HRMU, this prisoner felt that his honour and his honesty was, literally, all he had left. Although he spoke of his hopes for reduction in classification, he was not about to compromise his strict moral code for this. Having already experienced the worst that CSNSW has to offer, he could not be coerced in this way. He reserved his most contemptuous comments for the SORC, seeing them as wanting and encouraging prisoners to lie and obfuscate to achieve their ends, rather than accepting and appreciating his honesty about his character. Indeed, given the lack of any rehabilitative services experienced by this inmate, it is not surprising that he saw himself in this way.

A recent change in practice saw SORC recognising what prisoners already knew – that the requirement to review each serious offender every 6 months was not being achieved. It must be said that, while most prisoners who had dealings with SORC saw their intervention as more of a hurdle to be jumped rather than helpful sentence management, there was one prisoner who was appreciative of their intervention and appeared to have benefited from their support in terms of access to education and timely access to the therapeutic programme specific to his offence. (Andrew) He may have been unusual because of several features particular to his case and his experience was not really replicated.

> I've asked the SORC Board, for arguments sake, "where's my pathway? (They say) "Pathways, pathways no, no, no, we're not having pathways! (Leslie).

Several SORC prisoners mentioned "pathways" indicating that this terminology had been used to describe their progress through the prison system. This prisoner indicated that the jargon had changed, that SORC no longer conceived of the sentence in this way, and that he was given no information about what to expect in its place. It is difficult to assess the impact and effect of the workings of SORC. Their meetings are closed and they do not provide feedback to prisoners about the reasons for their decisions. It appears to many working in the system that their role is superficial and perfunctory, that they do not work with the prisoner early enough to achieve a case plan. Prisoners are often dismissive and disappointed that the Council does not perform more of a sentence management role.

> So you know and what annoys me is you've got these big wigs sitting in Sydney that don't deal with you every day (Ken).

This prisoner has the support of the gaol to progress to work release, however, SORC now want him to do a programme which will preclude him from working, move him from the gaol in which he has a trusted position and probably intrude into his parole period. Despite his reasonable and intelligent demeanour, he plans to refuse to participate and is resigned to serving most of his parole in custody rather than risk what he sees as his hard-won position in his current prison.

> They created this body to say we can focus on long termers . . . but they haven't shared a single thing of my pathway . . . I don't even know if I've got one . . . at the beginning . . . they said – we're going to create a pathway for you . . . I never heard anything (John has served 13 years out of a 14 year non parole period.)

The ability to provide adverse reports to the Parole Authority and intervene in classification decisions is usually seen as a negative by prisoners. The fact that SORC generally would not meet with the inmate until the last 4 years of the sentence and yet have input, which is neither reviewable nor even available to the prisoner, can only add to this mistrust. A press release from the then Attorney General John Hatzistergos, which stated that three-quarters of serious offenders failed to get parole, must cause some concern as to their efficacy in assisting prisoners and the prisons to prepare serious offenders for release at the EPRD (Attorney General's Department of NSW 2008). The NSW Ombudsman reflects the concerns of the serious offenders interviewed for this study. "In our view the current arrangements (for classification and case management of serious offenders) do not provide adequate independence and transparency in the decision making about these offenders." The Office urges a more 'transparent' system including the provision of reasons for decisions to inmates (NSW Ombudsman 2009/2010, p. 99).

5.8 Individualisation and the Responsible Prisoner

The frustrating combination of responsibilisation and powerlessness often results in an attitude of resentful compliance. The "get in the driving seat" comment mentioned by numerous prisoners exemplifies the type of correctional discourse which creates the "hall of mirrors" discussed in Chap. 7.

> You've got no say, you've got no control. There's an old saying in here – the pen is mightier than anything in the world, "cause one strike of the pen determines your future" (Chris).
>
> Again, this comment reflects the fact that every interaction is heavy with meaning, and prisoners know that they can be "written up" at any time (Crewe, p. 200)
>
> Abuses tend to occur not through hard means, in flagrant violation of the prison's rules, but through softer methods, within its bureaucratic folds. At their most damaging, they involve the tarnishing or neglect of prisoner reports – being "written off" on file (Crewe 2011, p. 465).
>
> In common with the experiences of the prisoners in the research for this book, Crew's interviewee's highlighted the insidious, hidden but quietly hegemonic "power of the pen," and the dominance of this mode of governance over more relationship-oriented personalised handling of prisoner management and interaction. He touches on an important dimension of this manifestation of "soft power," that it lacks personal embodiment and operates at a distance (Crewe 2011, p. 465). The absence of relational content and the depersonalising nature of these processes further disconnects the relationship of the prisoner with the mechanics of doing the sentence. "Paperwork" was clearly seen by prisoners as a weapon to be used against them: one negative comment or the absence of a crucial report having the potential to delay progression through the system and ultimately parole.

The Responsible Prisoner

> I've been in custody since I was 16 and a half. But you know there's no excuses for me about my history, that's my, you know, that's my doing. Youth and Community wasn't, that was family but my gaol history is my, my doing so I've got no one to blame you know, no fingers to point and I never do (Dennis).

This is not to say that prisoners do not want to be responsible for their contribution to their situation; however, a sense of lack of control over the progression of their sentence pervades the interviews. This prisoner, a long-term heroin addict, reflected the philosophy of self-responsibility often held by those who have participated in drug treatment. While he demonstrated a resigned compliance, he cannot be said to be one of Crewe's "enthusiasts" (Crewe 2009, p. 8), perhaps displaying more of a pragmatic attitude to the need to comply (Crewe, p. 17).

In what John Pratt calls the "new model of governance":

> the official version of the prisoner's progress through the penal system is, within certain clear constraints, a matter for them to decide, by making the appropriate choices from the assortment of possibilities the prisoners are thus to determine their own progress through the institution (Pratt 2005, p. 86).

When viewed retrospectively by Parole Boards, sentences are often seen in the ideal as an upward journey of progression through which the prisoner is expected to participate in available programmes, attend whatever services were recommended according to the sentencing remarks of the judge and generally prepare themselves for release in a series of logical steps. The assumption is often that the prisoner is a free agent and non-performance of any of these things is their fault, ignoring the fact that resistance is an integral part of the discipline and power exercised within the prison (Carlton 2007), as well as the practical barriers prisoners face in accessing programmes and services.

> I've played the game their way; I haven't got a single charge. You know, I'm not a drug addict so therefore I don't have that major little fault, which is a big one . . . they can use it later and nail you and not give you parole or anything . . . I pay attention to everything I do, you know (Steve).

By internalising the disciplinary nature of everyday practices within the prison, the long-term prisoners expressed the need to attend to all aspects of their behaviour, often as much to attend to their position within the gaol vis-à-vis other inmates as to complying with the authority of the gaol.

As Crewe expresses it:

> Power operates to a large degree "at-a distance", anonymously, and without the need for direct staff intervention. It works through psychological as much as physical means, via self-interest and self-regulation. It is less directly coercive or authoritarian than in the past, and in many ways it operates more lightly. However, it grips tightly, constrains effectively and is highly intrusive. (Crewe 2011, p. 456)

The high degree of self-regulation, "paying attention to everything I do", can be perceived as "playing" the system and draw negative attention to the prisoner. Most of those taking this stance, though, usually the more intellectually and socially adept prisoners, were able to successfully navigate the correctional landscape. For the vast majority of prisoners, however, this degree of self-awareness and self-control is beyond them.

5.9 Conclusion

This chapter attempts to illustrate some of the taken-for granted "correctional incidents" that are a part of the daily experience of prisoners. The official imperative of efficient management in a context of expanding numbers often leads to undesirable outcomes as far as the prisoner's progression through the prison system is concerned. The tendency to responsibilise the prisoner while failing to attend to the structural difficulties inherent in the serving of a sentence (Sotiri 2003, p. 238) contributes to the creation and perpetration of "risky systems", which rather than serving the Department's stated goal of reducing recidivism (however difficult that may be) perpetuates the negative aspects of imprisonment and hinders the transition back to the community.

Movements, whether dictated purely by security and managerial concerns or punitive motives, as many prisoners believe, provide extreme disruption unless part of a rehabilitative pathway. Classification, for many prisoners, is an ironclad barrier to the progression through the levels of security to the Holy Grail of minimum. For some categories of prisoner, such matters as behaviour in custody and willingness to rehabilitate are irrelevant compared to political considerations and the need to avoid undesirable publicity. Disciplinary practices and the application of rules are uncertain and often arbitrary. The strength of the official rhetoric of case management and Throughcare is matched by the equally vehement disavowal of its relevance to the prisoners in this study. A similar attitude prevailed to SORC. While this study did not address prisoner attitudes to the Parole Authority and to parole supervision, there was a general attitude of mistrust and apprehension about parole.

All of the "correctional processes" referred to in this chapter have an impact on the accessibility of programmes and services. While official pronouncements centre on the taking of responsibility by prisoners, in fact programmes and services will often be provided according to another set of often-conflicting, ever-changing priorities altogether. Changes in policy and implementation appear to be a constant in CSNSW (Sotiri 2003, p. 355). In addition to the micro processes affecting individual prisoners, changes on a macro level may well reflect current best practice, but clearly have a tremendous impact on the individual prisoner's ability to perform the obligations for which he will be accountable when seeking parole. Examples include moving programmes from the beginning to the end of the sentence, or changing the focus from treatment inside prison to the community.[8] For no longer is parole conceived as an entitlement but as a privilege to be earned by participating in programmes that are viewed as a magic bullet for reducing the risk of recidivism. The creation and maintenance of "risky systems" inside the gaol, rather than facilitating goals of rehabilitation and re-entry in prisoners, often merely continues the process of re-incarceration. The next chapter will continue developing some of these themes through the framework of prisoners' experience.

[8] Except for high-risk sex offenders for whom, contrary to the 'what works' evidence, treatment is only available in custody.

6

Relational Aspects of Imprisonment

6.1 Introduction

> And people ask me when I come in here, you know outsiders, Are you scared? And I go "No, I just get really sad, actually. I'm not scared of any of you in here, really, I'm more sad." That's what . . . it just saddens me that it's a wasted life (Jason).

The "waste" of personal resources which results from a term of imprisonment was often related by the prisoners to the absence of opportunities to have authentic relationships with other people. The presence of intense emotions in the interviews with prisoners (Liebling et al. 1999, p. 158) was often related to this feeling of loss of connectedness. Certain commonalities of experience were prominent, for example, despite the fact that this book focused more on the experience of sentencing and custody, the open narrative format of the interviews allowed prisoners to focus on what was important to them, and inevitably they wanted to talk about life outside prison, speaking unprompted about their families and loved ones. The previous chapter outlined some of the "correctional incidents" that constitute the managerial apparatus of the prison system

M. Hall, *The Lived Sentence*, Palgrave Studies in Prisons and Penology, DOI 10.1007/978-3-319-45038-4_6

and the effect these can have on the performance of the sentence. This chapter will provide a different lens to some of the most prominent themes raised by the prisoners. In describing aspects of everyday life in prison, the book relies upon the long tradition of prison research exemplified by the work of Sykes (1958) and, more recently, Liebling (2004) Crewe (2009) and Drake (2012).

Highlighting the way that prisoners relate to others reflects the priority given to issues of relatedness in the interviews. Elements of personhood such as sexuality and ethnicity fit within this framework as added factors in the negotiation of the prisoner with the sentence. The omnipresence of power relationships based on the idea that, as a total institution, all relationships within the prison are predicated on power, colours the interviews. As the focus of this book is on relating the lived sentence with the legal sentence which precedes it temporally, the categorisations in this chapter reflect the importance placed by prisoners on issues of relatedness. Perhaps it was to get away from the reality of power that prisoners often chose to focus on relationships characterised by the absence of these considerations. Prisoners often expressed their relief to be speaking to someone with no agenda. "I can let my guard down," "I pay attention to everything I do."

The constraints on interpersonal relationships form a considerable part of the pains of modern imprisonment and a significant barrier to the eventual re-integration of the prisoner into the community. The relevance of these issues to the overall argument of this book is that, to fully implement the aims of sentencing, the subjective experiences of prisoners must be addressed. Without an adequate understanding of the perceptions of prisoners of the experience of sentencing and imprisonment, systems and processes continue to perpetuate the kind of risky (Halsey 2006) and imaginary (Carlen 2008) features which may preclude proper reintegration or re-entry from prison into the community. The methods used by correctional management to control the tide of humanity coming into its prisons, as considered in the last chapter, begs the question of the effects of these processes on the relational aspects of imprisonment which are evidently so important to prisoners.

Criminal justice in NSW has come increasingly to exclude the subject. The complicated nature of legal proceedings and the secretive nature of correctional authorities in NSW combine to produce a peculiar disengagement with the prisoner about the sentence as a thing to be performed and endured. This performance aspect becomes important when approaching parole and the disengagement becomes apparent and is generally blamed on the prisoner.

The lack of respect and control felt by prisoners in the course of the processing and sorting outlined in the last chapter resonated through their accounts and informed many of their attitudes to their sentence. Halsey notes, "the disconnect between what is asked of young men in custody as against what is required of them when returning to the wider community" (Halsey 2006, p. 1210). Most prisoners are well aware of how ill equipped they will be when entering the community, prison having trained them for an altogether different life than will be expected of them outside. The way they relate to each other, to prison staff and to their families and friends has a determinative impact on the performance of the sentence and their success in remaining out of prison when released.

As an attempt to reflect some of the commonly expressed concerns of prisoners, this chapter, by necessity, includes a somewhat mixed bag of themes and issues, organised through the lens of prisoner relationships with other prisoners, with prison staff and with families. Each of the areas briefly analysed is deserving of a research project of their own, the dearth of research in Australia into the effect of the drug trade in prison, sexuality in prison, and ethnicity in prisons was another factor in the decision to present these findings. It is acknowledged, however, that such brief treatment can only identify potential areas for further enquiry and Australia awaits the type of intensive prison research currently undertaken in the UK.

6.2 The Relational Aspects of Life in Prison – Conceptions of Prison as "Community"

An examination of the interpersonal concerns of prisoners requires attention to the ways in which "community" is conceived within prisons by prisoners as well as by prison authorities. The absence of ethnographic research with prisoners in the USA in what Wacquant calls a period of "hyper incarceration" (Wacquant 2001) is reflected in the Australian context; apart from a few notable exceptions (including Goulding 2007; Baldry et al. 2008), few researchers in Australia have interviewed prisoners about anything, least of all their attitudes to their sentence and imprisonment. The long tradition of prison ethnography exemplified by Liebling, Jewkes, Crewe, Drake and others indicates that Wacquant's statement may not apply to the UK. Here, studies of the prison as community have a long pedigree and conceptions of "prison culture" have been utilised to explain the ways in which prisoners relate to each other and to workers in the prison environment.

The complexity of identifying what is meant by "prison culture" can lead to its use as a kind of omnibus concept without appreciation of the nuances of individual experience of prison life, and it lacks the subtlety to describe the variety of different manifestations of human behaviour inside prison. These conceptions therefore need to be tested against the accounts of prisoners. Halsey, in analysing the narratives of the young men in his study, notes the difficulty in reflecting "the nuances of each participant's situation" (Halsey 2006, p. 1214). This book shares that concern, as thematic analysis can only reflect broad outlines of individual situations, complicated as they are by ethnicity and citizenship status, mental health and intellectual disability issues, addiction and substance abuse, among other factors. Disputes about whether (so-called) prison culture results from the importation of cultural artefacts and practices from the outside world or engendered by the peculiar conditions of incarceration (Sykes's "pains of imprisonment" [Sykes1958/1999]) appear to be satisfied with the empirical conclusion that it is most likely that both factors have considerable influence (Berg and Delisi 2006, p. 633).

Despite the characterisation of the prison as a "total institution," the importance of negotiated order within prisons has also been long recognised, the compliance and cooperation of the majority of prisoners assisting in the maintenance of order. The importance of these theoretical paradigms for this book is that the further requirement that the prisoner undergoes a process of internal transformation and demonstrate (perform) it correctly, requires a high level of cooperation and commitment. The importance of the quality of relationships available to them in order to facilitate this process is widely recognised in the therapeutic literature, but noticeably absent from psycho-correctional discourse.

Crewe's intensive study of the prison society at Wellingborough takes the analysis of prison society further by centralising the notion of power and connecting the adaptations of prisoners to the manifold and insidious instances of "soft power," which has largely replaced the outright brutal regimes of the past (Crewe 2009).

> It (power) is tight and intrusive yet in some ways imperceptible, its grip is firm and enduring yet its character is soft and light, and while its scope is wide its source is diffuse (Crewe, ch. 9, p. 3).

No less intrusive, in fact, this "soft power" exemplified by the prominence of forensic psychology, arguably requires more of the individual than regimes of the past. The current model of rehabilitation, as will be argued in the next chapter, requires subjective transformations to be performed appropriately in a context of responsibilisation and accountability. This "soft power" then can be experienced as more intense, less predictable and truly baffling to some prisoners, who are often unable to respond appropriately to the underlying messages of criminal justice sanctioning due to personal and cognitive deficits.

Most studies view prison culture through the lens of violence, resistance and power (Berg and Delisi 2006; Carrabine 2005; Neuber 2011; Crewe 2009), which is certainly an ever-present concern for most prisoners. Viewing the relationships between prisoners and those they interact with exclusively on those terms, however, risks missing some important features such as positive aspects of so-called gang affiliations when younger prisoners rely on the protection of older prisoners. This tendency to view the relational aspects of prison life purely through the lens of violence or disorder is common to other areas of individual identity such as race and ethnicity and sexuality (see later discussion in this chapter). While this book relies to a substantial extent on the recognition of the ever-present exercise of power (Crewe 2009), it is hoped that the different focus taken highlights the essential humanity of prisoners. Rather than mere pawns in a power game or players who manipulate the system to their own ends, prisoners are viewed as people with the same relational needs as anyone else. In fact, given the expectation of internal transformation implicit in the sentence, their need for positive personal connections is perhaps more intense and deeply felt.

The way that the prisoners focused on the human elements of their sentence despite the research questions' concentration on the formal legal and managerial processes of imprisonment, demonstrates the centrality of this paradigm to the prisoners themselves. No matter what the topic, it was the way that the individuals involved related to the prisoner, and the impact on their interpersonal situation that framed their answers. These interactions, relationships and encounters constitute the performance of "prison culture" as it is played out in the life of the prisoner each day. That the requirements of the sentence demand fulfilment of certain internal transformative obligations make these relationships even more important.

Relationships with Others

Prison Officers and Prisoners

As front line staff, prison officers have the most immediate impact on the lives of prisoners. Their role has changed, officially at least, from mere turnkeys to a more human services role, although as discussed in the last chapter, the extent to which case management and Throughcare has been implemented is a moot point; and whether prison officers have the education or personal qualities necessary for such roles is arguable. The existence of considerable latitude in interpreting rules has also been canvassed in the last chapter, the holding of discretionary power over many areas of prisoner's lives places them as the most direct holders of power in the eyes of prisoners. Prisoners framed their answers about the content of the sentence and the difficulties involved in carrying out what was required of them with an appreciation of the actions and attitudes of staff.

Many other studies have emphasised the importance of prison officers. Alison Liebling's work on the moral content of imprisonment foregrounds relationships between prison officers and prisoners (Liebling 2004). Crewe's detailed study of Wellingborough prison in the UK explored the types of perceptions and attitudes held by prison staff towards prisoners. Drake candidly spoke of the need to engage with prison officers who otherwise had the power to disrupt or at least delay her research (Drake 2012, p. 191). What she calls "the habitus of maximum security" demonises and "others" the prisoners with whom they work (Greer and Jewkes 2004 in Drake 2012).

If there is little research with prisoners in NSW, there is even less with prison staff, despite their pivotal role in carrying out criminal justice policy around punishment. Prison officers in NSW have a history of resistance to attempts to introduce progressive policies. Ombudsman reports (Office of the NSW Ombudsman 2010), although couched carefully, indicate that prison officer/prisoner relationships continue to be problematic at times. The euphemistic "implementation issues" and "need for further training" is often shorthand for this problem. Given the "centrality of staff/prisoner relationships" (Liebling et al. 1999, p. 72), where the quality of the relationship is clearly a key consideration in the success or otherwise of policy change, it is puzzling that this issue has received little attention in Australia generally. In any case, "there is no satisfactory account of what a good or right relationship is" (Liebling et al. 1999, p. 74). Harding, highlighting the importance of prison environments in the success of programmes, reviews the literature on prison environments and concludes that "safe custody may be a necessary condition for effective treatment" (Harding 2000, p. 10). It must be recognised that power in prisons exists in a kind of dialectic, for most of the time prison officers rely for the legitimacy of their governance on the cooperation of prisoners (Liebling et al. 2005, p. 898). Therefore, the quality of the relationships between prison officers and prisoners is a key factor in preventing disorder.

The particular situation in NSW reflects an even greater importance of relationships between prison officers and prisoners as prison officer resistance has been an ongoing feature of the correctional history of NSW (see Chap. 3). The Department's new industrial relations strategy "The Way Forward" accompanied by the effective threat of privatisation is at least partly motivated by a strategic appreciation of the need to keep control of prison officers. The relationship between industrial action by prison officers and prisoner resistance by prisoners in NSW prisons (often caused by extensive lockdowns) is evidence of the importance of industrial issues to the treatment of prisoners. On the other hand, prisoner resistance, while historically a major element in the reform of NSW prisons, has been individualised and demonised. Prisoners who demonstrate defiance towards the system will suffer by being denied progression through classification and ultimately parole.

Taking It Personal and Playing Games

The problematic nature of the relationship of prison officers and prisoners was reflected in many of the interviews. Despite the official rhetoric of case management and Throughcare, examined in the last chapter, few prisoners saw any positive aspects in these relationships.

> There's prison officers . . . I don't know whether they're really bad like in character. But some of the prison officers are pretty bad to us (Xu).

This young prisoner had a perfect disciplinary record after eight years in prison (confirmed by a conversation with an officer who commended him as a polite helpful prisoner). He appeared bemused and puzzled as to the poor behaviour of some officers and could only attribute this to "poor character."

> Oh, some of them just take their job personal and it's not about rehabilitation to them. Some of them just like to play games and they take a dislike (Mick).

"Playing games" was referred to more than once in the interviews. The information vacuum inhabited by prisoners contributes to the feeling that, Alice in Wonderland – like, the prison operates in an arbitrary, contrary and dishonest way. The broad discretion possessed by front line prison staff, coupled with the lack of information discussed in the last chapter, contributes to this perception. "Taking the job personal" clearly refers to the adoption of punitive attitudes towards prisoners, that prison involves the infliction of punishment rather than imprisonment itself constituting the punishment. This prisoner clearly perceived that the philosophical orientation of some prison officers does not include a commitment to rehabilitation and that their role allows them to make this "personal."

Some of the comments in this study reflected positive relationships between staff and prisoners – one prisoner referred to "a beautiful officer" (Antony). It may be that, as Sparks and Bottoms discovered in the UK, "regimes operating in (different prisons) were markedly different"(Sparks and Bottoms 2006, p. 79) and certainly many of the prisoner comments reflected marked differences in regimes even between wings of the same prison. Vuolo and Kruschnitt found that "front line criminal justice workers are the critical players in determining whether innovations in prison policy are realized" and that "this effect is largely independent of the prisoner's characteristics and the institutions in which they are housed" (Vuolo and Kruschnitt 2008, p. 307). They point out that (the findings) "highlight the need to understand the environment from which (prisoners) are emerging, not just the communities into which they are released." The paucity of ethnographic research on prisoners in NSW is exceeded only by the lack of attention paid to the front line staff in our prisons and the way they operationalise official policy. The responses of prisoners in the previous chapter to questions about "Throughcare" and "case management" seem to indicate that the front line staff are poorly equipped for these roles.

Private Prison or New Opportunity for Change?

As interviews were conducted in the two privatised prisons in NSW, some of the comments by prisoners involved comparisons between the two systems. The debate about privatisation has largely receded and CSNSW was able to quietly privatise Parklea prison with little fanfare. Little is known about the differences between public and private prisons in NSW, despite the first private prison opening more than a decade ago.

Comments from prisoners indicate that a real change of culture may be possible; on the other hand, comments about the other private prison were less positive although, overall, those prisoners in privately run prisons (about a quarter of the prisoners interviewed) expressed more positive comments about the regimes there.

> "GEO are much better, they're nicer. I can't believe it." Interviewer: "Is it because they haven't got the culture in them yet, they haven't got that long history that the officers at Corrective Services have?" Prisoner: "No, because a lot of the officers here have come from Corrective Services. Here they respect you . . . and I respect them . . . If I have a bad day or they have a bad day they won't take it further whereas Corrective Services the next day they'll see you and do it again . . . if they hate you they hate you, but here, all right, fair enough you've had a bad day, I've had a bad day the next day it'll be good, you know" (Van).

Contact with prisoners at both of the privatised gaols reflected a different approach being taken by prison officers in the GEO-run prisons. The absence of a pre-existing culture of prison officers appeared to allow for a more reasoned approach to prisoner management, even among former CSNSW employees. This phenomenon has been noted in the British context and, as Shefer and Liebling point out, "may say more about the defects of traditional public sector prisons than about the advantages of privatisation per se," given the absence of proper evaluation and comparison (Shefer and Liebling 2008, p. 262).

An important caveat to this positive impression reflects findings in other prison studies (Schefer and Liebling 2008, p. 267; Hulley et al. 2012). Several prisoners reported that the regime in the private prison was more chaotic, less controlled and predictable and therefore less secure, in the personal sense.

> "Um, they (GEO) tend to make their own rules at times and they'll do kneejerk reactions against certain things and shoot everyone in the foot. You know, Corrective Services is simple . . . " Interviewer: "Because you know the rules?" Respondent: "Yeah, they stick by the rules, they try to treat you like dirt and kick the shit out of ya, you know? (Steve).

While his ironic comment about CSNSW "treat(ing) you like shit and kick (ing) the shit out of ya" reflected his status as a long-term prisoner who had experienced earlier regimes, he did reflect a common sentiment that the "devil you know" was sometimes preferable to the newer regimes where power was exercised in a more unpredictable and subterranean manner. Many older prisoners found the new regimes and requirements confusing and dishonest and preferred the more defined roles of the traditional prison.

Prisoners and Other Professionals

In keeping with the focus on interpersonal matters, prisoners often mentioned the importance of a good relationship with non-custodial staff. It was impossible not to be affected by the realisation that many yearned for personal connections which transcended the carceral boundaries and which made them feel more human. Thus, many of the comments highlighted particular individuals who had achieved this.

> I can't talk to blokes.... They find a weakness (Dave).

The position of female staff in the overwhelmingly male environment of the prison and the limited roles for women in the particular version of masculinity enacted by both custodial staff and prisoners constitutes an under-theorised area of prison criminology. As the majority of non-custodial staff tend to be females, constructions of women and gender clearly colour the interactions between male prisoners and female staff (Crewe 2006). Crewe intriguingly mentions that "relations with female staff were all the more volatile"(2009 ch. 4, p.15) in his intensive study of Wellingsborough Prison; his argument being that heightened emotional content arose from these different constructions of women. His findings that prisoners found female staff easier to talk to were reflected in the interviews for this book.[1]

It is no surprise that prisoners report that individual staff members, usually professional staff, made a difference to their prison experience

[1] Crewe, however, does not consider his own position as a male researcher as relevant to the types of attitudes expressed about female staff. The enactment of masculinity goes on between interviewer and interviewee, as much as between prisoner and staff member.

and in some cases to their general attitudes to their offence and their rehabilitation. Although largely ignored in the correctional context with the move towards group programming based on membership of "risk groups," the importance of the relational aspects of therapeutic contact, regardless of the modality used by the therapist, was reflected by many prisoner comments. Prominent were comments that indicated the importance of a true, authentic relationship, of a worker who was prepared to go beyond the confines of the job and who treated them normally, whether this involved confrontation and challenging or support and comfort. The increasing move away from one-on-one contact in prisons is therefore a concern.

> She actually cared you know what I mean, that was the difference . . . whereas other people are just doing their job, just writing reports. "Oh I seen him today" and then it'll say nothing about you. "He seemed angry" or whatever, no detail. Yeah if you have a bad day that's it you get bad notes, you know what I mean (Van).

This young prisoner, known to the interviewer through legal representation for his Court of Criminal Appeal matter, had been bitter, difficult to communicate with and very scared. Ten years on, he was still bitter about his sentencing. Despite sentence comments indicating that he had "No real chance at rehabilitation" (Van), he had clearly made significant changes to his attitude and behaviour, which he attributed mainly to his relationship with a psychologist.

Another aspect of this comment demonstrates the power of the written word, or "paperwork" over the lives of prisoners, "you have a bad day, that's it, you get bad notes," one bad day having the possibility to delay progression, security classification, and ultimately release. The "power of the pen" is a crucial element in the governance of prisoners, the insidious nature of such "soft power" (Crewe 2009) means that every interaction is potentially heavy with meaning and consequences. In previous regimes in NSW, those consequences would have been harsh physical treatment or deprivation. While these factors still operate, the consequences now are more likely to be related to reduction in classification, prison placement and timing of release on conditional liberty.

Prisoners and Prisoners

Relationships with other prisoners were not the focus of the interviews; however, in keeping with the general importance placed on interpersonal issues, prisoners placed these matters at the forefront when discussing how they were experiencing the sentence. The methodology of this research involved interviews in numerous prisons and therefore the types of broad evaluations available to prison ethnographers who study one prison intensively were not attempted. While there are similarities, each prison has its own unique habitus; despite a general trend towards highly centralised decision making in some areas, for a variety of reasons, historical, geographical and cultural, NSW prisons are each uniquely idiosyncratic.

There are, however, similarities across prisons in the way prisoners relate to each other. The tendency to "keep to yourself" among long-term prisoners was certainly detected in many of the interviews; indeed, the longer the sentence the more likely it was that the prisoner had largely withdrawn from interaction with others. "It is not solitude that plagues the prisoners but life *en masse*" (Sykes 1958 in Liebling and Arnold 2012, p. 414).

> You've got lots of friends in here but you've got no mates—know what I mean? (Chris).

This prisoner made the distinction between the necessity to get along with people and the formation of real relationships involving mutual trust. The necessity of making and keeping connections in prison is emphasised, but the underlying message is that these relationships are contextual and instrumental.

Relationships with other prisoners were often viewed as problematic due to the characteristics of the other prisoners, as "spinners" (mentally ill) or drug users.

> I'm one out now, medical one out. Because I fight really hard with my cellmates, I have bad thoughts about doing bad things to them because I can't stand the closeness. I was two out when I was in 13 wing and the

> officers must have thought I was a babysitter because they used to think I was a fruit loop and I'd get spinners and that. All the psych patients (Tom).

Many interviewees identified the pressure of living with strangers in crowded accommodation as one of the more stressful aspects of imprisonment. Although the official record may show that overall there are enough beds to accommodate prisoners, the long-standing CSNSW trend of building cells designed for one or two out and then modifying to accommodate more, appears to be continuing.

> Someone's gunna get killed in here, there's always fights in three outs, you know what I mean? It's alright to get along with one person but when you've got to get on with two people and put up with their bad habits (Ken).

This relatively newly opened prison, in true CSNSW tradition had already converted a number of cells designed for one or two prisoners to "three out" cells.

Rather than framing "violence" in prisons as an ever-present, discrete and individualised problem to be suppressed or managed, it may be more productive to attempt to understand the conditions in which it flourishes. While prisoners were quite matter of fact in their assumptions that violence would be a part of their experience, rarely was it described as a random occurrence. Most often, institutional or relational factors were presented as an explanation for the violence.

It is a truism in NSW that as "blue on green" violence declined; "green on green" took over (Brown, D. 2005, p. 31). Rates of assault are a key performance indicator (KPI) for prison performance and the rate of prisoner-on-prisoner assault in NSW at 13.3 per 100 prisoners is considerably higher than the national average of 9.14 (Australian Government Productivity Commission 2011, p. 8.14). The "dark figure" is probably higher due to powerful incentives not to report. In addition, the fear of assault (and sexual assault) may be a powerful factor shaping prison culture even in the absence of actual assault. The promulgation of popular media images of violent prisons may be as powerful a factor in the creation and maintenance of this climate of fear as it has been demonstrated to be in the wider community (Lee 2007). This is not to deny the actuality of violence in prison, rather that the situation is more nuanced than is often reported. Violence is more often implied and, rather than merely counting the numbers, attention should be paid to the situational and interpersonal factors which encourage such intimidation.

"Soft power" may not have completely replaced the old regimes of coercion and control in NSW. The unwavering focus on security (Drake 2012) evidenced by the importance of escape statistics as KPIs (Key Performance Indicator) for CSNSW indicates the priority given to such matters (see discussion on E category prisoners in the last chapter).

It is important to note in the context of high rates of prisoner-on-prisoner assault in NSW that some prisoners reported the use, at least of the fear of assault, by prison staff (Van reported that young "Asian" boys were threatened with transfers to Koori (Aboriginal)-dominated prisons). It is also possible and certainly implied by more than one prisoner that prison staff are tacitly allowing assaults to occur as a way of managing difficult prisoners. To some extent, this finding provides a caveat to the adoption of the "soft power" (Crewe 2009) concept to describe the exercise of power in relation to NSW prisons. While certainly operating "at a distance," the power to allow or even to create or encourage violence amongst prisoners is much more "in your face" than the ability to write notes in a file.

Neuber uses Pierre Bourdieu's work to explain the importance of violence for the stabilisation of prison order (Neuber 2011). Sykes's emphasis on institutional factors in engendering violence is supplemented by attention to the way individuals experience these factors, and Neuber's conclusion that "violence in the inmates' society is more than just action determined by the structure of the institutions or part of the social role each inmate adopts" points towards a more nuanced view of prison violence (Neuber 2011, p. 12). Neuber emphasises the close relationship between violence and biographical experiences of conflict using a "conflict oriented" concept of biography (Neuber 2011, p. 12). Absent from these accounts, however, is the valuable perspective on the relationship between masculinity, violence and prison culture derived from Connell (Connell 1995) and Messerschmidt (Messerschmidt 1993) and the post-Katzian work of Mark Halsey (Halsey 2006), which sheds more light on the complex relationship between biographical and institutional factors mediated by the need to do or perform the version of masculinity available to prisoners.

Violence as an expression of hegemonic masculinity in prison is illustrated by the ways that young men play out their version of status attainment. By challenging older prisoners to a kind of status-enhancing duel, they ensure their position both inside and outside of prison:

> Young blokes want to do things to get at me, you know, because there might be a bloke from the outside that they looked up to and they want to prove themselves in here to get into a little clique when they get out. It's a young man's place now. Not that I'm old, but you've got 18, 19, 20 year old kids in here now and when you've got status you become a trophy. So the last thing you want in the last couple of years is to become a trophy (Chris).

The two-pronged nature of the problem of the status accorded to those prisoners who had survived severe regimes of segregation such as Supermax is exemplified by this prisoner's experience. Because of his reputation as a "hard man," younger prisoners seeking to boost their status endeavoured to add his scalp to their belt, adding an extra layer of difficulty to his attempts to have his classification reduced after 14 years in maximum security and reinforcing his tendency towards solitude. The mixing of prisoners of different sentence lengths and conviction status provides a chaotic edge to daily prison life.

> In remand you've got blokes coming off the streets and because you're doing a long time you know you've got these blokes doing rubbish this, rubbish that, you don't want to listen to them . . . Look, I'm here to do my own time you know, I don't want be on anyone else's time (Frank).

There was a marked tendency for the prisoners interviewed to identify younger prisoners with short sentences or remand prisoners as the main threat to their ability to do their sentence "and not some other bloke's", as the saying goes.

> The funny thing is people who have done a long time, they have more common sense than people who are doing 6 months, a year, a couple of years.... Some people can say scary things.... for some long-term inmates they've changed a lot during those years, I will say that. Yeah. (Xu)

Getting involved in other people's dramas was universally seen as a risk to the possibility of the EPRD and most prisoners appreciated some time away from the yard. Some saw early lockdowns as a blessing and became stressed if out of their cells for longer than accustomed.

> I fret, honestly fret when I'm not locked in by 3.30, I start having a panic attack. (Kevin)

> I go to my cell early every day...I'm relaxed in my cell, I know that sounds strange/ (Chris).

The long-term prisoners in this study mostly expressed a preference for solitude, particularly those with long prison records. Interacting with others was seen as stressful and difficult and something to be avoided if possible. Harding, citing Zamble and Porporino's concept of the "deep freeze" coping mechanism of long-term prisoners, points to the consequent difficulties of engaging prisoners in rehabilitative programmes (Harding 2000, p. 10). It is of concern that so many of these men who have spent long periods in custody were voluntarily spending long periods in solitude in the years just prior to their release. Coupled with problems with maintaining contact with family, the interpersonal toll on long-term prisoners is considerable.

Drugs—"If You've Got the Powder You've Got the Power"

Drugs are clearly central to the unofficial economy of the prison. Crewe asserts, "it is impossible to understand the prison experience without understanding the role of drugs in penal culture, personal biography and criminal history" (Crewe 2009, p. 13 Ch.9). Many prisoners mentioned the drugs issue as problematic for them personally, not just because of personal use but the way the drug trade operates in prison as a source of power and influence over other prisoners.

> In really old times, I'm talking way back; there was honesty, integrity certain rules to stick by. We never had such things as drugs (Steve).

Interviews with the older inmates who participated in this study, many of whom had served multiple sentences, inevitably led to comparisons with the "old days." (Interestingly, long-term staff often express the same sentiments.) Paramount among the changes noted is the predominance of people with drug problems who bring to the prisons a new level of prisoner interaction. The existence of "drug-free wings" in prisons confirms the reality of the availability of illegal drugs in prison despite the concentration on security.

> "I don't know how . . . because everything's changed." Interviewer: "What has changed the most?" Prisoner: "It's all in the powder . . . . The powder rules . . . If you get hold of the powder you've got the power. Even Supermax isn't drug free" (Chris).

Many of the prisoners in the study spontaneously identified the presence of drugs, whether legal or illegal, as a cause of many of most difficult aspects of prison life as well as a way of coping. People are "stood over" for their medication; "bupe" (bupenorphine) in particular was identified as a substance which was highly prized for inducing a heroin-like "stone" if injected. Drugs also provide an easy and profitable way to earn money. Crewe highlights the centrality of drugs in the informal economy and power structure of the prison. His term "powder power" (Crewe, Ch. 6, p. 19) is remarkably similar to Chris's assessment that "if you've got the powder you've got the power." The other striking similarity is the proliferation of the "good old days" discourse, noted by Crewe, that the introduction of drugs like heroin disrupted the old order, where there may have been some prisoner solidarity. Of course, as Crewe points out, improvements in basic conditions also remove some the motivation to collectively organise.

This brief analysis reflects the fact that prisoners often spoke of the ubiquity of the drug trade in prison as a significant barrier to them performing what they saw as their obligations in the sentence. As a dominant force in the daily life of the prison, this unofficial web of relationships, almost opaque to outsiders, operates to control and determine prisoners lives both in prison and outside as the effect of drug debts incurred in prison can be a continuation of criminal activity on release.

The ubiquity of substance abuse amongst prisoners blends with the exercise of official power most notably in the use of methadone in NSW prisons.

Methadone

As a pragmatic response to high rates of hepatitis C and HIV and the reluctance of CSNSW to introduce needle exchange in prisons to combat the sharing of needles, methadone has been taken up enthusiastically by prisoners in NSW. Of the 3,647 prisoners on opiate substitution pharmacotherapy in Australia (8% of the national total of 46,078), 2,074 were in NSW prisons (AIHW report 2010). The following extracts highlight the concern expressed by prisoners that methadone has become another tool of control in prisons, too freely prescribed and not restricted to those with proven opiate addiction.

While there is good recent evidence of the benefits of opiate substitution in NSW prisons, which reduces death rates of prisoners on release (Larney et al. 2007) the evidence suggests that the programme may be better targeted at older users. Excessive use of medication among female prisoners has been characterised as an example of repression and official abuse; however, the harm minimisation perspective has no concern with these matters, public health trumping individual rights to choice over interventions and involvement in pharmacotherapy.

The relevance of this discussion to the overall questions of the book, which is the way that the in-court sentence is played out through the myriad of correctional incidents and experiences, is to highlight an aspect of a practice from the prisoner's point of view that challenges the official consensus. The overall benefits of opiate substitution in prisons should not blind us to the possibility of abuse in the non-consensual, coercive environment of the prison.

> There's boys in here that . . . they get sentenced to three months gaol they've never used heroin in their life, nothing. And they might have the occasional smoke but they give them morphine and the next minute they're on the methadone program (Kevin).

Many of the interviewees were on methadone because of long and intense histories of opiate use. Several prisoners, however, expressed concern that methadone was being used to control prisoners who may not have the clinical indications for inclusion on a methadone programme outside prison.

> It's the easiest thing to get on because what it does is control the inmate (William).

The benefits to correctional management of having prisoners sedated have been pointed out in relation to over-prescription of sedatives to female prisoners (Brown et al. 1988). While the battle to have methadone available in prison was partly motivated by a harm minimisation strategy, which recognised the dangers of intravenous drug use in prison, it is of concern that many comments from prisoners were in this vein. The absence of counselling and other support means that, contrary to the evidence on the effectiveness of methadone, "although methadone maintenance alone will be sufficient for small subgroup of patients, the majority will not benefit from a purely pharmacological approach" (Lowinson et al. 2005, p. 655) prisoners in NSW often receive pharmacological therapy alone.

The view that people are given methadone too freely is perhaps confirmed by the following statement from a prisoner, who, while having no opiate use history, had a long history of abuse of legitimately obtained pharmaceuticals such as valium.

> The real reason?—You do gaol easy... They offer it to you like lolly water. All you say is "I've been taking too many Panadols... (John)

While there is evidence that methadone can have positive benefits, these are restricted to use with people with opiate addiction. As an exercise of power, chemical constraint can assist in the maintenance of order and control and must therefore be scrutinised as part of an examination of prisoner life.

Prisoners and Others—Visits and Family, Contact with the Outside World

The next section examines the effect of some of the incidents of imprisonment on the maintenance of relationships on the outside. As vital supports for the prisoner on release, positive relationships with family are recognised by prisoners and authorities alike as rehabilitative necessities. Yet, for many prisoners, families are the site of significant conflict and difficulty; poverty and deprivation characterising the lives of many of the children and partners of prisoners.

It is not surprising, then, to find that visits for many prisoners are a mixed blessing. While missing their families and contact with the outside, visits serve to painfully remind prisoners of their inability to participate in everyday life.

> And I only just saw her (his mother) after 13 years... Because I spent a long time in Goulburn and I told my family don't worry about me in Goulburn... It's because it brings a burden on yourself as you're locked up and because if you see your family while you're in prison it stresses you out you know, because you're mother's crying and that and it just comes up on your head... (John).

The burden of imprisonment is vividly described "and it just comes up on your head" as if a physical burden weighs on the prisoner, made heavier not only for what they are missing, but also the stress of family conflicts which are played out without the prisoner having any agency.

Many families of prisoners are struggling and the knowledge that their behaviour has contributed to their struggle weighs heavily and can interfere with the maintenance of relationships.

> "This place is horrible. My own missus come here once and she couldn't believe it, she said she would never bring her daughter here." Interviewer: "What's so bad about it." Prisoner: "Just the way the officers . . . Because . . . they're associated with an inmate they don't get treated well" (Chris).

As expressed by Chris, the other prominent aspect of prison visits is concern for the difficulties and humiliations suffered by families and friends. The experience of visiting a prisoner is an exercise in patience and tolerance of degrading treatment, even for professionals. For families (most often young women with small children) who often travel long distances on public transport for very short visiting times (each institution has its own rules), the prison does not provide an environment which supports the maintenance of relationships.

> They want to come to see me but I don't want to bring them here to this place, you know . . . . Kills me when I ring them because (they say) 'can I come to see you Dad' I said 'Just not yet mate', you know 'But we want to see you Dad (Dave).

The involvement of welfare authorities in the lives of the children of prisoners is another aspect of imprisonment, which deepens the sense of alienation from family and lack of control over their lives. Many see their own childhood repeated in the lives of their children.

One prisoner had prevented his family, including his teenage daughter, from visiting him at the maximum security institution at which he had been confined for the past 8 years. As an example of the way visitors were treated, he expressed his concern at the way the visit for this interview had been announced to him:

> Oh it's just an interview by "some woman." You know, like, no names, just "some woman" (Chris).

He detected a lack of respect towards both interviewer and interviewee in the officer's treatment of the visit. (Crewe may also view this as an example of the "chivalrous" stance taken by some prisoners towards female staff (Crewe 2006)). The importance of respect and the ubiquity of its absence was a strong theme running through all of the interviews. Prisoners are rarely told who is visiting them, as if they have no choice and must speak to anyone with the official imprimatur of the prison. In addition, for prisoners being prepared for a visit in some institutions (especially those consisting predominantly of remand prisoners) means to be stripped down, searched and clothed in one piece "Guantanamo style" overalls not unlike a baby suit done up at the back, and held in small holding cells (if, on protection, often in full view of other non-protection prisoners) to wait to be taken for the visit, and the same treatment on the way back. The situation is further complicated if the prisoner is a protection inmate who must be kept away from other prisoners, ironically their very protection status serving as a red light to prisoners in the main. Several potential participants decided not to participate in interviews for this project after being kept in holding cells for long periods.

These concerns, which can lead to the severing of contact with significant others who may otherwise have provided support or accommodation on release, is clearly counterproductive when viewed through the Throughcare lens. Contact and support with families is widely recognised to have protective effects, as does a feeling of investment in the community. The isolation preferred by many of the prisoners interviewed is scarcely conducive to the conduct of normal relationships outside the prison and the regularity with which prisoners spoke of preventing family from visiting certain institutions demonstrates the possible magnitude of the problem.

> 17 year.... last year they come.... Yeah, first time in 17 years.

The distress felt by those prisoners with families overseas is unable to be expressed on the page, but this prisoner's anguished facial expression was enough to demonstrate this.

> I have no family here, plus I'm the only child in the family (Xu).

This young man who came into prison at 18 had not had any visits except recently from Kairos (a religious group) for the 8 years that he had been in custody. The burden of his incarceration on his elderly parents, who had invested all of their resources to send him to Australia, was so much the greater, and he expressed his deep shame at their suffering.

The casual cruelty of the institution is reflected in the attitude of prison authorities towards deaths in the family.

> My father died, not that I was close to him . . . they told me three days later . . . the bloke slowly died . . . and his own family was wondering why I hadn't been in touch with him (Chris).

This prisoner's failure to contact his family as a result of his lack of knowledge of his father's illness has further alienated him from his birth family. The difficulty in maintaining family relationships, often already riven with conflict and grief, is further exacerbated by imprisonment, the isolation from family further compounded by lengthy segregation and incarceration in the HRMU.

> My mother, she hated my father . . . . He raped her you know and she had me to that, I was born like a bastard . . . . And yeah, she told me when I was 15. She wanted to kill me when I was a baby . . . I met my old man once . . . . I found out he committed suicide (Andrew).

This indigenous prisoner was again in touch with his mother after some years of estrangement. The matter-of-fact way with which he reported the tragic story of his birth ("I was born like a bastard") not only illustrates his illegitimate status but his self-image as someone who was destined to participate in criminal activity. The tragedy of his family life was recounted in a matter-of-fact manner, common to many of the prisoners for whom grief and trauma is omnipresent. Blunted affect is a common side effect of post-traumatic stress, problematic when assessments of remorse are made.

Contact with some families can be difficult when it comes to complying with parole conditions and generally staying out of trouble.

> My brothers and that, they're all known to the coppers up there, my little brother, he just got home. He went to court for assaulting a police officer, so he just got put on house arrest, you know what I mean, and this is my little brother (Andrew).

As discussed subsequently, this man came into prison and was welcomed by an array of supportive male relatives who were not present during his childhood due to their frequent incarceration.

Conversely, having a partner and children provided some prisoners with powerful incentives to curb their behaviour and work towards release. "Doing the whole nine yards," that is, the whole of the sentence in custody was mentioned often, whether out of fear of lack of ability to comply with parole conditions or the need for independence from correctional authorities.

> "My first two lags in here . . . No girl, no kids." Interviewer: "So this is different?" Prisoner: "Yeah this is way different—like next door they said "you've been here 18 months not one charge not one mention what's going on, what are you up to" I said "Parole, I gotta get out of here . . . If I didn't have kids I wouldn't have bothered, I probably would have just done the whole nine yards" (Dave).

All of the prisoners interviewed spoke of the difficulties of maintaining relationships with family and friends. Institutional barriers, such as inconvenient and restrictive visiting times, remote locations, ugly and alienating visit areas and attitudes of staff, work towards a tendency to discourage visits.

The fact that prisoners foregrounded their relationships with others is considered an important finding in the research. Their responses indicate that the managerial and ideological milieu of the prison actively works to discourage positive relationships with others. Violence is individualised instead of being viewed as a rational response to situational factors such as overcrowding and the proliferation of mental health problems among prisoners. Relationships with staff are tainted by the reality of "hard" custodial power enveloped by the ever-present "soft power" of pyscho- correctional assessment. Prisoners' relationships with family are often already fractured and riven by grief and trauma and some have withdrawn completely from any meaningful human contact in the belief that their outsider status is permanent.

6.3 Dimensions of Personal Identity

The next section contains a discussion of two vital dimensions of personal identity which were raised by prisoners. In the first case, sexuality, it was not the ubiquity of responses but the unusual nature of this man's account, raising hitherto little examined dimensions of the experience of prisoners. The second dimension, ethnicity, was squarely raised by the sheer predominance of culturally and linguistically diverse (CALD) prisoners in the interview group and the obvious importance of ethnicity, uniquely perhaps, as a category for official sorting as well as a powerful element of personhood and identity. In addition, the particular position of indigenous prisoners in NSW prisons as part of the continuum of colonisation must be addressed in any analysis of imprisonment in NSW.

Sexuality

There is considerable disagreement about the role of sexuality and sexual relations in prisons, complicated by popular cultural representations of rape in prison and high levels of homophobia in male prisons (Donovan et al. 2011, Hensley et al. 2000). None of the interviewees in this study were asked directly about their sexual experiences in prison and only one chose to discuss the topic frankly, although several made oblique references to other prisoners (in one case as "cats", an old school synonym for homosexual). Analysis of sexuality in prison is almost always framed within an analysis of sexual assault and the exercise of power. There is an argument that, within such a total institution, all relationships must be viewed through the lens of power. High rates of sexual assault in prison have been a truism in NSW since Heilpern's groundbreaking study (Heilpern 1998) A recent Australian empirical study questions this popular assumption (Donovan et al. (2011).[2] The prevalence of high levels of homophobia, however, may suggest that it would be difficult to admit to having sex for men who do not identify as homosexual.

Citing the absence of research evidence about sex in prisons, and the "embarrassment, controversy and conflict" caused by the issue, The Howard League in the UK has recently initiated a Commission of Enquiry into Sex in Prisons. (Howard League 2013) The only mention of sexuality made by Ben Crewe in his extensive study of a UK prison was to report that the "hierarchy" in Wellingsborough prison was not expressed through sexual exploitation. He asserts that "(sexual exploitation) is not a central part of the prison experience for the majority of UK prisoners." (Crewe ch6 p54) Consensual sexual contact is not mentioned at all. Likewise, Drake, does not address the issue of sexuality and sexual relations despite her focus on power and security and the subjective experience of prisoners (Drake 2012)

There is, however, a tradition of research into sexual relations in prisons in the USA. Curiously (or perhaps pruriently), much of the evidence is about female prisoners (Hensley et al. 2000). Consensual sexual relations between male inmates are rarely included in such analyses (Hensley and Tewksbury 2002, p. 235). It is often assumed that coercion is a fundamental part of prison sexual relations; however, it is evident that, even in this context, the need for intimacy and relationship may be fulfilled (Kunzel 2008, p. 183). Some studies have referred to the tendency of female prisoners to form "family" type groupings (Hensley and Tewkesbury 2002, p. 231), but little attention has been paid to the positive aspects of consensual intimate relationships in male prisons. Intensely polarised traditional notions of what constitute sexuality for men and women –a need for intimacy and relatedness in women and for physical release for men have coloured much writing in this area. The possible existence of supportive, intimate relationships between male prisoners has not been acknowledged.

[2] The suggestion by Donovan et al. that the condoms handed out in prison were mainly valued for the use of the lubricant as free hair gel was supported by one of the prisoners interviewed for this book.

> I got some paperwork "not to be housed with inmate C"– my partner.... I've written numerous letters to SORC but they won't reply... to me, it's like are you vilifying us because we're gay? I don't want to go that angle because I've got to get parole (John).

This prisoner had been in a committed relationship with another long-term prisoner for some years. Prison authorities had wavered between tacit acknowledgement (they shared a cell for some years) to outright disapproval and separation. The obvious managerial benefits in settling down his partner, who had been a difficult prisoner, were recognised by one institution, leaving them happily ensconced in a type of domestic relationship for some years, albeit within a maximum security prison. As soon as the therapeutic wheels sprang into action towards the end of their sentences, it was perceived (in the opinion of the prisoner, by SORC) that the sexual nature of the offence committed by one of them meant that such an arrangement was unthinkable. His hesitation in invoking, for example, anti-discrimination legislation, illustrates the significant incentives for prisoners, when approaching parole in particular, not to "rock the boat" in any way.

In addition, the influence of fear of sexual assault and the perception of threat has been under-theorised here as in violence in prisons generally (see previous discussion regarding physical violence). While supportive sexual relationships do exist in prison, gay men are particularly vulnerable to sexual assault.

> But on the back of the, I'll never forget this, on the back of the escort truck this bloke wanted me to give him oral sex and um he was this scary big Lebanese bloke and um I didn't know that the um truck cameras worked and they did work they saw it all and they were trying to swerve the truck and all that." Interviewer: "So they didn't stop and stop him or anything?" Prisoner: "No they said they couldn't stop the truck and all that...And it's happened time and time again in gaol. I've learned to cope with it. One officer he just hated me, he hated us but he hated me because I was so flamboyant and proud" (John).

Openly identifying as homosexual, he repeatedly expressed the extra difficulty involved in being an outwardly identifiable gay man in prison.

He remarked upon the fact that he was dressed in visit overalls with a pink zip, using this as an example of the way that his sexuality, rather than being a private, personal matter, was constantly remarked upon and used as a reason to victimise him.

> See this thing at the back here, how it's pink, the officer out there when I was getting changed is going "Oh pretty pink . . . pretty girl you'll have a nice pink thing on your back (John).

Away from the protection of his partner, a "heavy" in the prison context, he felt vulnerable and spoke of repeated victimisation by staff and other prisoners throughout his imprisonment. When asked what was more difficult to handle, being gay or being a prisoner in a reviled group because of his offence, he expressed the view that being gay had made his prison experience more difficult.

> . . . it is hard especially when you get the petite skinny young 18 year old who comes into gaol and they're scared witless and you can see that you get the long termer who tries to take him under his wing and trying to make him his bitch (John).

Not only was he victimised by other prisoners, he reported several incidents of homophobic victimisation by prison officers.

> But it's the officers that are worse . . . One said "you're a fucking faggot aren't you, keep away from my fucking face or I'll fucking smash your head in.

On the other hand, this officer apologised later and the prisoner told a story, in which a female officer upbraided fellow officers for expressing homophobic views,

> and it's funny it's always a women who does it (challenges the homophobic culture) (John).

This brief account of one prisoner's experience of the disruption of a supportive consensual relationship by high-level prison authorities, not to mention incidents of sexual assault and homophobia, sheds light on the added burden of being a "flamboyant and proud" homosexual man in prison, an under-researched and poorly appreciated aspect of imprisonment. While it is important to identify commonalities in prisoner experiences, it important to avoid a totalising account and acknowledge the extra punishment suffered by some prisoners because of their sexual orientation.

Ethnicity

There is no doubt that the prison is an intensely racialised environment. Rather than a separate and discrete factor, race is a central paradigm in the correctional system and permeates all aspects of the criminal justice process, from the initial apprehension by police to sentencing and imprisonment. "It has even been argued that the new "master status trait" (Hughes 1971) for prisoners is racial affiliation, with no space for inmate loyalty as a generic class (Phillips 2007, p. 78). In 2008/2009, 21.8 per cent of prisoners in full-time custody were born outside Australia (NSW Department of Corrective Services 2010). Relevant to the Department's sorting and processing of prisoners, ethnicity is also a powerful factor in the experience of prisoners. The prisoners interviewed for this study broadly reflected the variety of ethnic groups in the prison system. Several had only learned English after entering custody. Many commented on the racially based groupings within the prison, both officially sanctioned and informal. Groups ally with other groups and on the positive side; older prisoners with shared cultural backgrounds provide support to new prisoners.

> It was good for myself because, I was just.... all older boys you know what I mean, we look after each other. That's our race, you know what I mean, if we don't have food then they give us food and try to um... that's how we were raised up, you know what I mean... (Van).

As a young man looking towards a long sentence, this prisoner was initially sent to Goulburn, where he remained for some years. While acknowledging its fearsome reputation, he found support among other prisoners of his ethnic background. The way that he identified qualities of caring and community with his "race" distinguishing this group from mainstream prisoners, where support is more difficult to obtain without some kind of "quid pro quo".

Seidler, in a qualitative study of prisoners convicted of offences of violence in an NSW prison, attempts to make some sense of the differing explanations given by Anglo Australians and those from other so-called individualistic societies with those given by inmates in "collectivist" cultural or ethnic groupings (Seidler 2010). While acknowledging the ideological nature of the criminalisation of ethnic minorities, the individual explanations of the prisoners are placed in a psychological context which largely ignores the official acceptance and use of these paradigms and the effect of institutional factors, in prison and the criminal justice system generally, on the maintenance of ethnic identities. Despite this, the study, as a rare example of ethnographic qualitative research with prisoners in NSW, provides an insight into the different perspectives of prisoners from differing ethnic backgrounds and reminds practitioners to attend to cultural matters when dealing with prisoners.

One of the (Anglo) interviewees for this research expressed in conversation the view that there was "reverse racism" in the prison environment. While he was reluctant to expand on his views, it was evident that he felt that prison was a racialised domain in which the accepted hierarchy may have been subverted (William). Phillips and Earle found that "white prisoners often reverted to narratives of white superiority to undermine and denigrate black prisoners, ventilating frustrations about the assertive black presence and official diversity policies through the language of racist victimization" (Phillips and Earle 2008, p. 1).

Choosing to ally oneself with those of similar background may be seen as one of the important adaptations to prison life.

> See I'm Italian, there's not that many Italians in prison . . . There's a lot of Lebanese, the way I got around it is I'm from Punchbowl and they're all from Punchbowl and Bankstown (John).

In common with many of the interviewees, the issue of race for this prisoner was the need to belong to a group for protection against perceived threat. The fact that he was of different ethnicity meant less than the fact that he was from the same geographic area; his non-Anglo background placed him in a natural alliance with other non-Anglo prisoners.

Officially Sanctioned Racial Sorting

Issues of race and ethnicity occupy a unique position as a powerful element of subjective identity for prisoners as well as one of the sorting and processing indices for correctional authorities. The segregation of prisoners by race has been a contentious issue in the USA. Following the 2005 US Supreme Court case of *Johnson v California,* decisions to racially segregate prisoners are to be reviewed "under the highest level of constitutional review, strict scrutiny" (Goodman 2008, p. 735). Such sensitivity to racial segregation in prison is absent in NSW jurisprudence.

> I'm happy that it was segregated cause I've seen a lot of violence in other gaols, know what I mean . . . (Van).

The official sanctioning of racial-based grouping of prisoners in NSW is exemplified by the practice introduced at Goulburn Correctional Centre in 2002. This was viewed as unremarkable and even desirable by many prisoners (reflected by an absence of academic or critical comment). In most accounts of this practice (mainly in the media), there is a direct connection made between high rates of violence amongst prisoners particularly at Goulburn and the necessity to racially segregate prisoners.

> At Goulburn, in response, they have taken to what is known as "ethnic clustering." Yard 6 has the Asians, Yard 7 the Islanders, Yard 8 the Arabic prisoners, and in varied yards, the many Aborigines. Separating the different ethnic groups requires close management. Even food is isolated. Intelligence is gathered to identify ringleaders, who are moved away from their power base (Masters 2005).

Prisoners also mentioned racial tensions regularly, one referred to "race wars."

> When I first came in it was a racial war back then . . . Asian against Koori. Asian and Islanders against Kooris and Lebanese. Same as in America- the Asians and the Islanders (Van).

Whether the mirroring of the race situation in US prisons by CSNSW was in response to unofficial groupings already present, or whether the US situation was copied by NSW authorities, the broad divisions of the groupings, for example, "Asians" as a generic grouping, reflect racist assumptions of sameness across nationalities which deny the nuances of culture. That these generic groupings are adopted also by inmates probably says more about the need to stick together and have allies in prison than it does about actual similarities between cultures.

One prisoner believed that the creation of racial and ethnic tension within prisons was a deliberate management strategy, a "divide and rule" approach.

> Fine, turn us against each other, and they've done that perfectly. I can't believe how well they've done that! (Dave).

Another pointed to the prominence of indigenous prisoners in many country gaols and the problems he experienced as an Asian prisoner.

> All right, if you have a fight with someone where do they send you? They send you straight to the Koori gaol and what happens there? The screws, I mean the officers they tell the . . . . they like to set you up, like us Asian boys (Van).

Apart from the use of the overt threat of violence – in this case, through other prisoners, the paradoxical, perhaps hypocritical, nature of official handling of race is evident. Evincing concern for the prevalence of gangs in the prison environment and then putting in place a system which sorts prisoners on the basis of racial characteristics encourages the formation and maintenance of ethnically based groups. The lack of attention paid to the possible impact of prison staff in exacerbating racial tension is also evident. The popular view seems to be that whatever was done at Goulburn did have an impact on what was an unacceptably high rate of violence amongst inmates.

> But now it's changed a bit, you know what I mean. We're much more safer now, there's no more war . . . Yeah, no-one wants dramas, you know what I mean, but that wasn't because of the system . . . that was just the inmates that were sick of it (Van).

This prisoner disputed the claim of the Department that segregation ended the "race wars" and attributed the decrease in tension to the inmates themselves. The idea that prisoners can achieve a reduction in hostilities themselves is barely recognised in the official record, any positive outcomes are always attributed to prison authorities.

On the whole, prisoners from CALD backgrounds were positive about their relationships with prisoners from the same background. As Phillips points out:

> An appreciation of the role of ethnicity as a resource, upon which prisoners may draw, either to endure the pains of imprisonment, or to more directly resist institutional control, or to assist with their resettlement in their home communities post-imprisonment, is also necessary (Phillips 2007, p. 83).

However, the question remains as to the long-term consequences of encouraging racial segregation in prisons, including ways to capitalise on the positive aspects of peer support.

The Futility of Imprisonment for Non-Citizens

> I've got C1 when I still had almost 4 years to go. Because I am on a deportation. That's why, um before like we couldn't get any further than C1 because we're not allowed to go outside and work. And later on, um someone took this to court . . . And now we can get C2. But I still won't be able to go outside and work (Xu).

Having been sentenced soon after his 18th birthday, having arrived in Australia only 3 months prior to his arrest, this young man with an exemplary disciplinary record had only just been transferred to medium security, after some years of prevarication by the Department about whether he needed to do the violence prevention programme. He provides an example of how other salient factors can mean that a "low-risk" prisoner (both in the sense of risk of re-offending and in a custodial management sense) can spend excessive periods in high security.

Non-Australian citizens serving long sentences are almost invariably deported at the expiration of their non-parole period. Access to the type of progression theoretically offered to other inmates is denied them since the Department changed its policy and practice on offering work and other release programmes to potential deportees in the late 1990s.

> The Department of Corrective Services has a policy of not allowing C3 classification for prisoners possibly subject to section 501. This means that unescorted day release and other pre-release practices routinely used by the Parole Authority to assess risk are denied to these prisoners (Grewcock 2009).

While ostensibly these prisoners are not treated differently, there is no doubt that this fact has a negative effect on their ability to access services and programmes due to a perceived inability to progress.

The philosophical implications of the law of sentencing and punishment are placed in sharp relief with this group of prisoners, as the prevailing paradigm of Throughcare simply does not apply to them at all. It is arguable that imprisonment, for non-citizens, is all about punishment and incapacitation without the tempering influence of concerns of reintegration and rehabilitation. For some prisoners, even the possibility of deportation means that the Department puts them in a type of holding pattern. It is doubtful that the commitment to Throughcare extends to these prisoners in a practical sense at all, as the effect of long-term lack of access to even the most rudimentary sentence planning available to other NSW prisoners arguably disadvantages them even further than just the lack of access to external leave programs.

An Indigenous Domain

As Blagg points out,

> It is necessary to separate Aboriginal justice issues from those affecting ethnic minority groups. Indigenous people were the subject of a specific set of colonial practices premised on the well-embedded belief that their evolutionary time was up and they were destined for extinction (Blagg 2008, p. 21).

The continuous nature of colonisation practices such as imprisonment as waste management (Blagg 2008, p. 21) belies many of the "rupture theories" and suggests that support for Wacquant's "carceral continuum" (Wacquant 2001) may be found in the Australian context.

> I used to class gaol as my home, you know. You know I've been in a lot of problems over the years since I've been free, you know, a lot of dramas in the family. I don't think it helped. Yeah, they treat the Aboriginals pretty well in here (Andrew).

The level of comfort exhibited by this prisoner who identified as indigenous was striking when compared to the other prisoners. While many others had resigned themselves through the passage of years to the situation, he was positive and thankful, seeing his sentence as fair, and fully embracing a "redemption script" (Maruna 2001). He spoke of coming into prison and finding the type of male family support not available to him as a child growing up with elderly female relatives.

> Like I learnt my tribe when I first came to gaol, I didn't know who my tribe was you know and you start to learn the Aboriginal languages as well, you know (Andrew).

Finding out about his heritage was directly related to his entrance to custody and he provides an archetypal example of Blagg's "paradox" in the conception of prison as Aboriginal domain, yet as a "damaging and disruptive influence" (Blagg 2008, p. 207). Having available in prison significant resources in the form of cultural support not accessible to him as an urban indigenous young person, he had fully engaged in rehabilitative and educational programming from the beginning of his sentence, with the help and support of SORC. The perception of prison and juvenile institutions as a refuge from problematic families ("I've been in a lot of problems over the years since I've been free") is indicative of the level of disadvantage suffered by the indigenous community in NSW.

More recently, as demonstrated by this prisoner, the "indigenisation" of criminal justice processes within prisons has "made the existing machinery simply more effective" (Blagg 2008, p. 88) as indigenous people are imprisoned at higher and higher rates in NSW as in the rest of Australia. Without addressing the structural causes of disadvantage, such initiatives are merely window dressing. Indeed, as Blagg points out, while prisons cause a deal of pain to indigenous people, the prevalence of imprisonment means that little shame is attached, raising the question of the relevance of deterrence as a sentencing aim.

Spivakovsky attempts to place the experience of indigenous prisoners in a Foucauldian framework, finding "post-colonial theory" wanting (Spivakovsky 2006). In a complex argument referencing governmentality theory, she attempts to foreground indigenous subjectivity by contrasting official discourse in New Zealand to that of the NSW Department regarding its indigenous prisoners. In NSW, what can also be seen as, consistently with the theme of the last chapter, responsibilisation, indigenous people are recognised as having the resources (or perhaps just the responsibility) to solve their own problems. In contrast, the language of corresponding agencies in New Zealand focuses on equality.

Further, even where recognition of structural inequality exists, the way correctional authorities operationalise this is by incorporation into a generic framework:

> the complex historical and cultural differences that Indigenous peoples experience can be boiled down to a few factors that can appear either alongside the existing criminal attributes of mainstream offenders, or as some internal or external factors that may vary between offender populations (Spivakovsky 2009, 222).

While some measures have improved conditions for Aboriginal prisoners, and in some prisons, according to some interviewees they constitute the dominant group in the prison, this apparent comfort with prison comes at a high price.

6.4 Conclusion

While relying substantially on theoretical accounts which emphasise the omniscience of power relations in prison, the importance of relational factors and personal characteristics such as sexuality, ethnicity and indigeneity in the performance of the sentence is highlighted in this Conflating "prisoners" together as a homogeneous group fails to recognise significant differences in the experience of the sentence. As an issue of personal identity, ethnicity is made even more powerful given its adoption as one of the indices of official sorting and classification like those discussed in the last chapter. Even more significantly, the over-representation of indigenous people in NSW prisons necessitates the development of unique thematic discussion given the continuous nature of colonisation.

As an opportunity to highlight a hidden aspect of a much-discussed issue, rather than a reflection of the frequency of discussion in the interviews, John's story demonstrates the importance of attention to other axes of disadvantage suffered by prisoners. More about prisoner sexuality than sex in prison, John's narrative was shot through with violence, sexual assault and fear. His long-term consensual relationship was nevertheless a prominent feature of his life.

Likewise, the brief discussion of drugs does not reflect their importance both in the unofficial economy of the prison and in its social organisation (Crewe 2009). The discussion about methadone highlights an issue particular to NSW prisons, which has received little attention given the conflicting issues of harm minimisation and personal agency raised by the extraordinary numbers of prisoners on the programme. From a public health perspective, the benefits of methadone are apparent however, in the context of the prison, the use of methods of chemical control should always be open to question.

The personal and interpersonal concerns of prisoners, while clearly as diverse as the prisoners themselves, nevertheless, have the potential to shed more light on the performance of the sentence and the factors conducive to what is sometimes called a "seamless" transition to the community. While reflecting elements of the omnipresence of power in prison, the focus of the analysis on the expectation that the prisoner commit to internal transformation means that acknowledgement and encouragement of the positive aspects of relatedness is essential. The way the prisoner relates to his peers, staff and family has a powerful influence on the ability of the prisoner to commit to performing the obligations of the sentence. The next chapter focuses on the sentencing aim and dominant correctional paradigm of rehabilitation, which is meant to be the means by which prisoners are to achieve this. Relationships have the potential to be a powerful influence over the ability of the prisoner to attend to the actions needed to fulfil the expectations of the sentence. Recognition of the harm caused to others and the will to have "no more victims" as one prisoner put it, is predicated on the ability to recognise and empathise with others. Positive, sustained personal relationships within and outside the prison can only assist in the achievement of these aims.

7

Rehabilitation

7.1 Introduction

> Yeah, yeah, pull it up. Stop all the gangster shit, okay. Encourage people, give people an honest chance. Gaols aren't set up to give people—that's why I laughed when you mentioned rehabilitation before. Gaol isn't about rehabilitation; it's about continuing the whole thing, okay, continuing the whole cycle (Antony).

Capturing the essence of the need to engage prisoners in the project of their own redemption and the essential fact that "gaols aren't about rehabilitation", Antony characterises the problem as "all the gangster shit". Surprisingly, he was not only talking about other prisoners, but also the "tough guy" stance taken by prison staff. His insight that gaol was about "continuing the whole cycle" epitomises the distance between the aims of sentencing and the reality of imprisonment—that for many it is not just one finite sentence, but a permanent cycle of release and return.

Linking the legal habitus of sentencing with the lived experience of a group of prisoners in the NSW, prison system uncovers some the processes and interactions which make up the sentence. The gaps between

M. Hall, *The Lived Sentence*, Palgrave Studies in Prisons and Penology, DOI 10.1007/978-3-319-45038-4_7

what is expected of prisoners and the means with which they can fulfil these expectations are thereby exposed. In an attempt to crystallise the main contention of the book—that strong subjective expectations of prisoners are imposed and reinforced throughout sentencing and imprisonment—the words of prisoners are again used to illustrate the barriers to fulfilment of this aim.

Limiting the scope to what prisoners say about how the requirement to rehabilitate plays out in prison, both reflects their main concerns and addresses a manageable aspect of this hugely complex and under-theorised area. Key theoretical arguments around the re-working of risk and rehabilitation are utilised to contextualise their experiences.[1] Although there is abundant evidence that educational programmes are valuable sites of rehabilitative energy,[2] this chapter will not focus on education or work programmes but only on those programmes that have been characterised as either offence focused or therapeutic. The question however, of the opportunity costs of pursuing intensive, costly offence-related programming at the expense of work release or education, or other sites of rehabilitative energy, is posed by some of the responses of prisoners.

This chapter will highlight the responses of prisoners when asked about the way that they understood rehabilitation as a part of the process of imprisonment (questions 8–13 Appendix 3, themes 2(b) Appendix 4). The chapter is organised in four sections, the first interrogating the meaning of rehabilitation. As a highly naturalised concept used by a range of different professional groups with different "habitus", it is surprising that more attention has not been paid to what it actually means. It is perhaps uniquely persistent in the discourse of law as well as corrections, but consequently the difference in conceptions of what it means is often elided.

[1] There are many aspects of rehabilitation, which have not been canvassed in this chapter. One of the most important, which is only touched on here, is the way that education and work, two basic needs which appear to be foundational to preventing re-offending and which do not arise from risk/needs assessment, are faring with this new focus on risk assessment and offence-specific programming.

[2] The irony of the rise of cognitive skills programmes at the expense of education is that the aetiology of "cog skills" is in education.

The second section, rehabilitation as subjectivity, captures one of the central contentions of this book: the persistence of expectations of subjective transformation throughout the sentence. While this conception of rehabilitation as a process of internal transformation and change is shared by some prisoners, for many it is a bridge too far and one that is nevertheless impossible in prison. The conception of rehabilitation as desistance from crime is the only real evaluation measure used to assess the success of criminal justice and the mission of CSNSW. This conception of rehabilitation flows from the idea that instilling pro-social behaviour in prisoners will result in them choosing to desist. Many of the prisoners expressed conventional goals of work, family and citizenship. Their focus was on these things and the insistence of the prison administration that they attend to goals of subjectivity and transformation was puzzling and bewildering for many.

The next section seeks to reflect the confusing, perverse combination of risk and responsibility, which creates a distorting effect when the reality of imprisonment is juxtaposed with the language of empowerment and personal development. What Drake calls "the duplicity of criminal justice" (Drake 2012, p. 133) dovetails with Indemaeuer's argument that there is a kind of "collusion" among criminal justice professionals to make the prisoner believe the sentence is about them and their needs. Carlen's (2008) conception of "imaginary penalities" also captures some of the atmosphere described by prisoners as "Alice in Wonderland" like. Adding considerations of "risk" to the already duplicitous, imaginary and confusing processes means that another level in the "hall of mirrors" has been added. No matter which way they go, no matter how many courses they do, the "hall of mirrors" reflects back on them keeping their risk levels static.

Lastly, the curious fit that characterises the new conceptions of rehabilitation arising from the risk/needs model, the managerial and security focus of the prison and prison-based cognitive skills programmes is examined. As the practical manifestation of the way risk blends with narrowing conceptions of rehabilitation, "cog skills" provides a perfect way to demonstrate compliance on the part of the correctional system with the requirements of the sentence. Conveniently packaged, short term and group focused, they are also ideal bedmates for the managerialist focus of modern corrections. This analysis brings together ideas about the new form of "rehabilitation" practised in NSW prisons.

7.2 What Does It Mean?

Rehabilitation is a highly contested concept with a range of meanings Inevitably, as a "buzz word" (Duff 2005) in common use by people with different professional training such as judges and social workers, rehabilitation has acquired a common sense meaning (often quite different from that held by the rehabilitatee). It is these taken-for-granted assumptions of shared meaning which must be interrogated and explained and which, when examined, often unearth sharp and significant differences in understanding.

As argued in Chap. 3, rehabilitation as an aim of sentencing underpins other important aims of sentencing such as the protection of the community.

> It must be remembered that the ultimate purpose of all punishment is the protection of society. It will often be in the best interests of society if emphasis is put on rehabilitation, particularly in cases where the offender can genuinely be said to be at the crossroads between a useless, drug-ridden and probably criminal existence and a relatively normal life in society, supported by a caring family (*R v Molina*).[3]

The fact that rehabilitation has a benevolent and humanitarian aspect (Bennett 2005, p. 20) when compared with some of the other aims of sentencing should not mean that the practices and policies should not be closely scrutinised for their intended and unintended effect. As part of an overall punitive approach, even the most positive programme can be used as a disciplinary, punitive tool. Goffman's classic 1961 work provides an enduring basis for examination and critique of rehabilitation regimes, complementary to a Foucauldian perspective.

> If Foucault's method flags the importance of noting relations between projects of rule and projects of self from the top down, then Goffman

[3] *R v Molina (1984)* 13 A Crim R 76 at 77

> gives us a means by which to invert this gaze, studying the same relationships but from the bottom up (Moore 2007, p. 13).

At the same time, it is important not to "repackage functionalism in a Foucaultian box" (Lacombe 1997, p. 333), instead "analyse the specificity of mechanisms of power" without constructing crude binary opposites or taking an unduly pessimistic stance (McMahon 1990, p. 144). While a critical view of part of what is called "rehabilitation" within the prisons of NSW is attempted in this book, the main contention is the importance of the lived experience of prisoners.

Understandably, much of the current emphasis on rehabilitation by practitioners and academic commentators is on the post-release period. While the importance of continued support after release must be acknowledged, this focus has contributed to a tendency to overlook what happens within prisons. Recent research demonstrating that rehabilitation is much more effective out of prison (as if that should be a surprise!) may have contributed to a lack of scrutiny as to what is called "rehabilitation" inside prisons. As Ward and Maruna point out, "in all the meta analytic number crunching around the 'what works' debate readers rarely get a sense of what is actually going on in rehab programs themselves" (Ward and Maruna 2007, p. 18). The view from the offender/client, that is, the subject of the criminal justice disposition/therapeutic intervention, is largely absent from the debate about efficacy. Indeed, prison administrators are cautioned about the dangers of using data on "consumer satisfaction" lest prisoners manipulate the data to induce popular programmes to remain (Parker 2004). In any case, no evaluation data of any kind is available regarding any of the programmes in NSW prisons (Heseltine et al. 2011).

At law, whether an accused has prospects of rehabilitation is a crucial factor in setting the non-parole period (minimum term) (see Chap. 3). It also underlies other important aims such as the protection of the community. While courts have some appreciation of the ongoing nature of rehabilitation, it is rare that they receive information on the operationalisation of the sentence. This can lead to a type of "imaginary sentencing" (Carlen 2008) where it is assumed that rehabilitative services will be available to the prisoner.

As a concept borrowed from human services, rehabilitation has been subjected to inevitable legal reductionism and distortion when it becomes just another item on the checklist, and where the meaning is rarely examined or problematised. As the responses of prisoners demonstrate, they may have different conceptions of what constitutes rehabilitation to either the courts or the prison system. Arguably, it requires more of the subjects of criminal justice processing than some of the other aims of sentencing. The expectation of transformation in the individual requires more of them than a passive serving of the sentence; repentance must be demonstrated or performed. Some level of congruence between all parties to the process as to the meanings and expectations thus invoked, is desirable and fair.

However, the discursive nature of penal and criminal justice processes (Wacquant 2009, p. 10) fragments and distorts the implementation of actual rehabilitative policies with the ever-present discourses of risk and dangerousness. Overlaid and underlying protestations of evidence-based practice are practices that ignore "evidence" and respond directly to populist currents in the media and elsewhere.

Rehabilitation as Subjective Transformation

One of the major contentions of this book is the existence of requirements of subjectivity, that is, the prisoner is expected as a result of the practical manifestation of the aims of sentencing, to feel punished, deterred, prevented from harming the community, rehabilitated, held accountable, denounced and manifest some recognition of the harm done. The way that these states are to be demonstrated, the way they are perceived and interpreted has great bearing on the disposition of the individual, from sentencing through imprisonment and to parole. Rehabilitation is the most obviously subjective and arguably the most relied upon in terms of measurement of outcomes (although paradoxically it is often measured using statistical measures of re-offending). Traditionally, it requires an active participation of the offender; rehabilitation is something that is done *with* the person *not* to them as in "treatment" in the medical model. The conflation of the two is most strikingly demonstrated in the area of drug rehabilitation where the medical model of addiction sits comfortably with a model of "rehabilitation" which relies primarily on diagnosis and treatment, that treatment being of a "rehabilitative" nature and often delivered by non-medical personnel.

In defining rehabilitation in a prison context, the obvious difference between the types of client-centred practice implied by the term is the element of free will or choice involved. For Duff (2005) prison rehabilitation is moral rehabilitation, distinct from therapeutic rehabilitation, which we may do with prisoners as well, but which must always be of their own choice. Moral rehabilitation can be imposed and inevitably involves trying to make prisoners see the error of their ways. Aside from philosophical arguments about freedom of choice, it is how to do this and how to measure success which is contentious and where most of the theoretical accounts of punishment fall down. As this view raises questions of subjectivity, of self-belief, moral rehabilitation must involve communication, which is a two-way process.

Prisoners spoke often of the fundamental difficulties of rehabilitation in prison. The following sections reflect some of the most important of the barriers identified, starting with the most fundamental: the damage done by imprisonment itself. The idea that such experiences can be transformational, but more fundamentally, the fallacy of a return to some former state of well-being not ever possessed by the majority of prisoners, is exposed immediately as fundamentally flawed.

Is It Possible in Prison?

> "How can you return me to me former self? It can't be done. You . . . say "Don't be violent"—you put me in a place that's violent. You say "Respect your laws"—you put me in a place where the laws aren't respected" (Tommy).

The contradiction between the requirements made of prisoners and the violence inherent in imprisonment is clearly demonstrated here. This prisoner cogently argued against the possibility of rehabilitation within the prison. His understanding of the formal meaning of the word is also clearly demonstrated, a return to some former better self:

> as restoration to social status and membership of society rather than simply as reduction in offending, which on this view is a means to rehabilitation rather than rehabilitation itself (Raynor 1997, p. 257).

The very meaning of the word "rehabilitation" in the sense of, as the prisoner says, "returning me to me former self" is here called into question, when the state of most prisoners is to be disadvantaged, uneducated and unable to participate in mainstream society to begin with. The damage done by incarceration is thus seen as precluding any positive effects. Thus the very paradigm of "rehabilitation" is of questionable benefit to the prisoner.

> Interviewer: "So, do you think rehabilitation happens in gaol? Prisoner: "There's not one god dammed bit of it! There's not!" (Chris).

For prisoners within certain categories, escapees in particular, risk-averse management delays re-classification and access to programming. For these prisoners, risk trumps rehabilitation and access to programmes and services.

> Interviewer "So what do you reckon we should do for rehabilitation? Prisoner: "I reckon sack them . . . The resources are just not here, so you being here there's no point, so you're just wasting money. You might as well not be there at all; you understand what I'm saying?" (Van).

This statement—"the resources just aren't here"—reflects a pragmatic appraisal of the services available to prisoners, as opposed to official rhetoric about "rehabilitation". It appears that workers in the system have the same perception: while the appearance of rehabilitation is necessary, the resources simply are not there (Mark Brown, in Cunneen et al. 2013, p. 88). To identify needs and then only "treat" those which are linked with recidivism, or not at all is to raise expectations in prisoners for assistance which may not be forthcoming. As rhetoric which has dubious reality for many of the prisoners interviewed here, "rehabilitation" was for them, something which had little to do with programme involvement. More important were the practical aspects of release—employment, accommodation and relationships, examined later in this chapter.

Remorse and Rehabilitation

It has been argued that the expression of remorse is a pivotal expectation of the prisoner both in the legal setting and while serving the sentence. In Chap. 4, a variety of perspectives were expressed by prisoners mostly puzzled by what was expected of them. In common with in-court sentencing, the relevance of remorse in this part of the lived sentence is unspoken and must be evident in the observable behaviour of the prisoner. In other words, the prisoner must continue to perform remorse appropriately in order to gain release. Mere good behaviour may not be enough. The extent of the expectation to conform to the official narrative of the offence and the psycho-legal narrative of themselves, as discussed in Chap. 4, is heightened in the period just before the EPRD, when the official gaze turns on the prisoner to assess his readiness for parole.

> "From the start they've been wrong about me . . . till now, they've been wrong" (Van)

Convicted of a violent offence committed in company, Van was demonised as an intractable violent offender at the age of 19. Complex legal issues leading to the acquittal and sentence reduction of his co-offenders contributed to his feeling misunderstood and vilified unfairly. His case exemplifies the difficulty of expressing remorse when the official narrative of the offence and of the self is at odds with the self-perception of the individual. Only recently had he been able to make sense of his situation, however his inability to express remorse early in his sentence had seriously delayed reduction in classification and access to programmes. The acceptance of the prisoner of the reasons and rationale of the sentence is damaged when the legitimacy of the legal process is questioned, as in Van's case.

Sabotage

Many prisoners spoke of the various ways that power is exercised through the imperative to rehabilitate. The meaning of rehabilitation as lived through the distorting lens of the prison is another dimension of control, scrutiny and of manipulation, an exercise in "soft power" (Crewe 2009), but one which is all pervasive and difficult to confront. Placing rehabilitative programmes in an environment characterised by mistrust allows the conventional power relationships of prisoner and guard to override the positive aspects. This may be why the more successful programmes have been isolated from the main prison, and as Mark Brown points out some jurisdictions have responded to this problem with the creation of the "dedicated boutique, treatment prison" (Cunneen et al. 2013, p. 88)

> Anyway he told me (a fellow prisoner who had done the VOTP) "It's crap. It does nothing for ya. And the officers try to sabotage you every chance they get" (Mick).

An emphasis on prison officers' awareness and support of the processes and goals of therapeutic programmes may require special selection and training as many prisoners expressed the view that prison officers often criticised and undermined programme involvement. The expectation that prisoners enter programmes that may allow private information to become public knowledge allows at least for the fear of manipulation, if not sabotage, as this prisoner expressed.

Coercion

As Crewe (2009) points out, coercion is one of the ways in which power is exercised in the modern prison. Without remissions to encourage prisoners to comply, the linking of release with the performance of rehabilitation through programme attendance, equips the prison with a powerful coercive tool. As the next quote demonstrates, the language and appearance of choice is counterposed with the reality of the power to continue imprisonment.

> They say they . . . they blackmail me with it, they said, oh we're going to get you to fill this in so if you fill this in we basically we can say to SORC about that that you have applied for it but we don't think you need to do it because of your history and that . . . And even filling out the form the first question is the inmate must voluntarily want to participate in this program and I said well I'm not voluntarily filling this out and they said oh just fill it out it'll be OK. What happened? It came back C3 restricted drug and alc. And I basically told them I'm not interested in doing it and now I've got parole threatening me that I won't get parole if I won't do it (Kevin).

Convinced that leaving prison with no money, as he had done several times before, was a recipe for disaster, this man had been in a trusted position in the regional prison, with many years of good behaviour and clean urines. The idea of regressing in classification, losing his opportunity for work release and again being released penniless for the sake of programme completion was unacceptable for him and he was prepared to resist and complete his full sentence in custody if necessary.

> This lady come out last week, and um that is another stick to beat people with "when you're in the last six months of your full sentence we can take you to court and extend your sentence. (Jack)

The ostensible benevolence of the idea of rehabilitation often precludes the type of scrutiny given to other more punitive aspects of criminal justice. Concerns that to critically analyse the purpose and meaning of the practices of rehabilitation will lead to a return to the bad old days of "nothing works" and a repeat of the unholy alliance between civil libertarians concerned about intrusions into freedom of choice and economic rationalists and punitive elements to make prison even more unpleasant has arguably silenced critique in this area.

As Fischer argues in relation to drug treatment courts, in a well-named article "Doing good with a vengeance", "DTCs (Drug Treatment Centres) obscure the fact that 'punishment' is the persistent and predominant mode of addiction control" (Fischer 2003, p. 244). The non-voluntary and coercive nature of programme involvement raises issues for the professional staff conducting these programmes: the proper basis for therapeutic intervention and the ethical frameworks of the professionals involved in making assessments which may result in punitive outcomes. Ward and Birgden (2009, p. 78) have argued that mandated, compulsory programmes are not inconsistent with a therapeutic approach. There is no doubt, however, that there is a fundamental change in the nature of the "therapeutic relationship" where coercion or lack of choice, lack of confidentiality, and an absence of the kind of primacy, agency and control which characterise the most successful therapeutic approaches are largely unexamined and unacknowledged in the delivery of services and treatment to certain stigmatised groups.

The absence of important therapeutic and human rights elements in prison programmes—for example confidentiality and pressure to make incriminating statements—must effect a change in the philosophical orientation of treatment. As Glaser notes,

> Ultimately sex offender treatment programs remain a form of punishment: the well-accepted principles justifying and limiting the role of punishment in Western legal systems may well be a better ethical guide for therapists in this area than conventional codes of mental health practice (Glaser 2003, p. 144).

This means that principles such as proportionality should apply here as elsewhere; for example is it proportionate to require a prisoner with a conviction as a juvenile to complete a program regardless of the nature of the index offence? Is it proportionate to require a prisoner with a five-year history of abstinence to complete an intensive drug programme which would extend his imprisonment? The ostensibly positive features of rehabilitation mean that these questions are rarely asked in relation to rehabilitative programmes. In a similar fashion to the use of methadone examined in the last chapter, it is important to pay attention to the ubiquity of the exercise of power in prisons and the potential for misuse of such power.

What They Want to Hear

The difficulties for prisoners in demonstrating remorse have been canvassed in Chap. 4. The performative aspects of criminal justice so prominent in the sentencing stage continue throughout the sentence with the expectation to rehabilitate. Prisoners must know how to perform rehabilitation as well as remorse without appearing to be calculating and rehearsed. It is proposed that the expectation of performance of remorse is what links the in-court sentencing stage with the sentence of imprisonment. The temporal gap between the powerful symbolic aspects of sentencing and the performance of rehabilitation means that by the time the programme is commenced, the prisoner is acculturated to the prison environment and is less receptive to the messages of redemption through responsibility. Giving the prisoner some idea of what to expect rather than "springing a programme" on them at the end of the sentence was clearly important to many interviewees.

> I don't know why they don't do it at the start and then do a life change as you're doing your time... By the time you get to that program you've learnt, uh, how the system runs and what they want to hear (Leslie).

"Doing a life change" is a good shorthand description of what rehabilitation requires, a process taking place over some years, not an event. To this man, giving him the tools to understand what had happened early in his sentence made more sense than allowing him to adapt to the prison first. It should not be surprising that the effects of incarceration can include the ability to adapt and deliver what is expected while participating in programmes. After serving a number of years prisoners may be more settled and easier to manage but they may also have developed an appreciation of the necessity to deliver an appropriate redemption narrative. Having learnt to adopt the official narrative of the offence, often a precondition for acceptance into programmes, they must then learn to perform the version of rehabilitation required by the sentence. The difficulties involved in assessing the genuineness of remorse discussed in Chap. 4 are reflected here, and several prisoners adverted to the need to "play the game".

Slipping the Guard

The necessity to "pay attention to everything (you) do", expressed by Kevin in the last chapter, illustrates the pervasiveness of "soft power" in the prison. The increased scrutiny of prisoners accompanying the psycho-correctional move to risk assessment, along with the case management model, puts some prisoners on the alert.

> I can slip my guard with you because you're not part of the system (Leslie).

Assessed and evaluated constantly, prisoners are often watchful of saying anything which could compromise their situation. Several prisoners expressed relief at the opportunity to speak without such constraints. The popularity among prisoners of religious-based organisations such as Kairos derives from their non-judgmental attitude to prisoners (and sometimes the fact that they are the only people who visit (Xu).

The Therapeutic Relationship

The importance of the therapeutic relationship to the success of any intervention is widely supported by research evidence. Several prisoners referred to the impact of a relationship of trust and confidence with a particular helping professional. For a person to be able to see through the official version of the prisoner and convey empathy and acceptance was commonly seen as the essential turning point for some of the prisoners. The willingness of the professional to "take on" the system, to adopt the perspective of the prisoner, critique the system, made their assistance valuable, is exceptional.

> (She said) "you're not the person they say you are, you're not the person they say you are . . . F, before she left, she called me up and said "I just want to tell you I'm leaving . . . I was like "Don't do that man, don't do that"—she was one of my friends you know . . . She goes "No, I've got to, I won't bend my morals . . . Look, they just want us to tick people off. I won't bend my morals. I'm leaving (Mick).

The reference to morality is also interesting; prisoners often express admiration for those staff and prisoners who display morally consistent behaviour, particularly when it placed them at odds with management. What may be characterised, in the current parlance, as "responsivity" issues also concern the quality of assistance made available to prisoners. Implementation issues such as the quality of staff training must be a concern. Moving staff out of prisons and into the community may accord with current research, but the result is a net loss for prisoners. The reference to "ticking people off" is eerily similar to the characterisation of some programmes as "tick and flick" (see later in this chapter) and seems to reflect the movement of the Department away from individual concepts of rehabilitation (incompletely implemented) to more generic programming.

Dazed and Confused

Competency issues were often raised in relation to other prisoners, the inadequacy of the language of responsibilisation and cognitive beliefs to explain or ameliorate the consequences of the severe disadvantage suffered by some prisoners. Here again, the glib language of CBT (Cognitive Behavioural Therapy) is used as an obvious example of the disjuncture between therapy and reality:

> This fellow who's having trouble is an Aboriginal, his education is about third class in primary school he can't express himself and he's getting frustrated and angry and he's starting to trip over his words—and people are saying "get into the driving seat" and he says "what the hell are you talking about" He doesn't understand and he's not the only one (William).

That cognitive behavioural programmes requiring group participation privilege more articulate and educated prisoners appears to be at least a possibility. Prisoners who can present an appropriately pro-social identity would appear to have quite an advantage in this setting.

> Let me tell you something about rehabilitation. This is, understand I don't have much of an education I went to school until year 7. So I'm not a very smart sort of person (Jack).

In common with many prisoners, this prisoner's lack of education was seen by him as a major barrier to participation in rehabilitation programmes. Much of what had been delivered to him in programmes merely bewildered him.

Rehabilitation as Desistance?

The prisoner quotes in this section are concerned with the way which the interviewees conceptualised rehabilitation and the differences between what they thought they required and what was in fact available to them.

Desistance theorists connect rehabilitation with the outcome most popular with politicians—desistance from criminal behaviour. Maruna acknowledges how much more complex this is to apply in practice but continues nevertheless to develop a theory which requires desisters to adopt a "redemption script" (Maruna 2001). Talk of "turning points" and "moments of clarity" in this model echo similar judicial language such as "at the crossroads". Many of the interviews for this book contained elements of what Maruna calls "redemption scripts".

The concepts and practice in desistance literature tend to be male-centred and fail to grasp the reality of the "weekend warriors" cluttering up the prison for the long termers, who are cycling through a "liminal marginalised and fluid community criminal justice space" (Baldry 2009, p. 20). The anthropological concept of liminality, derived from the work of Van Gennep (in Turner 1967) and revived by Turner (1967, p. 93), illustrates the way people cycle in and out of the justice system and remain in a permanent state of limbo created by these "liminal spaces" (Cunneen et al. 2013, p. 150). This idea complements the conception in this book of the continuous sentence.

While clearly the indigenous and intellectually disabled women of Baldry's study suffer multiple disadvantage and are totally locked out of the dominant paradigm of Risk/Needs/Responsivity (RNR), it is questionable whether these generalised approaches meet the needs of mainstream male prisoners either, given the preponderance of short sentences and the prevalence of mental illness, substance abuse and general educational and economic disadvantage in the general prison population. The position of indigenous male prisoners, who have little opportunity to gain the types of valued "desistance friendly" factors such as employment, is further complicated by the unique nature of their experience of imprisonment (Blagg. 2008, Cunneen et al. 2013, p. 144).

A "Good Life"

Consistent with the findings in Chap. 7, rehabilitation for the men interviewed was often conceived in interpersonal terms, being with people they cared for, in an intimate relationship, participating in "normal" activities. While prisoners were not always specifically asked what they meant by "rehabilitation", many accounts focused on the future, on their hopes to live a "good life", as Ward and Maruna call it (Ward and Maruna 2007).

> I'm not coming back, I want to do everything, I want to travel, you know what I mean (Van).

As a teenager when he was imprisoned, this young man was acutely aware that he had missed out of much of his youth. "I want to do everything" illustrates the breadth of what he had been denied. His exuberant physical actions—spreading his arms out wide, head thrown back with a big smile on his face—emphasised his enthusiasm for embracing the life he had missed.

The White Picket Fence

Many prisoners expressed their wish to be "normal", to have access to the same type of social capital valued by other members of society. While some were doubtful whether this would happen for them now, even the most alienated tended to refer to life outside prison in these terms.

> All I ever wanted to do, all I ever wanted out of life was to find a good girl get married and have kids. That's all I ever wanted even when I was young, that was all I ever wanted (Mick).

In common with many prisoners, this rather "white picket fence" version of life outside prison is at odds with common perceptions of prisoners as "outlaws". While the long-term prisoners interviewed struggled to maintain relationships with the outside world (as illustrated in the last chapter), the importance of these relational conceptions of the good life ran through their narrative. Many expressed mainstream goals—partner, children, house, job—as the ultimate that they could hope for from life. Few, however, were unrealistic enough to expect this.

That Little Block

Confronting the reality of the ongoing stigma carried by those who have committed violent acts, Chris acknowledged that the heinous nature of his crime placed him outside the realm of normal relationships with women. Whether justified or not, his actions have placed him outside the normal channels of social interaction and he demonstrated an acute awareness of this.

> You feel yourself that really honestly . . . I don't want to put, you know, you wouldn't want to have a relationship with me . . . Right, as a woman . . . You know because there is that in the back of the head there's that little block . . . (Chris).

Convicted of a violent sex offence as a young man and kept in solitary for a number of years, he was clearly yearning for some kind of personal connection, which he acknowledged he was unlikely to find given the nature of the offence. Intending to live in the outback he expressed the view that he was better off away from mainstream society, that his outsider status was permanent whether he wanted it or not. The uncomfortable nature of this interaction was outweighed by his obvious distress about this. It was clear that he was aware of the disastrous consequences of his choices in life on his ability to form relationships, particularly with women, and his awareness of this loss was palpable. Release for him was a life lived in a very limited way, never able to fully integrate with mainstream society. Rehabilitation had not been the focus of his sentence, his isolation merely confirming his status as outsider. Like many long-term prisoners, he had become compliant (ageing being one of most well-known factors in desistance) but found that his poor custodial record precluded him from access to the means to rehabilitate or redeem himself.

Debt

While the previous quote refers to an interpersonal barrier to rehabilitation as desistance, debt operates as a practical barrier. Another aspect of the ongoing nature of the punitive aspects of modern sentencing is the imposition of restitution, recovering money paid to victims for Victims Compensation under the new *Victims Rights and Support* Act NSW (2013) or the previous *Victim Support and Rehabilitation* Act (1996) (repealed)

> I thought I paid my debt to society being in gaol… (I've got to pay) $50,000. How am I supposed to pay that? They get out and they've got a debt and that plays on their mind "I've got to get ahead, I've got to get ahead." And what do they do? They reoffend (Van).

Debt is a major barrier to rehabilitation. Most prisoners have State Debt Recovery debts, many into thousands of dollars (Grunseit et al. 2008). In addition, recovery of victim's compensation often ensures that prisoners are repaying money during their lifetime. Bankruptcy is often the only option. This ongoing punishment is one of the ways that the sentence extends far beyond the prison and into the daily life and prospects of rehabilitation of the prisoner. While justifiable in terms of recognition of the harm done to the victim, ongoing debt becomes not just a practical barrier for the prisoner but an indication that the sentence never really ends even when they are released.

"Do the crime, do the time" is an oft repeated maxim in NSW prisons, but the "time" is now extended deep into the post release life of the prisoner. If restitution is accompanied by a real recognition for the need for reparation for the harm done to the victim, by truly linking the aims of the sentence with the pain of the sentence, an enhancement of the legitimacy of the system in the mind of the prisoner may result. As it is, restitution is experienced as an unfair extension of the punitive aspects of the sentence.

7.3 The Hall of Mirrors—Risk and Responsibility

In Chap. 6 the official discourse of the Department around correctional processing was contrasted with the effect on the lived sentence of these seemingly value-free and operational matters. The responsibilisation of the prisoner was placed at the forefront of the analysis and provides a backdrop to the words of prisoners, which concisely sums up the disjunction between the discourses of responsibilisation in an environment of limited personal freedom.

The transformation of the rehabilitative ideal into a tool for the risk management of offenders has resulted in some strange bedfellows indeed. The language of individual responsibility is married with the absence of any consideration of institutional and cultural factors. The decontextualisation of the prisoner, the violence inherent in incarceration, the casual cruelty of the institution (such minor matters as imperfect record keeping having sometimes catastrophic repercussions for individual prisoners), "the power of the pen" (Crewe 2009) give the whole process of incarceration a distorted "hall of mirrors" effect, with the prisoner always held responsible for any failure whatsoever.

The addition of another level in the hall—the need to negotiate the therapeutic expectation contingent on compulsory rehabilitation, linked to the imperative of risk reduction—allows and encourages manipulation and disappointment. The incorporation of the therapeutic ideal into the discourse and practices of risk has arguably distorted and modified any original ideal of personal redemption into a more static and institutionally determined process. As the slave of risk assessment, "therapy" (if that is what cog skills is), particularly mandated therapy, becomes an end in itself.

Prisoners expressed their bewilderment at the plethora of organisational and systemic barriers, overlaid by expressions of responsibilisation by therapeutic agents. The following section takes some of these comments and places them in the context of the reality of power in the prison context. (Crewe 2009) The expectations arising from sentencing outlined in Chaps. 3 and 4 are contrasted with the reality of powerlessness as regards the conduct of their everyday lives.

The Driving Seat

A common theme among prisoners in programmes was the incompatibility of the therapeutic ideas perpetuated in programmes with the reality of prison life. This problem is often overcome by separating prisoners in programmes from those in the main gaol.

> CM, who is the therapeutic manager berated people "You get in there you get in the driving seat and you drive your life.... And we go "Yeah that's fine until you try driving it and they go "who the hell do you think you are. We are the boss here you will do what you're told." And from one side you get this, from one side you get the other (Jason).

The obvious contradiction between the therapeutic imperative to control one's own destiny and the reality of prison life back on the wing gives rise to a degree of cynicism in prisoners who recognise the irony in requiring this of people who are unable to make even the most basic decisions about their life. The phrase "get into the driving seat" was mentioned often enough for it to be clear that it is a common metaphor, reflecting the responsibilisation of the prisoner discussed in Chap. 5. As Donahue and Moore put it

> Clients are the salvage of criminal justice . . . people in conflict with the law, as well as criminal justice personnel, are recruited into practices of punishment through the erasure of the punitive goals of the system in favour of a reinvention of criminal justice as venue for delivering social services (Donahue and Moore 2009, p. 320).

"The translation of offender into client serves to recruit people in conflict with the law into their own punishment by actively engaging them in their own correction" (Donahue and Moore 2009, p. 328). This perspective chimes with that of Indemauer who adverts to what he calls a "collusion" of participants in the criminal trial in duping the accused to believe that the process is about him, his needs, his subjectivity (Indemauer 1996). As one prisoner expressed it,

> It's me needs miss, me needs (Jason).

The plaintive way in which this prisoner pleaded for help with his significant social, intellectual and psychiatric deficits reflected the incorporation of the risk/needs discourse into the way prisoners conceptualise their imprisonment. Puzzled at the way his needs had been shoved out of the way by the nature of the offence (a sex offence) he could not verbalise his dismay in any other way, repeating this phrase again and again. Needs are transformed into markers of risk and, although they may be identified by the processes of modern correctionalism, unless they are connected to the risk of re-offending they will be ignored.

Responsibilisation positions the accused as master of his own destiny, and other aims of sentencing such as accountability reflect this. As discussed in Chap. 3, accountability, one of the newer aims of sentencing, needs to be explained and operationalised. If the prisoner is to be made accountable, does the responsibility cut both ways? Given the large proportion of the Corrective Services budget spent on imprisonment, and the adoption of the RNR model in CSNSW, one would expect that in accordance with RNR that prisoners who have been assessed as being in a group posing a high risk of re-offending would be provided with programmes and services whilst in custody in order to reduce that risk. Judicial comments made at sentencing often prescribe the type of rehabilitation necessary for the offender to address the problems viewed as contributing to the commission of the offence. At the end of the custodial part of the sentence, the Parole Authority reviews these comments and, most importantly, the prisoner's subsequent response to the judges' comments (as per s135(2) (e) of the *Crimes (Administration of Sentences)* Act 1999, NSW), which become an important part of their decision-making process. The prisoner is at this point made accountable for what he has done during his imprisonment.

Donahue and Moore see the drafting of the prisoner into his/her own rehabilitation as a political act. They note that the "client is nowhere to be found" in the court part of sentencing, but the transformation occurs through the operationalisation of the sentence. Their conceptualisation supports the major contention of this book that there is a significant and highly distorting disjuncture between the in-court phase of sentencing and the serving of the sentence itself.

As Raynor points out, "what works" entered Britain inspired largely by probation services searching for meaningful programme content (Raynor 1997). Apart from the justifiable need to ease the "pains of imprisonment" is there a need to ease the "pains of working with the imprisoned?" Despite convincing evidence that such gains that can be made from programme participation are better made outside prisons, there is an expectation, if only from the courts and the Parole Authority, that programmes will be provided.

> Ensuring reasonable access to offender management programs is of particular concern when dealing with sexual and violent offenders coming before the Authority . . . and continued availability and access of offenders to all these invaluable programs . . . is essential in order to provide the necessary opportunities to address offending behaviour (NSW State Parole Authority 2007).

Knowledge claims made by newly dominant groups in this area, mainly psychologists, require implementation of programs rather than provision of services to prisoners. The question of accountability to provide the means by which offenders can reduce their "risk" is exemplified by the number of cases, in particular, in relation to the *Crimes (Serious Sex Offenders Act) 2006 NSW* in which the absence of programmes or suitable accommodation is an issue. The strong relationship between the risk needs paradigm and rehabilitative treatment regimes is further cemented in the NSW cases where continuing detention or extended supervision is considered. The legislation requires the court to be satisfied that appropriate treatment is not available outside a prison for that particular inmate. Is it then open to the Department to simply refuse to provide such treatment as a way of limiting expenditure, when the result is further incarceration? The arbitrary nature of this provision "troubled" Mason J in *Winters*[4] (at 20). In one case a continuing detention order was made because there was no suitable accommodation available for an intellectually disabled man (*Davis*).[5] The "needs" of the prisoner have been transformed into risk factors to be controlled and manipulated.

In *Winters*[6] the Court of Criminal Appeal expressed the view that, despite the provision of funding for a private psychologist in two other cases, the Department was not expected to fund private counselling. The primary judge confirmed that "the practical effect is that legislation has been put in place which provides for the retention of persons such as Mr Winters beyond the completion of their sentence who, if appropriate community resources were provided could be released" (Hodgson JA at 147). That is, the policy choices of the Department result in continuing incarceration of at least some prisoners who, if all the evidence indicate would be better treated in the community. Mason P expressed concern about the potential for discrimination on the basis of means as regards access to programmes and services (Mason P at 36) and, on the basis of

[4] (2008) NSWCCA 33

[5] *New South Wales v Davis* [2008] NSWSC 862

[6] *Winters v Attorney General of NSW* (2008) NSWCCA 33

the decisions so far, it appears that a prisoner who can pay for his own treatment would be in a position to argue for release.

In *McGarry*[7], the Court emphatically rejected the idea that decisions about release were inappropriately left to the executive, reaffirming that "courts are not treatment institutions". "The absence of culturally appropriate treatment programmes results in systemic discrimination in that the outcome, irrespective of motive or intention, amounts to unfair discrimination within the prison" (Lindsay 2009, p. 45). There can be no assurance of accountability by the executive for the treatment of offenders who find themselves caught up in the bureaucratic system of prison administration that rigorously applies policies that make no allowance for ethnic and cultural factors.

The next section examines some of the institutional barriers to access to rehabilitative programmes identified by prisoners. By making explicit the way that naturalised practices operate to shape the form of the sentence, the responsibilised prisoner is placed in proper context.

Right to the Top

> They (the committee) justify their own existence by putting more people on, and it doesn't mean you have to be a really serious . . . and it's taken responsibility from parole officers and psychologists because they're limited in what they can do (Jason).

On one hand, prison officers have a high level of personal discretion in dealing with prisoners. Each prison has its own habitus, some very different from others, as Liebling has demonstrated (Liebling 2004). On the other hand, power in some cases is concentrated at very high levels in the Department even where relatively mundane decisions are concerned. Taking the management of "high risk offenders" right to the top of CSNSW bureaucracy ensures that prisoners who may cause problems (e.g. adverse publicity) for the Department can be identified well in advance. Unfortunately, this overly centralised decision making

[7] *McGarry v Western Australia* (2005) 31 WAR 69 at [36]-[39] (Wheeler J);

can lead to excessive delays, conflict between various decision-making bodies, and a high degree of frustration in prisoners. The extract which concludes this chapter (Kevin) demonstrates clearly the risk-averse, secretive and obtuse decision-making which characterises many prisoners' experience of imprisonment in NSW.

Availability of Programmes

A significant feature of the ideological dimension of the "bulky machinery" (Drake 2012, p. 34) of the prison apparatus is the appearance of choice. According to the official discourse of CSNSW prisoners have available to them "a suite of programmes", the implicit assumption being that prisoners who do not "choose" to participate in programmes are demonstrating their riskiness. The ideology of choice and responsibility in the unique context of the prison environment produces real and concrete consequences for prisoners.

> But I also know that a lot of gaols, that some things aren't available whereas some things are and it depends what your circumstances have been throughout. Cause they know you can't go to some gaols and they know, you know, so you're restricted to what you can do (Dennis).

Availability of programmes is often dependant on achieving a particular classification, and the rationalisation and centralisation of programmes has limited the ability of many prisoners to participate in programmes, particularly if on methadone or on protection. A "suite" of accredited programmes is said to be available through CSNSW, although only 14 of 45 positions to implement these were filled in 2008/2009 and the relegation of prisons to an add-on phrase—"as well as correctional centres"—(CSNSW Annual Report 2008/2009) does not augur well for the priority given to in-prison programmes. Correctional staff are aware of the fact that prison may not be the best place to do a programme (Howells and Day 1999, p. 4, Sotiri 2003) and most of the evidence supports this. It is interesting to speculate whether the Department, in adhering to evidence-based practice has privately conceded that in prison rehabilitation doesn't "work"—the withdrawal of psychologists from prisons is evidence of this. It may not be too cynical, then to propose that the provision of programmes in prisons, which appears somewhat half hearted in any case, may be good public relations and a way of satisfying the courts and Parole Authority.

In the next quote, William demonstrates his understanding of the disconnection between the judicial act of sentencing and the absence of accountability of the prison to provide the means to carry out the ensuing obligation. As a legally literate prisoner, he saw the lack of connection between the in-court sentence and what results in practice as a significant challenge to the legitimacy of the criminal justice system.

> Now society outside of the prison system expects Corrective Services to provide these programs and have inmates do it, but as I said to you before in terms of the judicial authority they are under no accountability to do these things (William).

A number of issues in addition to uneven provision of programmes are raised by the next extract. The dominance of the departmental line means that prisoners are, as always, "on the bottom of the hierarchy of credibility" (Baranek and Ericson 1982) adding to the Alice in Wonderland like feeling that their reality is, by default, suspicious and untrustworthy.

> Like a couple of the older heads got together the other week, oh in the last week, actually cause protection inmates in here can do a program right, called a SMART program and we (mainstream inmates) can't do it. Cause the counsellors won't run it for us . . . but because the protection inmates went and saw SORC first and told them they were doing the program when we went in and told them we didn't have access to it we got called liars to our face! . . . So the first thing I done is I . . . went to the counsellors and explained exactly what they were doing to me you know the long termers here . . . you cannot move on in the system where you get parole . . . without it (a program). So why do they choose to punish me? Chris).

This prisoner's feeling that by denying him participation in a programme that would facilitate his release, he was being punished unfairly and was pervasive in some of the other interviews. Programme provision is often uneven and inconsistent and contributes to the prisoners distrust when the means by which they can improve their situation is denied to them. Perverse and uncoordinated decision making around access to programmes and services accounts for a good deal of the mistrust felt by long-term prisoners interviewed for this book. Another element in this account was SORC's assumption that he was lying about the unavailability of the programme, related to the argument in Chap. 4 that prisoners are at the bottom of the "hierarchy of credibility" (Ericson and Baranek 1982). This comment also supports other prisoners' perceptions that SORC is out of touch and uninformed about what actually happens in individual prisons.

The connection between progression through the classification system and ultimately eligibility for parole and completion of programmes is well understood by most prisoners. Many expressed their frustration that because of their classification or placement they were unable to participate in the programmes that would assist them to be released and the earliest possible date. The importance of practical matters such as provision of programmes only at certain locations, strict rules about classification and entry to programs was emphasised. Prisoners on protection are also disadvantaged when it comes to access to programmes (although the quote above indicates that some programmes are restricted to protection inmates).

Empty Beds, Full Waiting Lists

The phenomenon of full waiting lists and empty beds in treatment programmes has been noted in the Audit Office's review of rehabilitation in NSW prisons (Audit Office of NSW 2004). While there appears to have been some recent improvements, long delays (as exemplified by the interview at the beginning of the chapter) characterise the processes involved in negotiating progression through the system. Many prisoners expressed their frustrations with the lack of opportunities for rehabilitation; rather than being unwilling to participate, they reported that opportunities were severely limited.

> You've got to wait till you're a C classo . . . and, um, the point is though when you're over there there's empty beds . . . there's 100's on the waiting list." Interviewer: "Are they not reducing people's classo quickly enough, do you think?" Prisoner: "Well if you're here you're a C classo anyway . . . and you're still waiting. I've been talking to different blokes who were waiting to go over. We've been waiting for months (Leslie).

Perhaps the most telling feature of the 2004 Audit of Rehabilitation Services was the response of the Commissioner of Corrective Services who, in response to a report which suggested that prisoners are being released without having been rehabilitated, suggested that the Audit Office "does not appear to have appreciated the full implications of this literature and its impact on our strategic approach". In other words, the implications for correctional management of the "what works" literature is the risk–targeting of programmes on the basis of who can participate, what "needs" will be addressed and non-provision to low-risk offenders. A "hierarchical approach" to assessment means that only targeted prisoners receive full assessments and referrals to programmes "where it can be demonstrated that the offender can benefit from the available interventions and services". Does this place the onus on the prisoner to demonstrate that they can benefit, a difficult task given the problems faced by the Department itself in demonstrating just that.

Legal Proceedings as Barriers to Management

The rise in the proportion of unsentenced prisoners offers a direct challenge to the out-dated paradigm which appears to view court appearances as an inconvenient anomaly rather than a normal part of the process of imprisonment. Despite the fact that ongoing legal proceedings must be par for the course with this population, and that Corrections has always had to deal with the court system, legal proceedings are seen as an inconvenience by correctional authorities.

> I'‘ve been here two and a half months as a C1 in a maximum security gaol, you know. Because I've got more court coming up for common assault. At MRRC they classo 'ed me X wing and I get here and the Dep says no you've got more court you can't go to X wing" (Dave). (X wing is minimum security).

Pending legal proceedings often prevent programme participation and reduction in classification.

> I actually had an appeal in . . . but because you can't do a program in here if you appeal. . . . Had to do the program to get out. . . . ." (so withdrew the appeal) (Jason).

Lengthy delays in this young man's case meant that his EPRD was rapidly approaching without him having been assessed. The practical reality of the "right of appeal" is demonstrated here in a similar way to protestation of innocence; engagement in legal proceedings does not endear prisoners to correctional authorities. There is a clear message that successful performance of the sentence with the appropriate demonstrations of rehabilitation, including remorse, is incompatible with recourse to legal proceedings.[8]

7.4 Rehabilitation + Risk = Cog Skills

As outlined in Chap. 3, the dominant paradigm in assessment and programmes in NSW prisons has shifted to a tight reliance on narrowly defined, offence-specific programmes heavily reliant on risk assessment instruments validated on other populations and delivering cognitive behavioural programmes to small numbers of prisoners. This has been a radical change for CSNSW where previously a plethora of small uncoordinated and unevaluated programmes existed.

---

[8] The problems faced by prisoners NSW in accessing legal services were canvassed thoroughly by the Law and Justice Foundation, see Grunseit et al (2008) *"Taking Justice into custody: The Legal Needs of Prisoners"* Law and Justice Foundation of NSW.

Several coexisting factors have transformed "rehabilitation" in prisons in NSW from a focus on the well-being of the individual to a means to reduce "risk" as conceived by actuarial measurement and clinical judgment. Additionally, this must be able to be measured and evaluated by the criteria of reduction of recidivism. Rehabilitation has always included a punitive or at least coercive element—"modern liberal penality even where in large part reformative and corrective, always included some element of deterrence and retribution" (Hutchinson 2006, p. 448). These elements have now been strengthened at the expense of other types of rehabilitative services such as education and basic social welfare support (Findlay 2004b). The ease with which needs can be turned into risk (Hannah Moffatt 2005) is demonstrated by the newly reinvigorated rehabilitative paradigms.

The strategic alignment of risk with narrowly defined intervenable needs contributes to the production of a transformative risk subject, who unlike the "fixed or static risk subject" is amenable to targeted therapeutic interventions. Newly formed risk/needs categorisations and subsequent management strategies give rise to a new politics of punishment, in which different risk/needs groupings compete for limited resources (Hannah Moffatt 2005, p. 31).

The "risk/needs" principle, panacea for "nothing works", has permeated correctional programming. The rise of the meta-analysis in the evaluation of psychological programming (Andrews et al. 1990) has allowed for the assertion that programs targeted to risk/needs are more successful at reducing recidivism, thus allowing for resources to be targeted and unnecessary expenditure limited. The resurgence of programmes arising from the "risk, needs, responsivity" paradigm has provided the link to another technology of control, treatment programmes. The logical imperative of risk-adverse rehabilitationism—the ability of professional groups to produce the goods in terms of written assessments and programmes which can be evaluated in terms of the recidivism paradigm—has created an enhanced role for these groups in criminal justice processes. Assessment and program delivery become ends in themselves, creating a self-referential legitimacy. As Gottfredson and Moriarty have pointed out:

> [u]sing risk assessment tools to predict treatment success or failure is a misapplication of the tool... properly constructed needs assessment

> devices...would prove to have greater validity (Gottfredson and Moriarty 2006, p. 192).

The view of reduction of offending as a scientific project (Sotiri 2003, p. 424) sits well with the "therapeutic bent" of the NSW Department and their obsession "with programs aimed at changing people" (Sotiri 2003, p. 425). The obvious congruence between this scientific approach and the need to provide evidence of efficacy as part of the managerialist imperative has assisted the rise of the cognitive behavioural programme, which by its nature is purportedly value neutral, short term, based on concrete behavioural gaols and emphasising the responsibility of the individual to rehabilitate himself.

Duguid, explaining the attractiveness of the cognitive skills model to prison authorities, points out the similarities to the medical model, in which "criminal tendencies are like a cancer" (Duguid 2000, p. 194). These programmes are able to provide evaluation data which assist the Department to manage the political imperatives of populist crime governance: "they (crimogenic need related programs) differ from past programs not only in terms of their claims to scientific objectivity but also in their ability to be empirically measured" (Sotiri 2003, p. 371). The attraction of such programmes in an era of budgetary restraint is that they "looked simple to use, relied on existing corrections staff, (were) modularised so that (they) could be shaped to almost any context and (they) had a solid research base". (Duguid 2000, p. 201) The result was what Duguid calls a "marketing maelstrom" as "cog skills" were imported around the world (Duguid 2000, p. 201). Programmes focusing on "crimogenic need" are therefore meant to be tightly focused only on those factors proven to be connected with the likelihood of recidivism.

The equation of rehabilitation with the performance and completion of psychologically based programmes based on risk assessment narrows and modifies the original concept of rehabilitation (Findlay 2004a, b). Roundly condemning "psychological determinism" in correctional programming in NSW, Findlay also states regarding risk assessment:

> If this diagnostic capacity (to identify future risk) was routinely available, and it is not, then such predictive wisdom would be more economically applied to crime prevention than correctional remedies" (Findlay 2004a, p. 61).

A concern is the fact that the treatment body may find it difficult to maintain appropriate "role boundaries" (Vess and Eccleston 2009, p. 281) as experts maintain dual roles in the context of their status as witnesses, either for the defence or for the prosecution. Another salient point is that there may be "a lack of risk assessment expertise available to offenders which is independent of the government department seeking a judicial decision against them" (Vess and Eccleston 2009, p. 281). Coupled with the possible tendency adverted to by Murphy and Whitty (2007) for lawyers not to challenge actuarially based risk evidence, there is a clear danger of prejudice to a person subject to these procedures.

Easton and Piper note, "[t]he conflation of risk management with rehabilitation conceptualises rehabilitation in a much narrower way" (Easton and Piper 2008, p. 415). Findlay agrees:

> [i]n the current "rebirth"' of the prison there has been a move away from basic, egalitarian inmate programs in preference for elite cognitive therapies. This shift has been justified, it is argued, by the misguided belief that prisoners with the greatest risk of serious re-offending can be identified, and on them limited correctional resources should be concentrated. In addition, this is again incorrectly supported by the conviction that, for these few inmates, their recidivism rates can be radically decreased through psychological intervention in gaol (Findlay 2004b, p. 1).

The growth of psychological power within prisons (Crewe 2009 Ch.4, p. 24) broadens and deepens the type of scrutiny of prisoners. Coupled with the "power of the pen", psychological assessments are often determinative of the prisoner's progression and ultimate release. As Crewe points out, "The consequences of rehabilitative deficiencies fell onto prisoners, who were held responsible for their "risk factors" whether or not means were available to address them." (Crewe Ch. 4, p. 28)

The way that risk can blend with other technologies of control leads to different practical applications when viewed through the lens of the kind of managerialism which pervades many correctional systems, including NSW. Risk has become a way of limiting expenditure on resources inside prisons, for now programmes only have to be provided to those at high risk of re-offending. Recourse to such quasi-scientific justifications allows for the development of broadly based programmes to "address" the risk. The fiscal advantages of targeting services and programmes are that expenditure can be limited to a relatively small group of prisoners.

While there is no necessary philosophical connection between the kind of cognitive behavioural programmes currently popular in corrections, and the risk paradigm, there is no doubt that the fit between risk assessment and the "magic bullet" approach to programming is a good one. Programmes purporting to provide empirical evidence of an effect on recidivism are clearly useful for correctional managers. The practical consequences of the adoption of the risk/needs model in the context of managerialism and management of scarce resources is that CSNSW have a quasi-scientific rationale for not providing resources to short-term or low-risk prisoners. Explicit recognition of this is found in the 2010/2011 Annual Report:

> a welcome emphasis on community corrections and diversionary programs ... has already seen resources such as psychologists and some programs moved from inside correctional centres out in the community (CSNSW Annual Report 2010/11, Commissioner's Foreword, p. 87).

Why Me?

The strict and formulaic reliance on risk assessments means that for many prisoners the nature of the index offence is of paramount importance. Behaviour in custody is a secondary consideration and any gains made by the prisoner in terms of improvements in behaviour and classification can be undone.

> I've seen a lot of people that are very violent you know what I mean and they don't have to do a program, they don't have to do anything and they still get parole (Van).

This young man was convicted of a serious violent offence that took place in an atmosphere of group violence that at the time was characterised as ethnically motivated. His narrative of the offence differed significantly from the official narrative and numerous complicating aspects including successful appeals by co-offenders left him with significant resentment at how he had been characterised. Non-violent throughout his sentence of ten years, he was still required to complete an intensive programme near to the end of his sentence, delaying and possibly precluding access to work release which he had been working towards.

> LSIR instruments may cover 5-6 domains and the department only responds to 1 or 2. . . . (there is a) risk that those resources will not be available when risk is identified." Interviewer "Much work on that?" CSNSW: "Thousands of LSIRS waiting to be processed. I worry about overriding, skewed data-more guys high risk than you would expect- fear that he will reoffend—and you're the one who said he was low risk. The culture here leads to this (Australian Prisons Project Interview, programme manager).

That the culture within CSNSW may lead to overrides by workers fearful of repercussions lends legitimacy to questions about the reliance on actuarial methods. Apart from the obvious and severe consequences for the wrongly classified prisoners this tendency has dire consequences for the ability of the system to adequately deal with those at sufficiently high risk of re-offending to warrant therapeutic intervention. Also, such programme involvement in lower risk offenders may actually have criminogenic consequences.

Rehabilitation as Certificate Collection—the "Tick and Flick"

The term "tick and flick" was used by one of the programme managers to refer to the short-term programmes, mainly drug and alcohol, (SMART in particular) offered by the Department. The disparaging tone of this comment is reflected by some of the interviews with prisoners who had completed large numbers of programmes with questionable benefits and little evidence of their efficacy.

> I've done about 20–25 (programs) yeah I've got about 20–25 certificates. So I've got a few. But they never really address my issues (Mick).

Collection of certificates is commonly believed by prisoners to impress the Parole Authority and is often seen as an end in itself. This prisoner, having served a number of sentences, expressed the futility of certificate collection and the imperative to keep doing programmes that were not really relevant to his offending.

If the Offence Was Drugs, Then You Must Be a Junkie

When the only programmes available are offence-specific there are significant numbers of prisoners who will not fit the criteria.

> When you're in gaol everyone just assumes that you're a junkie. Um and I've been mainly doing this program "Getting Smart". And, um I told them 'I'll tell you straight up—I've done a 100 programs and they're all the same or similar to this one.' And they said 'well if you want your classo you've got to do it.' I said "righto" and I went straight into class! (Mick).

Mick's comments reflect the pragmatic approach (Crewe 2009) taken by some prisoners particularly nearing the end of the minimum term. While Crewe's taxonomy of prisoner coping styles is a useful tool for understanding prisoner responses, it must be recognised that a change in coping styles can be expected at different stages in the sentence. When release becomes a reality for the prisoner adherence to personal beliefs and values may be sacrificed to a pragmatic response to institutional imperatives. Conversely, formerly compliant prisoners like Kevin (see below) often become frustrated by the illogical demands of risk-reliant programming and become disengaged and angry. Apart from the obvious waste of resources in badly targeted programming, the opportunity cost for the individual prisoner is potentially high.

A constant theme was the repetitiveness of many programmes. Prisoners often repeated programmes as if the aim was possession of as many certificates as possible (i.e. rehabilitation as certificate collection).

> And so I um did drug and alcohol so they brought it down to the wing to make—to get out of the cell a bit longer." Interviewer: "So you don't think you necessarily might have needed it?" Prisoner: "No I've never drunk, never taken drugs . . . I also did Anger Management to make up the numbers (Leslie).

In order to fill in time (7 years) before he was able to complete the sex offender's programme, this prisoner completed numerous short courses unrelated to his offending.

The often nonsensical outcome of the application of categorical sorting of prisoners on the basis of offences is brought into sharp relief in the case of people convicted of drug offences but with no drug and alcohol problems. One prisoner had served several sentences and had participated in a large number of treatment programmes, none of which had addressed what he saw as the precursor to his criminal behaviour, his experiences of neglect and abuse as a child. He was not a problematic substance abuser, and had committed the offences (allegedly) for pure financial gain. These prisoners pose a problem for correctional staff in the sense that that they do not fit the prevailing paradigm, and, although assessed as "high risk" there are simply no programmes available for them to reduce "their" risk. The absence of individually structured rehabilitative programmes leads to prisoners completing large numbers of possibly irrelevant programmes just to comply with requirements for classification or parole.

The Long and Winding Road—One Prisoner's Account

> Long termers lose a significant amount (when in programs) . . . takes them away from employment, remote gaols, hardship inflicted—re-entry takes more effort (Australian Prisons Project interview, programme manager).

What happens when a prisoner, although well behaved and trusted in their local environment nevertheless belongs to a category of prisoner where the risk imperative is heightened? or when the prisoner's ideas of what will assist them to live a "good life" conflicts with risk-based imperatives to complete programmes in custody prior to release? Does the evidence warrant such derailment from activities such as education and employment that have proven positive rehabilitative effects? The experience of the prisoners interviewed for this book seems to indicate that timing is everything when it comes to access to programmes and services to assist in rehabilitation. Much distress and confusion occurs at the beginning of the sentence, then a period of nothingness, then a frenzy of activity around parole.

Too little, too late is a common theme—as is the rigid application of the risk/needs paradigm in relation to certain categories of offenders. To demand that a prisoner who has managed to get himself into a relatively trusted position within an institution, near the end of his sentence voluntarily regress in classification to complete a programme, is to ignore the importance of the recruitment of the prisoner into his own redemption. The reduction of the period of supervised integration into the outside world in favour of intensive offence-specific programming appears to fly in the face of evidence as to "what works" in reducing re-offending. This is an excellent example of the way that mundane managerial factors can sabotage the fulfilment of the aims of sentencing. Proper sentence management of long-term prisoners in terms of the prevailing paradigm popular with the Parole Authority of NSW involves staged release with plenty of time for the prisoner to adjust and for authorities to monitor his response. This is often not possible with the privileging of offence-specific programming, delivered in a rushed way at the end of the sentence.

The next extract highlights a number of issues faced by inmates of NSW prisons, high-level, risk-based decision-making, the conflict between different conceptions of rehabilitation (work *v* programming) long delays caused by inefficient bureaucratic systems and the need for prisoners to be proactive in their sentence management. The similarity to the prisoners in Crewe's study is unmistakeable—they spoke of "hoops, hurdles and obstacles—a sense that the prison was deliberately making it hard for them"

(Crewe, Ch. 4, p. 18). In NSW this highly centralised power is heightened with certain categories of prisoner, mostly where there is a possibility of public or media interest. It is arguable that relative rarity of violence in NSW makes risk-averse decision-making far more likely as the smaller numbers cause a more concentrated focus.

A complicating factor—although not unusual—was that initially, until he began to request information about the reasons for refusal, Kevin says he was not made aware that he was required to complete a drug programme, this did not arise until he applied for a reduction in classification two years before the end of his minimum sentence. It is interesting to note that, despite the absence of an appeal process, a personal appeal to the relevant senior bureaucrat resulted in action. It is also interesting to note the control at very senior levels at which decision making about certain types of offenders occurs.

Interviewer: "So where you were, at Prison A you were recommended a C3?" Prisoner: "Yeah . . . I got knocked back . . . And I appealed the decision." Interviewer: "How did you do that?" Prisoner: "Um I wrote to the Director of Classification and I put my case to him and I said, you know, it's nice throwing me out of goal after years in goal and all my history with no money basically . . . Three times they recommended me . . . in two years . . . Come back C3 Ngara Ngura (they said) (drug program at Long Bay) and I said 'Waste of time.' . . . You know, I don't need to address any drug issues I've got the history, the runs on the board all the clean urines."

Interviewer: "Was it SORC that was pushing the Ngara Ngura option ?" Prisoner: "Yeah, oh, PRLC" (Pre Release Leave Committee -a division of SORC). Interviewer: "And how long had you done in gaol by that point?" Prisoner: "5 years, well I've done 7 now. Anyhow, I've had no charges, no dirty urines or anything like that." Interviewer: "And you were in a really trusted job weren't you?" Prisoner: "Yeah—no one could understand why I kept getting knocked back."

Interviewer: "Do you know why?" Prisoner: "No, no I got . . . I applied for the last lot of information from PRLC under Freedom of information . . . And I found out it was the Assistant

Commissioner that was knocking me back... SORC had recommended it, PRLC recommended it but the Assistant Commissioner was saying no." Interviewer: "So it goes right up to that level?" Prisoner: "And he kept saying no. He was the one who kept saying no and when H (another Assistant Commissioner) got involved apparently the Commissioner signed off on it. He pushed it all through, come back approved and I was out of there a week later"

Interviewer: "So you've been in work release all this year." Prisoner: "Yeah." Interviewer: "Doing what?" Prisoner: "Oh, I haven't been working... by the time they get you here and do a... so they've got to reassess you here for programs and all that stuff." Interviewer: "How long does that take?" Prisoner: "Weeks." Interviewer: "Really? Weeks?" Prisoner "Which I can't understand that process -and its gone as far as the Assistant Commissioner why in the world... Why does it have to come here and then be approved by the GM here? It seems senseless to me and I spent probably eight or nine weeks waiting for that to come through. Sitting in here doing nothing."

Interviewer: "So what do they have to do here?" Prisoner: "Well it has to go before the... they call it um giving you programs, so the case management here and the classification here make another... do another classification thing... and they make a recommendation whether you're approved for works release whether you're approved for day and weekend leave... TAFE and it goes to the GM and then goes to Regional and they've all got to sign it before it comes back through the process."

"And then you go for your job interview and, like, CCG (Community Compliance Group) they take you out for your interviews it then takes like, another, um, four weeks for the paperwork to be processed and the worst part about it is that a lot of blokes go for job interviews get jobs and employers want someone now they don't want somebody in 4 weeks time... so a lot of bloke will get jobs and by the time the paper work's put through the job is gone."

Interviewer: "So you go for the job what do they have to do after that?" Prisoner "Well they have to do an assessment of the company, they have to check them out . . . um you have to have two sponsors at your work location so they've got check them out, make sure they've got no criminal history. Interviewer: "So how long did that all take?" Prisoner: "Well, six weeks."

" . . . Another problem is that—normally anyone who gets employed you've sort of got have a minimum 3 months left . . . so unless you've got a minimum of the 3 months left a lot of employment agencies won't take you on because they don't get anything out of it . . . I was just under the three months" (Kevin).

7.5 Conclusion

The experiences of these prisoners demonstrate that considerable barriers exist to the fulfilment of rehabilitation as an aim of sentencing. These barriers often arise from the way that CSNSW organises itself and the managerial imperatives and priorities that shape the sentence. In the case of the serious offenders interviewed, overly centralised, risk-averse and agonisingly slow decision-making and implementation, poor timing, and overall a failure to communicate with prisoners about a plan for their rehabilitation characterised the responses. Drafting prisoners into their own redemption requires an understanding of the processes and relationships that facilitate their understanding and response to their imprisonment.

Rehabilitation in NSW prisons has, in official discourse and arguably in practice, become inextricably linked to dominant practices of actuarial risk assessment. While factors peculiar to NSW criminal justice—for example, the close relationship between psychiatry and criminal justice—have seen the retention of significant faith in clinical judgment in the courts, the prisons have embraced the technology of risk as it relates to the delivery of services to prisoners. NSW, lacking the same respect for the professional judgment of social workers in legal matters evident in the UK and relying more heavily on psychologists, has arguably a weaker base for the retention of the broader view of rehabilitation evident in the UK.

Coupled with the managerialist tendencies examined in Chap. 5, the form of rehabilitation currently practised bears little resemblance to those factors which prisoners believe will help them. Exemplifying Crewe's "soft power" (Crewe 2009 Ch. 4, p. 37), the psychological "habitus" is felt by prisoners as an ever-present, totalising discourse that can be used against them throughout their sentence. The constant need to self-regulate, to adhere to the official narrative both of their crimes and of their lives (Crewe, Ch. 4, p. 37) constitutes, for Crewe, a new "pain" of imprisonment, one characterised by "tightness".... the grip exercised by "soft power" (Crewe, p. 37). Constant judgment was felt as punishment (Drake 2012, p. 100)

In any practical sense, quite apart from considerations of fairness and equity, the need to draft prisoners into their own redemption clearly requires an appreciation of the way that they conceive of and experience the sentence. The minutiae of prison life as illustrated in previous chapters often becomes what the sentence is about. Overarching themes of redemption and rehabilitation are subsumed into the managerial apparatus of the prison until close to the end of the sentence when accountability for the performance of the subjective expectations of the sentence becomes the dominant paradigm.

8

Conclusion

The central challenge for this book has been to identify and analyse the relationship between legal sentencing and the lived experience of the sentence. Trying to make sense of "what prison is like" as well as "what it is for" (Crewe, 2009 Ch. 9:15) the research and theoretical propositions relate two different macro spheres of operation (courts and prisons) while simultaneously moving between the general and the specific in each man's experience.

In order to avoid abstracting the lived sentences from the socio-political context in which they are experienced, Chap. 2 attempts to ground these accounts with an illustration of the complex currents of criminal justice in NSW over the past 40 years. Rapid and substantial change in sentencing, bail and parole legislation has been accompanied by other developments, usually on the fringes of criminal justice, which emphasise notions of restoration and accountability. Alongside this, however, has been a perceptible move towards more punitive criminal justice dispositions and longer sentences.

It is arguable that, as the trial becomes relegated to the very small minority of criminal matters the sentencing process has become the focus of legal attention in NSW. Its prominence as the dominant paradigm in

M. Hall, *The Lived Sentence*, Palgrave Studies in Prisons and Penology, DOI 10.1007/978-3-319-45038-4_8

the court system given the high rates of pleas of guilty has been demonstrated by the intensity of attention shown by the flurry of legislative activity in NSW over the past 40 years (as outlined in Chap. 2). The importance of an examination of the context in which the sentence is experienced (Chaps. 2 and 3) is highlighted. Without this focus, the individual is de-contextualised and the sentence is uncoupled from its historical and socio-political habitus.

There has been a significant absence of attention to the subjective aspects of sentencing and imprisonment both in traditional legal accounts of sentencing and even in more broad ranging socio-logical and socio-legal theories of penality. As Crewe puts it "Prisoners as people become increasingly invisible in debates about imprisonment" (Crewe Ch. 9, p. 14). This leaves not only an empirical gap, in that the actions and reactions of the subjects of criminal justice processing are absent from evaluation studies but further, a significant theoretical aspect of the operation of penality is subsequently omitted or inadequately theorised.

> [t]here is a significant disjuncture between the symbolic delivery of punishment by a long prison sentence, the experience of serving such a sentence and the question of its utility in making amends for harm or preparing an individual for their return to society. It is thus argued that neither victim nor prisoner needs are fully addressed . . . (Drake, 2012: 75)

It is this disjuncture with which this book is concerned: the gap between legal sentencing and the lived sentence. The complexity in the forms of governance in the prison (where, for example, movements can be used as a disciplinary mechanism and classification can preclude rehabilitation) necessitates a careful untangling of the various threads of prison experience. Crewe's insights into the way the modern prison exercises power emphasises the way that "power can operate at a distance" (Crewe Ch. 9: 5). What he calls "soft power" (p. 7) can harden and become "deeper and heavier" prisoners describing "less in terms of weight than tightness". "Instead of brutalizing . . . it grips, harnesses and appropriates . . . " (Crewe, Ch. 9, p. 7).

A new basis for theorising sentencing is proposed in this book. The theoretical and methodological imperative to consider the subjective aspects of sentencing by talking to prisoners is highlighted. The expectation that the prisoner undergo internal transformation, performed appropriately, is linked to the earlier discussion of remorse, which, it is argued, persists throughout the sentence. The conflicting currents of penal managerialism, individualisation and risk are examined to show how the "devil is in the detail" in incarceration. The effect on legitimacy in the mind of the prisoner is foregrounded, with the additional insight that the internal transformation required of the prisoner requires a high level of acceptance of legitimacy. Overall, the idea that the "lived sentence" is ongoing and may persist far beyond incarceration is emphasised.

8.1 Theorising the Gap—Legal Sentencing and Penal Practices

No attempt has been made to produce a general account of penality nor to propose a direct connection between the legal habitus of sentencing with the managerialist, risk-focussed environment of corrections. Garland and Young's assertion that the socially mediated nature of the practices of imprisonment necessitates a detailing of the empirical practices that constitute the reality of the penal process informed the research. Further, an important insight is that the philosophy of punishment arises from and is mediated by these same social processes:

> [p]olitical, ideological, economic, legal and other social relations do not merely 'influence' or 'shape' or 'put pressure upon' penality they *operate through it* and are materially inscribed in its practices (Garland & Young, 1984: p. 21).

provides the basis upon which the theoretical perspectives have been developed.

Thus, while acknowledging the indirect nature of the relationship between the legal habitus and that of corrections, it is contended that, nevertheless, this perspective supports an analysis of these philosophical principles as they relate to real and concrete expectations by and of the prisoner that arise from them. Some assessment of the practical application of the sentence in the light of what is expected and as regards the recipient of the communication is therefore necessary. In other words, if we are to represent to sentenced people that sentencing is meant to achieve X, Y and Z, and that you, the sentenced person are meant to undertake F, G and H, it is incumbent on the system to ensure that first, this has been appreciated by the person and secondly that there are sufficient means to at least attempt to achieve these goals.

Even if not in a straightforward instrumental way, the philosophical concepts expressed in s3A of the *Crimes (Sentencing Procedure) Act* that arguably underpin our entire criminal justice system, inform and shape the types of actions and reactions which constitute the operationalised sentence. Just because the aims of sentencing are expressed in broad philosophical terms does not mean that real and concrete expectations of actions do not arise from them. It is easy to use the recognition of the separation of powers to justify the gap between the sentence in court and the sentence as served to excuse the system from accountability, however, the failure of the prisoner to likewise respond is not similarly excused. The constant scrutiny and assessment of the prisoner and the importance of the assessment of compliance with sentence comments at the point of parole consideration clearly demonstrate the importance of these expectations.

The implication of this for the development of theories of penality is that, though they are socially mediated and constructed, it is not sufficient to dismiss the aims of sentencing as irrelevant to sentencing outcomes as they are applied to the prisoner. This is not a normative argument, in the sense that it would be argued that the aims of sentencing should guide the processes of imprisonment and punishment, but recognition of the reality of the situation for the sentenced person. Taking this point further, and again relying on an argument usually made in a normative way, if the assumption is made that sentencing is a communicative enterprise (Duff, 2004) then it is necessary to identify to whom and by whom the communication is made, what it means and what practical consequences arise from it.

Weaving through the lived sentence are expectations of the sentenced person—of behaviour, of attitude, and most problematically, of internal transformation. The theoretical argument in this book attempts to provide a new basis for enquiry into the connection between the aims of sentencing and the way the criminal justice system operates, in a way that resonates more strongly with the actual, the empirical and the experiential rather than merely the discursive. Punishment can never be a purely instrumental process of implementing the goals of sentencing. The subjective aspects of each person's reaction means that the aims of sentencing may never be able to be balanced or truly proportionate. This does not mean that we should stop asking what the prison is for, nor accept the high rates of failure to fulfil what it says it sets out to do. Of course, as Drake convincingly demonstrates the prison is "for" other things than the control of recalcitrant individuals (Drake, 2012).

While Garland and Young see sentencing as:

> part of an extended process which begins when police and prosecution authorities decide how to process suspects and which extends beyond the formal stage of sentencing at trial to such matters as the allocation of prisoners to different prisons and decisions on early release (Garland & Young, 1984: 26)

the argument in this book takes this conception one step further in that, rather than forming "part" of this extended process, sentencing is, to the sentenced person at least, a continuous process which can often extend beyond the period of formal contact with the criminal justice system.

> Sentencing has largely been treated as a static, unitary act of punishment, the validity of which can be judged the moment the gavel falls (Biersbach, 2012: 1748).

To speak of the utilitarian, forward reaching aims of sentencing in terms of static, event-based analysis is inconsistent with their very nature. The important aim of rehabilitation which, it has been argued, underpins many of the other aims, such as protection of the community, clearly requires a perspective which encompasses more than the single, static event of the court portion of the sentencing process. Even the so-called 'just deserts' aspects of sentencing such as punishment and denunciation persist in a temporal sense beyond the courtroom, despite the philosophical characterisation of them as 'backward looking'. Only by ignoring the reality of the sentenced person's experience can this perspective be sustained.

The artificial separation between the in-court phase of sentencing and the lived sentence derives from the influential habitus of the legal profession that dominates the criminal justice system. That this perspective does not accord with the reality of the lived sentence means that most theorising about sentencing occurs from a limited base. This distorts and undermines a proper examination of sentencing. When viewed through the lens of the sentence as served, the requirements of the sentence acquire a different flavour altogether and require consideration of all the elements of the sentence, philosophical, substantive and procedural.

The recognition of the increasingly porous nature of the prison in its extension into some communities (Berg & Delisi, 2006: 633) noted by Baldry et al. (2008), Peacock (2008) and Weelands (2009a) in Australia, has forced a re-examination of the previously accepted perceptions about the nature of prison culture and its aetiology. Sparks, Bottoms and Hay (1996) (in Neuber, 2011, p. 3) point out that the boundary between prison and outside is "far more permeable than it appears". The ways that criminal justice processes contribute to the "cycling in liminal space" of the intellectually disabled prisoners in Baldry's study (Baldry et al., 2008) demonstrates the fluidity and non-fixed nature of the boundaries of the prison. The emergence of COSPS, electronic monitoring and surveillance of parolees all extend the carceral net. These conceptions necessitate the development of new ways to describe and explain "prison culture" which transcend the artificial boundaries imposed by the organisational aspects of criminal justice. In common with the attempt in this book to link sentencing and imprisonment, there is an increasing emphasis on the need to disregard institutional boundaries when examining the ways that carceral power is manifested. Continuous and enduring in its effects, the sentence of imprisonment is a visceral, lived experience where, on a daily basis, the 'sentence as served' as opposed to the sentence as legal artefact, constitutes a myriad of interpersonal encounters and deficits.

In conceiving the sentence as a continuous, experiential and concrete collection of processes, attention must shift from the accepted habitus of law and corrections onto the reality of the nature of the experience of sentenced people. For the prisoner, it is nonsense to conceive of sentencing as a discrete process that is over when they leave the courtroom. In accepting these artificially drawn boundaries theorists and practitioners are faced with an incomplete basis upon which to theorise about penality or implement criminal justice policy. Bridging the gulf between the habitus of legal sentencing and the lived experience of the sentence can only be possible through attention to the experiences of sentenced and imprisoned people.

From both a theoretical and a methodological point of view, this book has demonstrated the necessity of attending to the experiences of prisoners themselves. Theoretically, the subjective expectations arising from sentencing require it. Methodologically, the only person who is part of all of the different processes is the sentenced person. While it may seem trite and stating the obvious to assert that the prisoner is the only common denominator in all the stages of criminal justice processing, from arrest to sentencing and beyond, this fact alone necessitates a different perspective when theorising about penal practices and punishment.

The emphasis on the minutiae of imprisonment reflects both the prisoners' emphasis on such matters and the theoretical importance of interrogating naturalised and "taken for granted" practices in criminal justice. The devil really is in the detail when it comes to incarceration. Recognition of the pains and frustrations of imprisonment embedded in the thousands of disciplinary processes embedded in every relationship and interaction in the correctional environment is necessary for a realistic appraisal of the sentence. The role of mundane, processual and procedural incidents of sentencing and imprisonment in the fulfilment of the aims of sentencing and indeed of punishment itself is highlighted by the requirement to respond to the sentence.

8.2 The Interviews

Subjective, Internalised, Transformative Sentences

Understandably, given the temporal nature of imprisonment 'listening for the number' in court was a primary concern of the prisoners interviewed. Time—the doing, wasting or killing of it, becomes the main game—"concern for time is 'a constant and painful state of mind'" (Galtung in Jewkes, 2002, p. 10). Despite the images of imprisonment as a kind of death, like entering a deep freeze, in NSW, significant expectations are placed on prisoners to perceive and act upon the sentence, to earn their release.[1]

What happens in the courtroom has a significant, if ill appreciated relationship with the serving of the sentence in the sense that the definition and narrative of the offence, the nature of the offender, what steps need to be taken to fulfil the strictures of the sentences, are all largely defined and confined by the legal process. Comments from the sentence will form a part of a 'checklist' for consideration of conditional liberty. This construction of reality confines and defines all of the subsequent behaviour and actions of and towards the prisoner.

Despite the importance of the remarks on sentence, the interviews demonstrate that, outside this preoccupation with the number of years to be served, very little of what is said by the judge is heard or understood by the subject of the sentence. What may be meant to be a ritual of condemnation tempered by the possibility of redemption can often be heard and experienced as condemnation alone. "I'm not that bad man" as Van says in Chap. 4. Drake (2012) recognises that words of censure and judgment can be difficult to hear. Opportunities for meaningful communication about the reason for the sentence, and what the prisoner must now do to make amends, are lost.

Despite this, many prisoners internalise a sense that more is required, both of them and of the correctional system than just 'doing time'. This becomes a reality when they are assessed for release on conditional liberty. Messages of punishment and condemnation alongside more compassionate messages of forgiveness and guidance are meant to be and often are taken seriously by the sentenced person. While the goals of sentencing are often lost in the 'it's only the number' mentality fostered by the legal process, the sentenced person feels, hears and experiences the effects of the sentence through the prism of their own experience.

[1] The total reversal of the paradigm of parole in NSW has been discussed earlier.

The misperception by the sentenced person that the sentence is about them and their needs, arguably perpetuated by a kind of "collusion" between the court and legal and ancillary professionals, such as probation officers, may militate against this process of acceptance (Indemauer, 1996, p. 144). The prisoner, subjected to correctional sorting and processing, may gradually realise that the risk/needs paradigm transforms needs into risk and then ignores those needs not directly connected to the risk of re-offending. Rehabilitation becomes as depersonalised as the other correctional processes experienced by the prisoner. The negative effect on the legitimacy of punishment of the uncoupling from its philosophical base (as discussed below) often contributes to confusion and negativity on the part of prisoners.

Transformation and Responsibilisation

The process of responsibilisation, which arises as part of the managerialist project and is also highly compatible with the modern psycho-correctional discourse, overlies the requirement of subjectivity/transformation. Responsibilisation, exemplified by the phrase uttered by a programme coordinator, much quoted by interviewees "put yourself in the driving seat", coupled with the often arbitrary, complex decision-making around correctional procedures such as classification, transfers and movements can lead to the prisoner's disengagement. Even those prisoners with a positive attitude to their rehabilitation are often alienated by the sometimes illogical and obtuse decisions made.

The requirement that the sentenced person undergo an inner, subjective process of transformation in order to comply with the sentence is the unspoken bedrock of the criminal justice and correctional industry.

If sentencing and imprisonment are part of a communicative enterprise that relies on "the offenders capacity to understand and respond to her imprisonment as punishment" (Duff in Weaver and Armstrong, 2011: 29), it makes sense to identify those factors and processes that have either a negative or a positive effect, down to the minutiae of prison life. If transformation is to be expected then consideration of the conditions under which this is expected to take place attains paramount importance.

The Other Side of Responsibilisation: Entitlement

As Donahue and Moore point out "clients are managed, to be sure, but they are also **entitled**, an important and underexplored feature of the managerial empowerment oriented enterprise" (Donahue & Moore, 2009: 319) (emphasis added). Responsibilisation produces expectation. For some prisoners reconciling the disparity between the expectations of what the sentence will be about with the reality of imprisonment is part of the process of adjustment to the pains of imprisonment.

The invitation to rehabilitate may also be taken seriously, leading to despair and often hostility when the means to achieve this are not available. "It's me needs, miss, me needs" (Jason). Sparks (2002: 552) has argued that prison conditions by definition restrict and limit choice on the part of both custodian and prisoner. The high level of discretion possessed by correctional authorities is compounded by confusing, unclear messages of compliance with the managerial and security needs of the prison complex. This leads to uncertainty when paradoxically juxtaposed with the language of self-reliance and self-actualisation. "Giving up rather than giving in" as Crewe says "liberates the individual from . . . the potential for disappointment" (Crewe, Ch. 9 p. 7).

Performance

Brownlee characterises the state's communication of censure to the offender as a "performative act" (Brownlee, 2011, p. 57). The requirements of the sentenced person arising from the sentencing process are not only internally transformative but also performative (Leader, 2007). Remorse and thus the potential for rehabilitation must be performed in a socially acceptable way both at the in-court phase of the sentence but also throughout the sentence and most especially at the point of consideration for parole (Hall & Rossamanith, 2015 forthcoming). To require that evidence be demonstrated of compliance with the strictures of the sentence raises even more questions—what is an appropriate demonstration or performance (Leader, 2008), or of internal transformation? It has been argued that remorse as a mitigating factor in sentencing persists as a primary concern throughout the sentence, manifesting in the requirements that the sentenced person demonstrate (or perhaps perform) that they feel denounced, punished, deterred, made accountable, recognise the harm done to the victim and, in the light of this, that they endeavour to rehabilitate. Tied up in the expression of remorse is acceptance of punishment and denunciation and perhaps an element of self-punishment and self-denunciation. Remorse, as an important element in the court stage of the sentencing process, continues as a central part of the expectation that the sentenced person will undergo and demonstrate certain internal transformations. As with many under-interrogated assumptions about human behaviour adopted in criminal courts, sentencing bodies largely act as if they understood what it means and how to discern it (Rossmanith, 2009, 2015 forthcoming). Rossmanith's recent interviews with judicial officers in NSW demonstrate the complexity of this assessment. Even if on some level the person knows that a credible performance of remorse is required of them, at the same time they must display it spontaneously. Those maintaining their innocence are completely outside the frame of reference of this idea of redemption.

Thus, although imprisonment remains disconnected in many ways from the legal processes of sentencing, this primary and fundamental requirement continues throughout. In the transformation of the legal into the lived sentence, the requirement that the sentenced person undergo an internal subjective process of transformation rests on their acceptance of the messages of reproach. The 'remorse' spoken of during the in-court sentencing phase and the ongoing demonstration of contrition is a continuous theme which connects the in-court sentencing process with the processes of assessment throughout the sentence but in particular prior to conditional release. Some of the interviews highlighted the fact that remorse may be a gradual process, the effect of being charged, held on remand and enduring a trial, for many precluded the acceptance of responsibility until sometime into the serving of the sentence. Despite the diversity in prisoner responses, the findings strongly support the contention that remorse or the lack of it is a central concern in the processes of sentencing and imprisonment, despite the lack of academic and legal attention.

The meaningfulness of the sentence requires not only clear communication about what is required and provision of the means to achieve it, but it also requires an internal commitment on the part of the sentenced person (Weaver & Armstrong, 2011). To be able to be "receptive to (the) reproach" requires a significant degree of internal acceptance. Furthermore, the response must also be appropriately demonstrated. Feigned remorse or redemption is perceived as unacceptable (Hawkins, 2003, p. 202). The charade is that, as much as it is expected, it is valued more highly if given freely rather than coerced or even required. This results in a complex situation for the punished person who must appear spontaneously remorseful.

The psychological implications of this doublethink are complex enough without then transposing this on the complex jurisprudential aspects of sentencing. The question of the level of understanding of and reaction to the messages of sentencing and punishment by the recipient is a crucial part of the recruitment of the individual into the project of redemption. This is an implicit and powerful requirement of our goals of sentencing. As Ward and Maruna point out, "If participants themselves do not engage with or commit themselves to an intervention the 'treatment' cannot really claim to be of much help" (Ward and Maruna, 2007, p. 19). Sentenced people must be convinced that their wrongdoing requires action on their part. Privileging the importance of the commitment of the participant to redemption requires attention to the subjectivity of the person, to their hopes, wishes and aspirations to live what Ward and Maruna call a "better life" (Ward & Maruna, 2007, p. 24).

It has been suggested in Chap. 3 that acceptance of the official narrative may arise as an obligation from the sentencing aim of 'accountability', the requirement that the sentenced person not only accept it but also be able to weave his own acceptable "redemption script" around it (Maruna, 2001, p. 87). Arguably, the recent introduction of restorative justice concepts adds yet another layer of expectation to the sentence; restoration may underpin some of the newer aims such as accountability and recognition of harm to the victim. Arising from this is the expectation that the prisoner will not only accept the official narrative but also take steps to demonstrate it. Likewise, the prisoner must demonstrate appropriately, recognition of harm to the victim. In this way, the often-conflicting aims of sentencing persist in the performance of the sentence. While being punished and denounced by imprisonment, the prisoner must also demonstrate that he has responded adequately to the other sentencing aims expressed by the judge.

The men interviewed demonstrated their confusion and lack of personal skills to successfully perform such a transformation, even it were possible in the environment of the prison. They must conform to the official narrative of both the offence and their own personal deficiencies, despite the difficulty of accepting such negative assessments of themselves. These struggles are pathologised instead of being viewed as a normal reaction to criticism of fundamental aspects of the self.

Legitimacy and the Aims of Sentencing

The disconnection of the sentencing process as legal artefact from the lived experience of the sentence, while dominant in both legal and correctional discourse, results in damage to the legitimacy of both systems, particularly from the point of view of the sentenced person.

> legitimacy . . . demands reference to standards that can be defended externally in moral and political argument. In the first instance this stipulates attention both to procedural and relational dimensions of prison regimes; in other words, to the recognition of prisoners in terms both of their citizenship and their ordinary humanity. More ultimately it also calls for accounts both of the justice of the laws and procedures which put them in prison, and of the rationales which claim to justify their confinement. (Sparks and Bottoms, 1996: 59)

These "rationales", it has been argued, are the aims of sentencing as applied in the individual case. The uncoupling of the theoretical basis of sentencing from its visceral manifestation has a negative effect on the legitimacy of our criminal justice system (Sparks & Bottoms, 1996). Prisons may "perform legitimacy but do not achieve justice" (Crewe, 2009, Ch. 9, p. 6). Relegating legal sentencing to static, event-based analysis misses the point of the sentence and may lead to a form of "imaginary sentencing" (Tombs, 2008). Conversely, the isolation of the sentence as served from the philosophical aims of sentencing may result in mere warehousing of prisoners. As Liebling points out, "questions of *exterior* legitimacy . . . can only be satisfactorily addressed if we develop a fuller understanding of the *interior* quality of the prison" (Liebling, 2004, p. xxi).

If legitimacy is important as regards the daily functions of the prison, it is even more important in relation to the expectations of personal transformation implicit in the sentence. It seems clear that the type of internal transformation that arises from the aims of sentencing requires, or at least is greatly facilitated by, the commitment of the sentenced person. People need to be drafted into their own redemption. This requirement that the sentenced person accepts the official narrative, both of the offence and of himself is taken for granted, but arguably requires a high level of insight and personal acceptance. It could be argued that the adversarial legal process itself militates against such an acceptance, with its emphasis on contestation. To drop this stance and accept negative assessments of character and morality while complying with confusing prison regimes is often a bridge too far for the prisoner.

8.3 The Impact of Risk Focused Managerialism—Imaginary Sentences?

Examination of the increasing dominance of actuarial calculations of risk, introduced in Chap. 2 as an important development in the socio-political history of NSW criminal justice, is continued in Chap. 3 in relation to sentencing. These discussions form the basis for further theorising about the new form of "rehabilitation" which has resulted in Chap. 7. In an era of growth in prison numbers, including huge rises in unsentenced prisoners, risk as it applies to security concerns and the exigencies of managerial correctionalism overrides the need for sentence and pre-release planning (Drake, 2012). Action is taken in arbitrary and counterproductive ways with little concern to the needs of the prisoner to fulfil the strictures of the sentence until the last 6 months before the prisoners EPRD.[2] The concept of "imaginary penalities" as expounded by Carlen (2008) and by Tombs (2008) in relation to sentencing provided an important theoretical underpinning to the main contentions of this book. The prisoners interviewed reported experiences which uncannily resonated with this conception, both in relation to their in-court experience, where Tombs' insights into sentencing were particularly apposite, and in their experience of imprisonment, where the 'imaginary sentence' is the one being constituted and thereafter examined by the Parole Authority.

The disconnection of the aims of sentencing from the sentence can lead to the "dystopian vision" counselled against by Zedner (2002) and Brown (2005), in action. Correctional managerialism on its own becomes empty and meaningless without a clear vision of the aims of the sentence and what it entails for both the sentenced person and the state. The interview data tends to indicate that much of the communication at sentence, flawed though it is, becomes subverted through the process of correctional managerialism and risk-averse decision making into a distorted version of rehabilitation. Programme participation is the only way to reduce 'risk' and gain conditional liberty, as Crewe explains:

> [t]his is a particular version of rehabilitation. It has authoritarian as well as humanitarian features. It is more paternalistic than maternalistic... It eschew conventional methods of paternal power... It polices indirectly and anonymously (Crewe, 2009, Ch. 9, p. 2).

The coexistence of the rhetoric of rehabilitation with the reality of risk-averse and cost-conscious correctionalism has resulted in a form of 'rehabilitation' privileging completion of cognitive behavioural programmes. These factors, allied with a strengthened role for psychologists in corrections following their predominance of the 'what works' movement, have

[2] The CSNSW has recently created an assessment unit for "serious offenders". It is hoped that some evaluation of this service will occur (including interviews with prisoners) to assess whether there has been any improvement in this regard.

further strengthened this dominance.[3] Conflicts between other no less legitimate paths to rehabilitation (e.g. work) are arguably compromised by the predominance of psychological programming. Concomitantly, the "prisoner as client" (Donahue & Moore, 2009) is responsibilised for his or her own redemption through the managerial actuarialism of the modern correctional project (Donahue & Moore, 2009: 324). The mismatch between the expectation of personal agency and the ability of the individual to negotiate the prison system with its lack of choice and arbitrariness contributes to the pains of imprisonment and undermines legitimacy.

It has been demonstrated (in Chap. 3) that, while a varied approach is evident in the practice of judges, risk assessment dominates correctional practices. The pervasive nature of the use of these instruments may herald an increased role in criminal justice generally. For correctional staff the sentence is all about the reality of managing bodies. Shot through with conceptions of correctional managerialism, risk, and new conceptions of rehabilitation, transformation and redemption, correctional management must also take place in a context of severe budgetary constraints. Chapter 5 examines this managerial apparatus, what Drake calls "the bulky machinery" of the modern prison (Drake, 2012) and the effect on the lived sentence. The shaping of conceptions of risk by the correctional environment has in turn fed into new conceptions of risk and rehabilitation.

While insidious and highly relevant to the experiences of each of the men interviewed, risk as a paradigm of assessment and management of bodies operates in the shadows of criminal justice and in a somewhat uneasy alliance with the psychiatric medical model. Much of the data in the interviews is only obliquely about the risk of the individual, implicitly, the friendly tone of the interviews contained the assumption that the interview subjects were not 'risky people' that the interviewer would treat them as people of worth whose opinion was sought and valued. For professionals it is the language du jour, for the prisoner, another imposed categorisation which must be negotiated. As the prisoner is subject to a range of sorting procedures, it may well blend into the

[3] It is not suggested that these programmes may not be beneficial for some prisoners.

background until parole, when risk of re-offending becomes of primary concern to the authorities. Frustration was expressed about the static nature of risk, particularly for sex offenders. Despite compliance with the strictures of the sentence, often nothing could be done to reduce the perception of risk. This sense of powerlessness seemed to conflict with the expectation of some prisoners that rehabilitation would be rewarded by redemption. Hence, the attribution of risk status can represent a significant and permanent barrier to redemption.

8.4 Conclusion: The Lived Sentence as Communication: The Devil in the Detail

The contention that punishment and therefore sentencing has meaning that reflects the goals of sentencing is a more controversial proposition than it may appear. The perception that sentencing is only or primarily what happens in the courtroom is constantly perpetuated by legal analysis. For sentencing to have meaning beyond the symbolic, performative and expressive pronouncements of the courtroom, it makes sense that its effect should flow through the operationalisation of the words spoken by the judge into the serving of the sentence, and sometimes beyond. Implicit in the processes and discourses of sentencing, correctionalism and parole is the proposition that sentencing involves 'more than a number', more than a courtroom pronouncement and that its effect continues outside the courtroom. While it is clear that the punitive and denunciatory aspects of imprisonment continue sometimes far beyond the sentence, it appears much less clear that the more positive rehabilitative aspects of the sentence do the same.

The logical consequence of the acknowledgement of this is a different theoretical focus on the sentence as a lived, visceral experience, continuous and containing prescriptions for action on the part of both the sentenced person and the state. Woven together in the experience of living the sentence are the experiences of being sentenced, of being denounced, punished and told to rehabilitate. All of this is to be assessed by way of a set of actuarial practices that have distorted the basic approach of rehabilitation to become an exercise in risk management.

Discretionary decision-making involving moral judgments about remorse and the willingness to make amends still operates in the shadows of this scientific approach to risk.

The manifold diverse systems of governance that characterise the prison have fostered the formation of new structures of power and legitimacy which, while "softer" than the old regimes of physical punishment, are no less confining and controlling. (Crewe, 2009, Ch. 9, p. 4) Prisoner responses demonstrate that every interaction in prison is heavy with meaning. Prisoners must know without being told clearly what they must do or say in order to demonstrate their eligibility for conditional liberty or release. If they have failed to meet expectations before as in the case of the 40% of prisoners who have been there before, then the screws are tightened still more, the bar raised still higher.

This book has sought to demonstrate that the divergence between the contradictory official discourses and the inner experience of the punished person not only exists but is important. The sentence contains requirements that go far beyond the confines of the courtroom and which need to be made explicit and communicated clearly. The effect of the disconnection between the aims of sentencing is a reduction in the legitimacy of sentencing from the perspective of the prisoner. This has a clear detrimental effect on the performance of the sentence and thus its efficacy in carrying out these aims.

Bibliography

Cases

Attorney General's Application under s37 of the Crimes (Sentencing Procedure) Act 1999 (No 2 of 2002) (2003)137 A Crim R 196
Bugmy v The Queen (1990) 169 CLR 525
Bugmy v The Queen (2013) HCA 37
Butters v *The Queen* (2010) NSWCCA 1
Cornwall v NSW (2007) NSW CA 374
Curtis v The Queen (2007) NSWCCA 11
Fardon v The Queen (2003) 223 CLR 575
Featherstone v The Queen (2008) NSW CCA71
Kable v Director of Public Prosecutions (NSW) (1996) 189 CLR 51
Knight v The Queen (2006) NSWCCA 292
Lyons v The Queen (1987) 2 SCR 309
McGarry v Western Australia (2005) 31 WAR 69
Miles v The Queen (2002) NSWCCA 276 2002/199
New South Wales v Tillman (2007) NSWSC 605
New South Wales v Davis (2008) NSWSC 862
Power v The Queen (1974) 131 CLR 623
R v Benbrika & Ors (Ruling No 20) [2008] VSC 80
R v Curtis (2007) NSWCCA 11

M. Hall, *The Lived Sentence,* Palgrave Studies in Prisons and Penology, DOI 10.1007/978-3-319-45038-4

R v Dodd (1991) 57 A Crim R 349
R v Fernando (1992) 76 A Crim R 58
R v. Gladue (1999) 1 S.C.R. 688
R v Henry (1999) 46 NSWLR 346
R v Jurisic (1998) 45 NSWLR 209
R v Mailes (2004) 62 NSWLR 181
R v M.A.K., R v M.S.K. (2006) NSWCCA 381
R v Molina (1984) 13 A Crim R 76 at 77
R v Previtera (1997) 94 A Crim R 76
R v Ponfield (1999) 48 NSWLR 327
R v Robinson (2002) NSWCCA 359
R v Schlenert (2008) NSWCCA 481
R v Scott (2005) NSWCCA 152
R v SLD (2002) NSWSC 758
R v Thomson; R v Houlton (2000) 49 NSWLR 383
R v Way (2004) 60 NSWLR 168
R v Wong (1999) 48 NSWLR 340
R v Lian (1990) 47 A Crim R 444
R v Way (2004) NSWCCA 60 NSWLR 168
Pfitzner v The Queen (2010) NSWCCA 314
Radford v Parole Board (2002) NSWCCA 70
Ryan v The Queen (2001) 206 CLR 267
Stricke v R (2007) NSWCCA
Winters v Attorney General of NSW (2008) NSWCCA 33
Veen v The Queen (No 2) (1988)164 CLR 465
Yardley v Betts (1979)1 A Crim R 329
Wong v The Queen; Leung v The Queen (2001) HCA 64

Legislation

Bail Act 1978 (NSW)
Bail Amendment (Repeat Offenders) Act 2002 (NSW) (repealed)
Crimes (Administration of Sentences) Act 1999 (NSW)
Crimes Amendment (Diminished Responsibility) Act 1997(NSW)
Crimes Amendment (Mandatory Life Sentences) Act 1996 (NSW)
Crimes (Criminal Organisations Control) Act 2009 (NSW)
Criminal Legislation Amendment Act 1996 (NSW)
Crimes Legislation Amendment (Sentencing) Act 1999 (NSW)

Crimes (Sentencing Procedure) Act 1999 (NSW)
Drug Court Act 1998 (NSW)
Mental Health Act 1990 (NSW) (repealed)
Mental Health (Criminal Procedure) Act 1990 (NSW)
Optional Protocol to the Convention against Torture and Other Cruel, Inhuman or Degrading Treatment or Punishment, opened for signature 4 February 2003, UN Doc A/RES/57/199 (entered into force 22 June 2006)
Probation and Parole Act 1983 (NSW) (repealed)
Sentencing Act 1989 (NSW) (repealed)
Victim Support and Rehabilitation Act 1996 (NSW) (repealed)
Victims Rights and Support Act 2013 (NSW)

Articles/Books/Reports

Aas, K. J. (2005). *Sentencing in the age of information—from Faust to Macintosh*, London: Glasshouse Press.

Ackland, R. (2005, April 22). Where pure evil is no longer the correct label. *Sydney Morning Herald*, 2005.

Alder, M., & Longhurst, B. (1994). *Discourse, power and justice: Towards a new sociology of imprisonment*, London: Routledge.

Andrews, D. A., Zinger, I., Hoge, R. D., Bonta, J., Gendreau, P., & Cullen, F. T. (1990). Does correctional treatment work? A clinically relevant and psychologically informed meta- analysis. *Criminology, 28*, 369–404.

Anthony, T. (2008) Late modern developments in sentencing practice for indigenous offenders: Beyond David Garland's framework. *Proceedings of the 2nd Critical Criminology Conference* (pp. 2–27). Sydney: Crime and Justice Research Network.

Arrigo, B., & Bullock, J. L. (2008). The psychological effects of solitary confinement on prisoners in Supermax units: Reviewing what we know and recommending what should change. *International Journal of Offender Therapy and Comparative Criminology, 52*(6), 622–640.

Armstrong, S., & McAra, L. (2006). *Perspectives on punishment—The contours of control.* New York: Oxford University Press.

Ashworth, A. (2010). *Sentencing and criminal justice.* Cambridge: Cambridge University Press.

Attorney General & Justice Department of NSW (2008, July 13,). Highest number of serious offenders in prison. *Ministerial Media Release.*

Audit Office of NSW (2006). "Prisoner Rehabilitation" (Auditor-General's Report of Performance Audit of the Department of Corrective Services) *Report No 151*, Sydney: Audit Office.

Australian Broadcasting Commission (2005). "Goulburn Supermax". *Four Corners 7/11/2005 reporter Chris Masters.*

Australian Broadcasting Commission (2010). *Lateline,* broadcast 2 March 2010.

Australian Bureau of Statistics (2011). *Prisoners in Australia.* Commonwealth of Australia, Canberra.

Australian Productivity Commission (2010). *Report on government services—corrective services.* Australian Government Printer.

Australian Government Productivity Commission (2011). *Report on government services.* Commonwealth of Australia, Canberra.

Bagaric, M. (2000). Incapacitation, deterrence and rehabilitation: Flawed ideals or appropriate sentencing goals. *Criminal Law Journal, 24,* 24–48.

Bagaric, M., & Amarasekara, K. (2003). Feeling sorry? Tell someone who cares: The irrelevance of remorse to sentencing. *Howard Journal, 40*(4), 364–376.

Baldry, E. (2004). Women in prison—25 years after Nagle. *Current Issues in Criminal Justice, 16,* 101–105.

Baldry, E. (2007). Throughcare: Making the policy a reality. *Keynote Address, The Reintegration Puzzle Conference,* Sydney, 7–8 May 2007.

Baldry, E. (2009). Prisons and vulnerable persons: Institutions and patriarchy. In M. Segrave (Ed.), *Proceedings of the Australian & New Zealand Critical Criminology Conference 2009.*

Baldry, E., Brown D., Mark Brown, Cunneen, C., Schwartz, M., & Steel, A. (2011). Imprisoning rationalities. *Australian and New Zealand Journal of Criminology, 44*(1), 24–40.

Baldry, E., Dowse, L., Snoyman, P., Clarence, M., & Webster, I. (2008). Reconceptualising disability in the criminal justice system: People with mental health disorders and cognitive disability. *Paper Presented at ANZSOC Annual Conference,* Canberra 26–28th, November 2008.

Baldry, E., McDonnell, D., Maplestone, P., & Peeters, M. (2006). Ex-prisoners, accommodation and the state: Post-release in Australia. *ANZ Journal of Criminology, 39*(1), 20–33.

Barnes, L. (2001). Protective custody and hardship in prison. *Sentencing Trends* 2, Judicial Commission of NSW.

Barnes, L. A., Poletti, P., & Potas, I. (2002). Sentencing dangerous drivers in New South Wales: Impact of the Jurisic guidelines on sentencing practice. *Research Monograph 21, Judicial Commission of NSW* Sydney.

Bennett, C. (2005). On the right to be punished: Responsibility and the critique of the rehabilitative ideal. *Criminal Justice Matters, 60*(1), 20–21.

Bennett, C. (2008). *The apology ritual: A philosophical theory of punishment.* Cambridge: University Press.

Berg, M. T., & Delisi, M. (2006). The correctional melting pot: Race, ethnicity, citizenship and prison violence. *Journal of Criminal Justice, l*(43), 621–634.

Bibas, S., & Bierschbach, R. (2004). Integrating remorse and apology into criminal procedure. *Yale Law Journal, 114*, 85–148.

Bierschbach, R. (2012). Proportionality and parole. *University of Pennsylvania Law Review, 160*, 1745–1788.

Bird, G. (2002). Prisoners of difference. In Brown & Wilkie (Eds.), *Prisoners as citizens.* pp. 65–76. Annandale: Federation Press.

Blagg, H. (2008). *Crime, aboriginality and the decolonisation of justice.* Annandale: Hawkins Press.

Booth, T. (2012). 'Cooling out' victims of crime: Managing victim participation in the sentencing process in a superior sentencing court. *The Australian and New Zealand Journal of Criminology, 45*(2), 214–230.

Bourdieu, P. (1980). *The logic of practice.* Palo Alto, California: Stanford University Press.

Bourdieu, P. (1990). *The logic of practice.* Stanford, California: Stanford University Press.

Bourgois, P., & Schonberg, J. (2009). *Righteous dope fiend.* Berkley: University of California Press.

Brignell, G. (2002). Bail: An examination of contemporary issues *Sentencing Trends and Issues* no. 24 Judicial Commission of NSW.

Bronitt, S. (2008). Balancing security and liberty: Critical perspectives on terrorism law reform. In M. Gani & P. Mathew (Eds.), *Fresh perspectives on the 'War on Terror'* ANU E-Press.

Brown, D. (1991). Battles around truth. A commentary on the *Sentencing Act* (1989). *Current Issues in Criminal Justice, 3*, 329.

Brown, D. (1995). Prison policy: Where to now? *Current Issues in Criminal Justice, 68*, 1995–1996.

Brown, D. (2002). The politics of law and order. *Law Society Journal, 67*, October 2002.

Brown, D. (2003). 'Contemporary comment: The Nagle Royal Commission 25 years on' Speech delivered to the NSW Council of Civil Liberties, NSW Parliament House, 5 September 2003. *Current issues in Criminal Justice, 15*, 170–175.

Brown, D. (2005). Continuity, rupture, or just more of the 'volatile and contradictory'? Glimpses of New South Wales penal practice behind and through the discursive. In J. Pratt, D. Brown, M. Brown, S. Hallsworth, & W. Morrison (Eds.), *The new punitiveness: trends, theories, perspectives.* London: Willan.

Brown, D. (2008). Current imprisonment rates, future forecasts and security issues—Implications for Australian prison systems. Paper delivered at *Correctional Security 2008 Conference*, Swissotel, Sydney, 18–19 August 2008.

Brown, D. (2009). Cruel, inhuman & degrading treatment: Prison inspections in Australia following the proposed ratification of OPCAT. *Human Rights Defender, 18*(3) pp. 9–12.

Brown, D., Kramer, H., & Quinn (1988). Women in prison—Task force reform. In M. Findlay & R. Hogg (Eds), *Understanding crime and criminal justice.* Melbourne: The Law Book Company Ltd.

Brown, D., & Quilter, J. (2014). Speaking too soon: The sabotage of bail reform in NSW. *International Journal of Crime, Justice and Social Democracy, 3*(3) 73–97.

Brown, D & Wilkie, M (2002). *Prisoners as Citizens: Human Rights in Australian Prisons.* Sydney: Federation Press.

Brown, D., & Wilkie, M. (2004). *Prisoners as citizens.* Sydney: Federation Press.

Brown, M. (2000). Risk in contemporary penal practice. In Mark Brown & J. Pratt (Eds.), *Dangerous offenders.* Abingdon, Oxon: Routledge.

Brown, M. (2008a). Risk, punishment and liberty. In C. Cunneen & T. Anthony (Eds.), *The Australasian critical criminology reader.* Sydney: Federation Press.

Brown, M. (2008b). Toward a new economy of suspended rights: Sex offenders and post-sentence confinement and control. School of Social and Political Science, Melbourne University, Australia.

Brown, Michelle. (2008). *The culture of punishment: Prison, society, spectacle.* New York: New York University Press.

Brownlee, K. (2011). The offenders' part in the dialogue. In R. Cruft, M. H. Kramer, & M. R. Reiff (Eds.), *Crime punishment and responsibility: The jurisprudence of Antony Duff.* Oxford: Oxford University Press.

Bull, M. (2010). *Punishment and sentencing: Risk, rehabilitation and restitution.* Australia: Oxford University Press.

Campbell, M. (1990). Changing horses. *Current Issues in Criminal Justice, 3*(3), 300.

Carlen, P. (Ed.) (2008). *Imaginary penalties.* Cullompton, Devon: Willan Publishing.

Carlton, B. (2007). *Imprisoning resistance: Life and death in an Australian Supermax*. Sydney Institute of Criminology, Series no 25.

Carrabine, E. (2005). Prison Riots, social order and the problems of legitimacy. *British Journal of Criminology, 45*, 896–913.

Chan, J. (1990). Decarceration and Imprisonment in New South Wales: A Historical Analysis of Early Release. *University of New South Wales Law Journal, 13*(2), 303–416.

Chan, J. (1992). *Doing less time: Penal reform in crisis.* Sydney: Institute of Criminology, Sydney University.

Cheliotis, L. (2006). How iron is the iron cage of the new penology? The role of human agency in the implementation of criminal justice policy. *Punishment and Society, 8*, 313–340.

Christenson, M (2009) *NSW Public Sector Accrual Accounting: Why did it happen and has it mattered?* Phd thesis, University of Adelaide.

Clark, J., Corben, S., Heggie, K., & Stone, L. (2006). Trends in escape from department of corrective services custody. *Department of Corrective Services Research Bulletin*. 22.

Clement, M., Schwarzfeld, M., & Thompson, M. (2011). *Addressing recidivism, crime, and corrections spending,* National Summit on Justice Reinvestment and Public Safety, Council of State Governments Justice Center, USA.

Clemmer, D. (1940, 1958) *The prison community.* New York: Holt, Rinehart &Winston.

Connell, R. W. (1995). *Masculinities.* St Leonards: Allen & Unwin.

Coulter, J. (1999). *Case management in New South Wales correctional centres.* Independent Commission against Corruption NSW.

Crewe, B. (2005). Prisoner society in the era of hard drugs. *Punishment and Society, 7*(4) pp. 457–481.

Crewe, B. (2006). The orientations of male prisoners towards female officers in an English prison. *Punishment and Society, 8*(4), 395–421.

Crewe, B. (2007). Power, adaptation and resistance in a late modern men's prison. *British Journal of Criminology, 47*, 256–275.

Crewe, B. (2009). *The prisoner society: Power, adaptation and social life in a English prison.* Oxford: Oxford Scholarship Online.

Crewe, B. (2011). Depth, weight, tightness: Revisiting the pains of imprisonment. *Punishment and Society, 13*(5), 509–529.

Crewe, B., & Maruna, S. (2006). Self-narratives and ethnographic fieldwork. In D. Hobbs, & R. Wright (Eds.) *The handbook of fieldwork*. New York: Sage.

Crouch, M., Gorta, A., Mahony, K., McLennan, K., Porritt, D., & Simmons, D. (1987). Bathurst Gaol evaluation study: Research findings January 1983-January 1986. *NSW Department of Corrective Services, Research Publication, 12.*

Cullen, B., Dowding, M., & Griffin, J. (1988). *Corrective services in New South Wales.* Australia: Law Book Company Limited.

Cunliffe, E. (2007). (This is not) a story: Using court records to construct judicial narratives. *Australian Feminist Law Journal, 27,* 71–95.

Cunneen, C. (1997). *The Royal Commission into Aboriginal Deaths in Custody: An overview of its establishment, findings and outcomes.* Aboriginal and Torres Strait Islander Commission, Canberra.

Cunneen, C. (2001). *Conflicts, Politics and Crime: Aboriginal Communities and Police.* Allen and Unwin Sydney.

Cunneen, C. (2004). Indigenous imprisonment since the Nagle report. In 'The Nagle report—25 years on Symposium'. *Current Issues in Criminal Justice, 16*(1), 98–101.

Cunneen et al. (2013). *Penal Culture and Hyper- Incarceration: The Revival of the Prison.* Routledge Abingdon, Oxon.

Cunneen, C., Baldry, E., Brown, D., Brown, M., Schwartz, M., and Steel, A. (2013). *Penal Culture and Hyper- Incarceration: The Revival of the Prison.* Oxon: Routledge Abingdon.

Dambach, M. (2008). Kariong Juvenile correctional centre: Countless contraventions of international law. *Australian Journal of Human Rights, 14*(1), 181.

Day, A., & Casey, S. (2009). Values in forensic and correctional psychology. *Aggression and Violent Behaviour, 14,* 232–238.

Day, A., & Ward, T. (2010). Offender rehabilitation as a value laden process. *International Journal of Offender Therapy and Comparative Criminology, 54,* 289–306.

De Graaff, P. (2005). Should education in corrections be publicly required and compulsory? In *Inside learning for outside living Conference.* Australian Corrections Education Association.

Department of Attorney General of NSW (2008). Highest number of serious offenders in prison. *Press Release 13 July 2008.*

Department of Corrective Services NSW (1968). *Annual report.* Sydney: NSW Government Printer.

Department of Health New South Wales (1983). *Inquiry into health services for the psychiatrically ill and developmentally disabled.* NSW Government.

Department of Corrective Services NSW (1974–1975). *Annual report.* Sydney: NSW Government Printer.

Department of Corrective Services NSW (1982–1983). *Annual report.* Sydney: NSW Government printer.

Department of Corrective Services NSW (2008). *Annual report.*

Department of Corrective Services NSW (2008). Summary of affairs. *Freedom of information government gazette NSW.* December 2008.

Department of Corrective Services NSW (2010). *Offender population report* 3 October 2010.

Department of Corrective Services NSW (2010). *Facts and figures.* 10th edition Corporate Research, Evaluation and Statistics

Donahue, E., & Moore, D. (2009). When is an offender not an offender? Power, the client and shifting penal subjectivities. *Punishment and Society, 11*(3), 319–336.

Donovan, B. Richters, J., & Butler, T. (2011). Prison sex, don't believe what you see on TV. *HIV Australia, 9*(1) pp. 12–14.

Douglas, H., & Touchie, J. (2006). Maximum security: Being in the belly of the beast. *Criminal Law Journal. 30*, 73.

Doyle, D. J., & Ogloff, J. R. P. (2009). Calling the tune without the music: A psycho legal analysis of Australia's post—Sentence legislation. *The Australian & New Zealand Journal of Criminology, 42*(2).

Drake, D. H. (2012). *Prisons, punishment and the pursuit of security.* UK: Palgrave Macmillan.

Duff, A. (2004). Punishment, retribution and communication. In G. Bruinsma, H. Elffers & J. W. Keijser (Eds.), *Punishment, places and perpetrators: developments in criminology and criminal justice research.* Cullompton, Devon: Willan.

Duff, R. A. (2005). Punishment and rehabilitation: Or punishment as rehabilitation. *Criminal Justice Matters, 60*(1), 18–19.

Duff, A., & Garland, D. (1994). *A reader on punishment.* Oxford: Oxford University Press.

Duguid, S. (2000). *Can prisons work?* Toronto: University of Toronto Press.

Eades, D. (2008). Telling and retelling your story in court: Questions, assumptions and intercultural implications. *Current Issues in Criminal Justice, 20*, 209.

Easton, S., & Piper, C. (2008). *Sentencing and punishment: The quest for justice.* Oxford: Oxford University Press.

Edney, R. (2002). Judicial deference to the expertise of correctional administrators—the implications for prisoner rights. *Australian Journal of Human Rights, 7*(1).

Edney, R., & Bagaric, M. (2007). *Australian sentencing: Principles and practice.* Cambridge: Cambridge University Press.

Ericson, R. V., & Baranek, P. (1982). *The ordering of justice: A study of accused persons as dependants in the criminal process.* Toronto: University of Toronto Press.

Feeley, M. (1979). *The process is the punishment: Handling cases in a lower criminal court.* New York: Russell Sage Foundation.

Fernandez, L. (2003). Fundamental aspects of sentencing. Legal Aid Commission of NSW.

Findlay, M. (2004a). The demise of corrections 15 years on: any hope for progressive punishment? *Current Issues in Criminal Justice, 16*, 57–70.

Findlay, M. (2004b). Prisons as progressive punishment: The state of corrective services. *Evatt Journal, 4*(3).

Findlay, M., & Henham, R. (2011). *Transforming international criminal justice: Retributive and restorative justice in the trial process.* Cullompton, Devon: Willan.

Finkelstein, C. (2004). A contractarian approach to punishment. In M. Golding & W. Anderson (Eds.) The *Blackwell guide to the philosophy of law and legal theory*. Wiley - Blackwell, Oxford.

Finnane, M., & Woodyatt, T. (2002). Not the king's enemies—Prisoners and their rights in Australian history. In D. Brown & M. Wilkie (Eds.), *Prisoners as citizens.* Annandale: Federation Press.

Fischer, B. (2003). Doing good with a vengeance. *Criminology and Criminal Justice, 3*(3), 227–248.

Foucault, M. (1977). *Discipline and punish: The birth of the prison.* New York: Pantheon Books.

Freiberg, A. (2000). Guerrillas in our midst? In M. Brown & J. Pratt (Eds.), *Dangerous offenders: Punishment and social order.* London: Routledge.

Frieberg, A. (2002). Affective vs. effective justice. *Punishment and Society, 3*(2).

Freiberg, A. (2005). Managerialism in Australian Criminal Justice: RIP for KPI's?' *Monah University Law Review, 31*(1).

Funnell, N. (2006). Where the norm is not the norm: The Department of Corrective Services and the Harm- U. *Alternative Law Journal,* 3(1), 2.

Garland, D. (1990). *Punishment and modern society: A study in social theory.* Oxford: Clarendon Press.

Garland, D. (2001). *The culture of control: Crime and social order in contemporary society.* Chicago: University of Chicago Press.

Garland, D. (2010). *Peculiar Institution: America's death penalty in an age of abolition.* Belknap Press, Harvard University Press, Cambridge Massachusetts.

Garland, D., & Young, P. (Eds.) (1984). *The power to punish.* Aldershot, Hants: Ashgate.

Garland, D., & Young, P. (1984b). Towards a social analysis of penality. In D. Garland & P. Young (Eds.), *The power to punish.* Aldershot, Hants: Ashgate.

Glaser, B. (2003). Therapeutic jurisprudence: An ethical paradigm for therapists in sex offender treatment programs. *Western Criminology Review, 4*(2), 143–154.

Glaser, B. (2009). Treaters or punishers? The ethical role of mental health clinicians in sex offender programs. *Aggression and Violent Behaviour, 14*(4), 248–255.

Goffman, E. (1961). *Asylums: Essays on the social situation of mental patients and other inmates.* Garden City New York: Anchor Books.

Goodman, P. (2008). It's just black, white or Hispanic: An observational study of radicalizing moves in California's segregated prison reception centers. *Law and Society Review, 42*(4), 735–770.

Gorta, A. (1982). Parole in NSW: Benefits, dangers & opportunities. *Research Bulletin* No. 10 NSW Department of Corrective Services.

Gorta, A., & Eyland, S. (1990). Truth in sentencing. Impact of the *Sentencing Act* (1989). *Research Publication* No. 22 NSW Department of Corrective Services.

Gottfredson, S. D., & Moriarty, L. J. (2006). Statistical risk assessment: Old problems and new applications. *Crime & Delinquency 52,* 178–200.

Goulding, D. (2007). *Recapturing freedom.* Annandale: Hawkins Press.

Grant, D. (1992). *Prisons: The continuing crisis in NSW.* Australia: Federation Press.

Gray, D. C. (2010). Punishment as suffering. *Vanderbilt Law Review, 63*(6), 1619.

Grewcock, M. (2009). Multiple punishments: The detention and removal of convicted non-citizens. *UNSW Law Research Paper 2009–41* Paper presented to the Australian and New Zealand Critical Criminology Conference Monash University July 2009.

Grey, G. C., & Salole, A. T. (2006). The local culture of punishment: An ethnography of criminal justice worker discourse. *British Journal of Criminology, 46,* 661–679.

Griffin, J. (1988). Probation and parole part II. In Cullen et al. (Eds.), *Corrective services in NSW,* Law Book Company of NSW.

Griffith, G., & Edwards, T. (2009). Privatisation of prisons update. *E-Brief* No 3/09 NSW Parliamentary Library Research Service.

Groves, M. (2002). The purpose and scope of prison discipline. *Criminal Law Journal, 26,* 10–27.

Grunseit, A., Forell, S., & McCarron, E. (2008). *Taking justice into custody: The legal needs of prisoners.* New South Wales: Law and Justice Foundation of New South Wales.

Hall, M., & Rossmanith, K. (2016). Imposed stories: Prisoner self narratives in the criminal justice system. *International Journal of Crime, Justice and Social Democracy, 5*(1), 38–51.

Halliday J., French, J., & Goodwin, C. (2001). *Making punishments work: Review of the sentencing framework for England and Wales.* London: Home Office.

Halsey, M. (2006). Assembling recidivism: The promise and contingencies of post release life. *Journal of Criminal Law and Criminology, 97*(4).

Halsey, M. (2007). On confinement: Resident and inmates perspectives on secure care and imprisonment. *Probation Journal, 54*(4), 338–367.

Halsey, M. (2008). Risking desistance. In P. Carlen (Eds.), *Imaginary penalities.* pp. 218–252. Cullompton, Devon: Willan Publishing.

Haney, C. (2006). *Psychological limits to the pains of imprisonment.* Washington, DC: APA Books.

Hannah-Moffatt, K. (1999). Moral agent or actuarial subject: Risk and Canadian women's imprisonment. *Theoretical Criminology, 3*(1), 71–94.

Hannah-Moffatt, K. (2005). Criminogenic needs and the transformative risk subject. *Punishment and Society, 7*(1), 29–51.

Harding, R. (2000). The psycho-social environment of prisons and its relationship to recidivism. *Criminology Research Council of Australia* Australian Institute of Criminology, Canberra.

Hargreaves, J. (2009). Beyond rehab: Where does prison fit? *Current Issues in Criminal Justice, 21*(1), 148–153.

Hartman, K. (2008). The absent voice of prisoners. *J Journal: New Writing on Justice, 1*(1).

Hawkins, K. (2003). Order, rationality and silence: Some reflections on criminal justice decision making. In L. Gelsthorpe, & N. Padfield (Eds.), *Exercising discretion: Decision making in the criminal justice system and beyond.* Cullompton, Devon: Willan Publishing.

Hebenton, B., & Seddon, T. (2009). From dangerousness to precaution: Managing sexual and violent offenders in an insecure and uncertain age. *British Journal of Criminology, 49*(3), 343–362.

Heilpern, D. (1998). *For fear or favour: Sexual assault of young prisoners.* Lismore: Southern Cross University Press.

Henham, R. (2000). Problems of theorising sentencing research. *International Journal of the Sociology of Law, 28,* 15–32.

Hensley, C., Struckman-Johnson, C., & Eigenberg, H. M. (2000). Introduction: The history of prison sex research. *The Prison Journal, 80,* 360.

Hensley, C., & Tewksbury, R. (2002). Inmate to inmate prison sexuality: A review of empirical studies. *Trauma, Violence and Abuse, 3*, 226.

Heseltine, K., Day, A., & Sarre, R. (2011). *Prison-based correctional offender rehabilitation programs: The 2009 national picture in Australia.* Research and Public Policy Reports, series 112, Australian Institute of Criminology.

Hochstetler, A., Copes, H., & Williams, P. (2010). That's not who I am: How offenders commit violent acts and reject authentically violent selves. *Justice Quarterly*, *27*(4) pp. 492–516.

Hogg, R. (2002). Prisoners and the penal estate in Australia. In D. Brown & M. Wilkie (Eds.), *Prisoners as citizens: Human rights in Australian prisons* Annandale: Federation Press.

Hogg, R., & Brown, D. (1998). *Rethinking law and order.* Australia, Annandale, New South Wales: Pluto Press

Horn, R. (1997). Not 'one of the boys': Women researching the police. *Journal of Gender Studies*, *6*(3), 297–309.

Howard League (2013). Briefing Paper: Consensual sex in prisons. *Commission into sex in prisons*. Howard League.

Howells, K. (2000). The psycho social environment of prisons and its relationship to recidivism. *Criminology Research Council of Australia* Australian Institute of Criminology, Canberra.

Howells, K., & Day, A. (1999). The rehabilitation of offenders: International perspectives applied to Australian correctional systems. *Trends and Issues in Crime and Criminal Justice, No 22* Australian Institute of Criminology

Hughes, E. C. (1971). *The sociological eye: Selected papers.* Chicago, IL: Aldine Atherton.

Hulley, S. Liebling, A., & Crewe, B. (2012). Respect in prisons: Prisoners' experience of respect in public and private sector prisons. *Criminology and Criminal Justice, 14*(1) 3–33.

Hutchinson, S. (2006). Countering catastrophic criminality: Reform, punishment and the modern liberal compromise. *Punishment and Society, 8*(4), 443–467.

Hutchins, W. (2010). Update on Parole and the state parole authority. *Criminal Law CLE.*

Hutton, N., & Tata, C. (2002). *Sentencing and Society: International Perspectives.*

Indemauer, D. (1994). Offenders' perceptions of sentencing. *Australian Psychologist, 29*(2), 140–144.

Indemauer, D. (1996). Who owns sentencing? A reply to Bartholomew (1996). *Australian Psychologist, 39*(1), 63–65.

Independent Commission Against Corruption New South Wales (1993) *Police informants- A discussion paper on the nature and management of the relationship between police and informers.* NSW Government.

Irwin, J. (2004). *The warehouse prison.* Oxford: Oxford University Press.

James, G. (2007). *Review of New South Wales Forensic Mental Health Legislation.* Department of Health New South Wales.

Jewkes, Y. (2002). *Captive audience: Media, masculinity and power in prisons.* Cullompton, Devon: Willan.

Johansen, R. (2008). The ruse of rehabilitation: The Supreme Court's misconception of coercion in sexual offender rehabilitation programs. *Lewis & Clark Law Rev*iew, *12*, 763.

Johns, R. (2002a). Sentencing law: A review of developments in 1998–2000. *NSW Parliamentary Library Research Service,* Briefing Paper 2/02.

Johns, R. (2002b). Bail law and practice—recent developments in NSW. *NSW Parliamentary Library Research Service,* Briefing Paper 15/02

Johnson, P. (2003). Reforms to NSW sentencing law: The *Crimes (Sentencing Procedure) Amendment (Standard Minimum Sentencing)* Act 2002. Judicial Commission of NSW.

Jones, C., Hua, J., Donnelly, N., McHutchison, J., & Heggie, K. (2006). 'Risk of re-offending among parolees' Bureau of Crime Statistics and Research NSW. *Crime and Justice Bulletin* No. 91.

Keane, J., Potas, I., & Donnelly, H. (2004). *Sentencing Trends and Issues no 30: Common Offences and the Use of Imprisoment in the District and Supreme Court in 2002.* Judicial Commission of New South Wales.

Kemshall, H., & McGuire, J. (2001). Public protection partnership and risk penality—The multi-agency risk management of sexual and violent offenders. *Punishment and Society, 3*(2), 237–264.

Kilty, J (2010). Gendering violence, remorse and the role of restorative justice: Deconstructing public perceptions of Kelly Ellard and Warren Glowatski. *Contemporary Justice Review, 13*(2), 155–172.

Kirchengast, T. (2008). Sentencing law and the 'emotional catharsis' of victim rights in New South Wales homicide cases. *Sydney Law Review, 30*(4) 615–637.

Kolber, A. J. (2009). The subjective experience of punishment. *Columbia Law Review, 109*, 182.

Kunzel, R. (2008). *Criminal intimacy,* University of Chicago Press.
Lacey, N. (2008). The prisoners' dilemma: Political economy and punishment in contemporary democracies. In *The Hamlyn Lectures 2007*. Cambridge: Cambridge University Press.
Lacombe, D. (1996). Reforming Foucault: A critique of the social control book. *British Journal of Sociology, 47*(2) 332–352.
Lacombe, D. (1997). Reforming Foucault: A critique of the social control thesis. *British Journal of Sociology*, *47*(2), 332–352.
Larney, S., Matthers, B., Dolan, K. (2007). Illict drug treatment in prison: Detoxification, drug free units, therapeutic communities and opioid substitution programmes. *National Drug and Alcohol Research Centre University of New South Wales.*
Laster, K., & O'Malley, P. (1996). Sensitive new age laws: The reassertion of emotionality in law. *International Journal of the Sociology of Law, 24*(1) 21–40.
Leader, K. L. (2007). Bound and gagged: The performance of tradition in the adversarial criminal trial. *Philament*, no. 11.
Leader, K. L. (2008). *Trials, truth telling and the performing body.* PhD book, University of Sydney.
Lee, M. (2007). *Inventing fear of crime: Criminology and the politics of anxiety.* Devon: Willan.
Legislative Council of NSW (2000). *Select committee on the increase in prisoner population: Interim report: Issues relating to women.* Legislative Council of NSW.
Legislative Council of NSW (2001). *Select committee on the increase in prisoner population: Final Report* Parliament of NSW, Parliamentary Paper No. 924.
Legislative Council of NSW (2010). *Inquiry into Privatisation of Prisons* Final Report, Paper no. 21, Parliament of NSW.
Liebling, A. (2001). Whose side are we on? Theory, practice and allegiance in prisons research. *British Journal of Criminology, 41*, 472–484.
Liebling, A. (2004). *Prisons and their moral performance: A study of values, quality and prison life.* Oxford: Oxford University Press.
Liebling, A., & Arnold, H. (2012). Social relationships between prisoners in a maximum security prison: Violence, faith and the declining nature of trust. *Journal of Criminal Justice, 40,* 413–424.
Liebling, A., Price, D., & Elliott, C. (1999). Appreciative inquiry and relationships in prison. *Punishment and Society, 1*(1) 71–98.
Liebling, A., Tait, S., Stiles, A., Durie, L. (2005). Revisiting prison suicide: the role of fairness and despair. In A. Liebling & S. Maruna (Eds.), *The Effects of Imprisonment.* Willan Cullompton.

Lincoln, Y., & Guba, E. (1985). *Naturalistic inquiry*. Newbury Park, CA: Sage Publications.

Lindsay, R. (2009). Punishment without finality: One year in the life and death of Alan Egan. *Criminal Law Journal, 33*(1), 45–54.

Loughnan, A. (2010). Drink spiking and rock throwing: The creation and construction of criminal offences in the current era. *Alternative Law Journal, 35*(1), 19–21.

Loukas (2008). "Court of Criminal Appeal Update 2007" Public Defenders Office, Department of Justice New South Wales.

Lovegrove, A. (2007). Public opinion, sentencing and lenience: An empirical study involving judges consulting the community. *Criminal Law Review*, 769–781.

Lowinson, J. H., Ruiz, P., Millman, R. B., & Langrod, J. G. (2005). *Substance abuse—A comprehensive textbook*, 4th edition. Philadelphia: Lippincott Williams & Wilkins.

Lumby, C. (2002). Televising the invisible: Prisoners, prison reform and the media. In D. Brown & M. Wilkie (Eds.), *Prisoners as citizens*. Sydney: Federation Press.

Lynch, M. (1998). Waste managers? The new penology, crime fighting, and parole agent identity. *Law and Society Review, 32*, 839–869.

Lynch, M. (2000). Rehabilitation as rhetoric: The ideal of reformation in contemporary parole discourse and practice. *Punishment and Society, 2*(1), pp. 40–65.

Mackenzie, G. (2004). *How judges sentence*. Annandale: Federation Press.

Mackenzie, J. (2005). *How Judges Sentence*. Annandale: Federation Press.

Marinos, V. (2005). Thinking about penal equivalents. *Punishment and Society, 7*(4), 441–455.

Martel, J. (2006). To be, one has to be somewhere: Spatio-temporality in prison segregation. *British Journal of Criminology. 46*, 587–612.

Maruna, S. (2001). *Making good: How Ex-convicts reform and rebuild their lives*. Washington, DC: American Psychological Association Books.

Maruna, S., & Mann, R. E. (2006). A fundamental attribution error? Rethinking cognitive distortions. *Legal and Criminological Psychology, 11*(2), 155–177.

Matthews, R., & Young, J. (2003). *The new politics of crime and punishment*. Cullompton, Devon: Willan Publishing.

Messerschmidt, J. (1993). *Masculinities and crime: A critique and reconceptualisation of theory*. Rowman and Littlefield.

MacKenzie, G., & Stobbs, N. (2010). *Principles of sentencing*. Annandale: Federation Press.

Mackinnell, I., Spears, D., & Tackachi, R. (1993). 'Special circumstances' under the *Sentencing Act* 1989 (NSW) *Judicial Commission of NSW.* Research monograph no.7

Martel, J. (2010). "Remorse and the production of truth" *Punishment and Society, 12*(4), 414–437.

Masters, C. (2005). 'Supermax' Australian Broadcasting Commission television. *Four Corners,* 7 November 2005

McAra, L. (2005). Modelling penal transformation. *Punishment and Society, 7*(3), 277–302.

McConville, M. Sanders, A., & Leng, R. (1991). *The case for the prosecution.* London: Routledge.

McCulloch, T., & McNeil, F. (2007). Consumer society, commodification and offender management. *Criminology and Criminal Justice, 3*(1).

McCullough, J., & Pickering, S. (2009). Pre crime and counter terrorism: Imagining future crime in the 'war on terror'. *British Journal of Criminology, 49*(5), 628–645.

McGowen, R. (2000). Revisiting the hanging tree: Gatrell on emotion and history. *British Journal of Criminology, 40,* 1–13.

McGuire, J. (2005). Deterrence in sentencing: Handle with care. *Australian Law Journal, 79,* 448.

McMahon, M. (1990). Net-widening: Vagaries in the use of a concept. *British Journal of Criminology, 30*(2), 121–149.

McNeill, F., Burns, N., Halliday, S., Hutton, N., & Tata, C. (2009). Risk, responsibility and reconfiguration: Penal adaptation and misadaptation. *Punishment & Society, 1*(14), 419–442.

McSherry, B. (2005). The introduction of terrorist related offences into Australia: Comfort or concern? *Psychiatry, Psychology and Law, 12*(2), 279–288.

Mihailides, S., Jude, B., & Van den Bossche, C. (2005). The LSI-R in an Australian setting: Implications for risk/needs decision making in forensic contexts. *Psychiatry, Psychology and the Law, 12*(1).

Minogue, C. (2008). Review essay: Recapturing freedom: Issues relating to the release of long term prisoners into the community. *Alternative Law Journal, 33*(3), 185–188.

Miralis, D. (2007). Law and order 2007. *Law Society Journal, 54,* March 2007.

Miralis, D. (2008). Law and order 2008. *Law Society Journal, 60,* April 2008.

Moore, D (2007). *Criminal artefacts: Governing drugs and users,* Vancouver: UBC Press

Murphy, T., & Whitty, N. (2007). Risk and Human Rights in United Kingdom Prison Governance. *British Journal of Criminology, 47*(5), 798–816.

Neuber, A. (2011). Understanding violence in the society of captives: Sykes meets Bourdieu in prison. *Howard Journal, 50*(1) 1–16.

New South Wales 1978, Report of the Royal Commission into New South Wales Prisons, (Justice J. F. Nagle, Royal Commissioner), Government Printer, Sydney.

New South Wales Attorney General's Office (2009). Report backs NSW approach to serious sex offenders. Press Release, July 2009.

New South Wales Audit Office (2004). *Performance audit: Prisoner rehabilitation: Department of corrective services.* NSW Government.

New South Wales Coroner's Office (2006). *Inquest into the death of Scott Ashley Simpson* (unreported, Magistrate D. Pinch, 17 July 2006).

New South Wales Department of Prisons (1965). *Annual report.* New South Wales: Government Printer.

New South Wales Government (2006). *A new direction for NSW: State Plan.* Premier's Department.

New South Wales Law Reform Commission (1996). *Report no. 79—Sentencing*

New South Wales Law Reform Commission (2012). *Report no. 133—Bail*

New South Wales State Parole Authority (2008). *Annual report.* New South Wales Government, Department of Justice.

New South Wales Women in Prison Task Force (1985). *Report of the NSW women in prison task force.* Sydney: Government Printer

Nutley, S., & Davies, H. (2000). Criminal justice: using evidence to reduce crime. In S. Nutley (Ed.). *What works? Evidence based policy and practice in Public Service.* UK: The Policy Press, University of Bristol.

Office of the NSW Ombudsman Annual Report 2007/8

Office of the NSW Ombudsman Annual Report 2009/10

O'Malley, P. (1999). Volatile and contradictory punishment. *Theoretical Criminology, 3*(2), 175–196.

O'Malley, P. (2008). Neo-liberalism and risk in criminology. In T. Anthony & C. Cunneen (Eds.) *The critical criminology companion.* New South Wales, Australia: Hawkins Press.

O'Neill, J. (1990). The punishment salesman. *Independent Monthly,* October 1990.

O'Toole, S., & Eyland, S. (2005). *Corrections criminology.* Leichardt: Hawkins Press.

Parker, R. (2004). Program evaluation. In *What works in offender rehabilitation conference.* Australia: NSW Department of Corrective Services Sydney

Pratt, J, Brown, M, Brown, D, Hallsworth, S, Morrison, W. (2005). *The New Punitiveness* Willan, Cullompton.

Peacock, M. (2008). Third space between the prison and the community: Post release programs and re-integration. *Current Issues in Criminal. Justice, 20,* 307–312.

Phillips, C. (2007). Ethnicity, identity and community cohesion in prison. In M. Wetherell, M. Lafleche & R. Berkeley, (Eds.), *Identity, ethnic diversity and community cohesion* (pp. 75–86). London: Sage.

Philipps, C., & Bowling, B. (2003). Racism, ethnicity and criminology: Developing minority perspectives. *British Journal of Criminology, 43,* 269–290.

Phillips, C., & Earle, R. (2008). Ethnicity, identity and social relations in prison. *Identities and Social Action Project,* Economic and Social Research Council

Phillips, J. (2001). Cultural construction of manhood in prison. *Psychology of Men and Masculinity, 2*(1) 13–23.

Poletti, P. (2005). "Sentencing Tends and Issues" No. 34. *Sentencing Council of New South Wales.*

Poletti, P. (2010). The impact of the standard non-parole period sentencing scheme on sentencing patterns in New South Wales. *Judicial Commission of NSW,* Research Monograph No. 33.

Poletti, P., & Barnes, L. A. (2002). Conviction and sentence appeals in the New South Wales Court of Criminal Appeal 1996–2000. *Judicial Commission of NSW* Sentencing Trends and Issues No. 22.

Potas, I., & Traynor, S. (2002). Sentencing methodology—Two tiered or instinctive synthesis. *Judicial Commission of NSW* Trends and Issues in Sentencing No. 25.

Powell, M. B. (2000). Practical guidelines for conducting investigative interviews with Aboriginal people. *Current Issues in Criminal Justice, 12,* 181–200.

Pratt, J. (1998). *Governing the dangerous: Dangerousness, law and social change.* Annandale: Federation Press.

Pratt, J. (2008). Penal populism and the contemporary role of punishment. In T. Anthony & C. Cunneen (Eds.), *The critical criminology companion.* Annandale: Federation Press.

Productivity Commission (2009). *Report on Government Services* Committee for the Review of Govenment Services, Commonwealth of Australia.

Raynor, P. (1997). Some observations on rehabilitation and justice. *Howard Journal, 36*(3), 248–262.

Rinaldi, F. (1977). *Australian prisons.* Canberra: F & M Publishers.

Robertson, J. (2009). Parliament of NSW, Legislative Council 29 October 2009.

Robinson, G. (2008). Late modern rehabilitation: The evolution of a penal strategy. *Punishment and Society, 10*(4), 429–445.

Robinson, P. H., & Darley, J. M. (2003). The role of deterrence in the formulation of criminal law rules: At its worst when doing its best. *Georgetown Law Review, 91*, 949.

Robinson, G., & Shapland, J. (2008). Reducing recidivism. *British Journal of Criminology, 48*(3), 337–358.

Rogers, L. R., & Erez, E. (1999). The contextuality of objectivity in sentencing among legal professionals in South Australia. *International Journal of the Sociology of Law, 27*, 267–286.

Rossmanith, K. (2009). The Magistrate and Mr. Moore: Storytelling, narrative forensics, and a judge's experience of sentencing, *TEXT*, Special Issue 18, October 2013, 1–13.

Rossmanith, K. (2015) "Feeling and judging remorse" *Body and Society, 21*(2), 167–193.

Roth, L. (2007). Law and order Legislation in the Australian States and Territories 2003-2006. *NSW Parliamentary Library Research Service* Briefing Paper No. 12/06

Ruschena, D. (2003). Determining dangerousness: Whatever happened to the rules of evidence? *Psychiatry, Psychology and the Law, 10*(1), 122–139.

Ryan, G. W., & Bernard, H. R. (2003). Data management and analysis methods. In N. K. Denzin & Y. S. Lincoln (Eds.), *Collecting and interpreting qualitative materials.* California: Sage.

Sales, L (2010). Holcroft's custody death 'nothing new' Broadcast: 02 March 2010, *Australian Broadcasting Corporation.*

Sarre, R (2001). A 25 year jubilee retrospective of Robert Martinson's famous article. *The Australian and New Zealand Journal of Criminology, 34*(1), 38–46.

Schwartz, D., & Propper, I. (1988). Special care unit—Development of Australia's first penal therapeutic community. In B. Cullen, M. Dowding, & J. Griffin (Eds.), *Corrective Services In New South Wales.* North Ryde: The Law Book Company Limited

Seidler, K. (2010). *Crime, culture and violence: Understanding how masculinity and identity shapes offending.* Bowen Hills, QLD: Australian Academic Press.

Sentencing Council of NSW (2008). 'An intensive corrections order for NSW: consultation paper'

Serious Offenders Review Council of New South Wales (2008). *Annual report*

Shefer, G., & Liebling, A. (2008). Prison privatization: In search of a business-like atmosphere. *Criminology and Criminal Justice, 8*, 261–278.

Silver, E., Miller, L., (2002). A cautionary note on the use of actuarial risk assessment tools for social control. *Crime and Delinquency, 48*(1), 143.

Simon, J. (1993). The ideological effects of actuarial practices. *Law and Society Review, 22*(4), 771.

Simon, J., & Feeley, M. (2003). The form and limits of the new penology. In T. G. Blomberg & S. Cohen (Eds.), *Punishment and Social Control.* New York: Walter de Gruyter.

Simpson, R. (1997). Bail in New South Wales. *Briefing Paper No 25/07 NSW Parliamentary Library Research Service.*

Simpson, R. (1999). Parole: an overview. *Briefing Paper No 20/99 NSW Parliamentary Library Research Service.*

Simpson, R., & Griffith, G. (1999). Law and order legislation in the Australian states and territories 1995–1998: A comparative survey. *Briefing Paper 7/99 NSW Parliamentary Library Research Service.*

Sotiri, M. (2003). *Punishment and Imprisonment in New South Wales: Towards a conceptual understanding of purpose.* Doctoral thesis, UNSW.

Sparks, J. R. (2002). Out of the digger: The warrior's honour and the guilty observer. *Ethnography, 3*(4), 556–581.

Sparks, J. R., & Bottoms, A. E. (1996). Legitimacy and order in prisons. *British Journal of Criminology, 46*(1) pp. 45–62.

Sparks, J. R., & Bottoms, A. (2006). Legitimacy and order in prisons. In Y. Jewkes & H. Johnston (Eds.), *Prison readings: A critical introduction to prisons and imprisonment.* Cullompton, Devon: Willan Publishing.

Spivakovsky, C. (2006). Theoretical passages and boundaries: The indigenous subject, colonialism and governmentality. *Passages: Law, aesthetics, politics.* Melbourne: Melbourne University July 2006.

Spivakovsky, C. (2009). The construction of the racially different indigenous offender. In M. Segrave (Ed.), *Proceedings of the Critical Criminology Conference 2009.* Melbourne: Monash University Melbourne.

Steel, A. (2009). Bail in Australia: Legislative introduction and amendment since 1970. In M. Segrave (Ed.), *Proceedings of the Australian & New Zealand Critical Criminology Conference 2009.* Melbourne: Monash University Melbourne.

Sykes, G. (1958/1999). *The society of captives: A study of a maximum security prison.* Princeton, New Jersey: Princeton University Press.

Tait, D. (2002). Sentencing as performance: Restoring drama to the courtroom. In C. Tata & N. Hutton (Eds.), *Sentencing and society: International perspectives* (pp. 469–482). Burlington VT: Ashgate.

Tata, C. (2002). Accountability for the sentencing decision process: Towards a new understanding. In N. Hutton & C. Tata (Eds.), *Sentencing and society: International perspectives* (pp. 399–428). Aldershot: Ashgate.

Tata, C. (2007). Sentencing as craftwork and the binary epistemologies of the discretionary decision process. *Social and Legal Studies, 16*(3), 425–447.

Tata, C. (2002). Accountability for the sentencing process. In N. Hutton & C. Tata (Eds.), *Sentencing and society: International perspectives.* Aldershot: Ashgate

Tombs, J. (2008). Telling sentencing stories. In P. Carlen (Ed.), *Imaginary penalities.* Cullompton, Devon: Willan Publishing.

Turner, V. W. (1967). *The forest of symbols.* Ithaca, New York: Cornell University Press.

Vess, J., & Eccleston, L. (2009). Extended supervision of sexual offenders across Australia and New Zealand. *Psychiatry, Psychology and Law, 16*(2), 271–287.

Vinson, A. (1982). *Wilful obstruction: The frustration of prison reform.* Australia: Methuen Australia.

Vinson, A. (1999). Reforming prisons: A 1970s experience. In Paper presented at the *History of Crime, Policing and Punishment Conference Convened by the Australian Institute of Criminology in conjunction with Charles Sturt University,* Canberra, 9–10 December 1999.

Vinson, A. (2004). Implementing the key principles of the Nagle Commission' in 'Nagle: 25 years on Symposium'. *Current Issues in Criminal Justice, 16*(1), 93–98.

Vinson, A., Cunneen, C., & Baldry, E. (2004). Nagle: 25 years on Symposium *Current Issues, 16*(1), 93–98.

Von Hirsch, A., & Ashworth, A. (1998). *Principled sentencing: readings, theory and policy.* Oxford: Hart Publishing.

Von Hirsch, A., & Maher, L. (1992). Should penal rehabilitationism be revived? *Criminal Justice Ethics, 11*(1), 25–30.

Vuolo, M., & Kruttschnitt, C. (2008). Prisoner adjustment, correctional officers, and context: The foreground and background of punishment in late modernity *Law and Society Review, 42*(2), 307–336.

Wacquant, L. (2001). Deadly symbiosis: When ghetto and prison meet and mesh. *Punishment & Society, 3*(1), 95–133.

Wacquant, L. (2002a). The curious eclipse of prison ethnography in the age of mass incarceration. *Ethnography,* 3(4), 371–397.

Wacquant, L. (2002b). Scrutinizing the street: Poverty, morality and the pitfalls of urban ethnography. *American Journal of Sociology, 107*(6), 1468–1532.

Wacquant, L. (2009). *Punishing the poor.* Durham and London: Duke University Press.

Walsh, T. (2006). Is corrections correcting? An examination of prisoner rehabilitation policy and practice in Queensland. *The Australian and New Zealand Journal of Criminology, 39*(1) 109–133.

Ward, A., & Birgden, A. (2009). Accountability and dignity: Ethical issues in forensic and correctional practice. *Aggression and Violent Behaviour, 14,* 227–231.

Ward, A., & Maruna, S. (2007). *Rehabilitation.* London: Routledge London

Ward, T., & Salmon, K. (2009). The ethics of punishment: Correctional practice implications. *Aggression and Violent Behaviour, 14,* 239–247.

Warner, K. (2003). The role of guideline judgments in the law and order debate in Australia. *Criminal Law Journal, 27*(1), 8–22.

Warner, K. (2006). Sentencing scholarship in Australia. *Current Issues in Criminal Justice, 18*(2).

Weatherburn, D., Wan, Y., & Corben, S. (2014). Why is the NSW prison population growing. *Bureau of Crime Statistics and Research, Crime and Justice Statistics Bureau Brief* Issue paper no. 95, April 2014.

Weaver, B., & Armstrong, S. (2011). User views of punishment, the dynamics of community based punishment: insider views from the outside. *The Scottish Centre for Crime and Justice Research,* Research report no. 3, 2011.

Webb, J., Schirato, T., & Danaher, G. (2002). *Understanding Bourdieu.* London: Sage.

Weelands, D. (2009a). Residential centre or day prison? The case of COSP. *Current Issues in Criminal Justice, 20*(3), 485–489.

Weelands, D. (2009b). Punitive rehabilitation in New South Wales: New developments in community corrections. In M. Segrave (Ed.), *Proceedings of the ANZ critical criminology conference.* Melbourne: Monash University.

Weisman, R. (2009). Being and doing: the judicial use of remorse to construct character and community. *Social Legal Studies, 18,* 47.

White, R. (2008). Prisoners, victims and the act of giving. *Parity, 21*(9).

Witton, J., & Ashton, M. (2004). More than just methadone dose-enhancing outcomes of methadone maintenance treatment with counselling and other psychosocial ancillary services. *Research into Practice Briefings.* London UK: National Treatment Agency for Substance abuse London UK.

Woodham, R. (2005). Security in correctional centres. In S. O'Toole, & S. Eyeland (Eds.), *Corrections criminology*. Sydney, New South Wales: Hawkins Press.

Wright, P., & Collis, W. (2010). State unit accused of spying on parolees. *Sydney Morning Herald*, 9 August 2010.

Yannoulidis, S. (2002). Negotiating 'dangerousness': Charting a course between psychiatry and law, *Psychology and Law, 92*, 151–162.

Yap, L., Richters, J., Butler, T., Scneider, K., Grant, L., & Donovan, B. (2011). The decline in sexual assaults in men's prisons in NSW: A 'systems' approach. *Journal of Interpersonal Violence, 26*, 3157.

Yates, P. (2009). Is sex offender denial related to sex offender risk and recidivism? A review and treatment implications. *Psychology, Crime and Law, 15*, 2–3.

Zdenkowski, G., & Brown, D. (1982). *The prison struggle: Changing Australia's prison system*. Australia: Penguin Books.

Zedner, L. (2002). Dangers of dystopias in legal theory. *Oxford Journal of Legal Studies, 22*(2), 341–366.

Index

M. Hall, *The Lived Sentence,* Palgrave Studies in Prisons and Penology, DOI 10.1007/978-3-319-45038-4